A BROADER VISION

107 Years of Interesting Anecdotes in the Life of a Canadian Physicist

who Changed the World with Spectroscopy

and Analytical Chemistry.

JOHN E. BURGENER

Copyright © 2014 by John E. Burgener
First Edition – January 2014

ISBN
978-1-4602-0632-4 (Hardcover)
978-1-4602-0633-1 (Paperback)
978-1-4602-0634-8 (eBook)

All rights reserved.

No part of this publication may be reproduced in any form, or by any means, electronic or mechanical, including photocopying, recording, or any information browsing, storage, or retrieval system, without permission in writing from the publisher.

Produced by:

FriesenPress
Suite 300 – 852 Fort Street
Victoria, BC, Canada V8W 1H8

www.friesenpress.com

Distributed to the trade by The Ingram Book Company

TABLE OF CONTENTS

Foreword v
Acknowledgements..vii
Chapter 1 How It Started 1
Chapter 2 My Grandfather's Cheese Factory 8
Chapter 3 The School Years 14
Chapter 4 The 1930s – Farming to Survive the Depression 30
Chapter 5 Cars...41
Chapter 6 High School Years 49
Chapter 7 After High School and My Jet Engine................56
Chapter 8 The Lab at Alcan, Arvida..........................68
Chapter 9 Married..81
Chapter 10 The Early TSL Years 91
Chapter 11 Our First House..................................99
Chapter 12 Growth in the Company..........................116
Chapter 13 A Bigger House 133
Chapter 14 Again the Lab Moves - and Our Daughter Arrives......141
Chapter 15 The ThermoCarb 150
Chapter 16 The Middle Years................................170
Chapter 17 Corporate Battles over Wear Check 182
Chapter 18 Moving On after Wear Check - Family Events –
the Kids Grow Up..193
Chapter 19 New Techniques, Mobile Labs, Growing the Business.....207
Chapter 20 The Later Years.................................218
Chapter 21 Retirement......................................223
Chapter 22 Cruises...240
Chapter 23 Medical Complications...........................247
Chapter 24 Reflections.....................................254

Foreword

I was born in World War I, went to school during the Great Depression, graduated from university, and was married in the middle of World War II. I made some important changes to aluminum production in Canada in the forties, then raised a family and developed a business in the fifties. I also established on-site labs in many places, greatly aiding mineral exploration. I developed assay techniques, which are now universally used. I had an effect on steel production and developed a scientific means of engine maintenance, now in use around the world. I raised two million dollars for a charitable cause, and raised four children who are changing the world today. I published a book in 2010, and subsequently published this book in 2013. It all happened because I strove for excellence in everything I did, and was constantly in communication with God, who blessed me with many gifts. The support of my loving wife, family, and friends were all a tremendous help in making it possible.

My parents told me many stories of their lives, but they were all verbal and most of them were told when I was young. Sadly, most of their stories are only faintly remembered. Details of their lives, such as when and where they were born, had to be found out by asking others. There are many more details I wish I knew; the information I have currently collected is sketchy and possibly erroneous.

I decided that I would write my story while I am still around. I did not attempt to write a biography, but rather chose to write a collection of stories that might be of interest to our children, grandchildren, and others. The stories of my earlier life are of my direct family. The later stories cover the years of my adulthood, my married life, and my children.

John E. Burgener

I have been unusually blessed with wonderful parents and siblings. The opportunity of good education and a good grounding in religion gave me a road map to a peaceful, and, I believe, a reasonably useful life. I have been even more blessed by God's gift of a wonderful wife, four wonderful children, eleven grandchildren, and so far, five great grandchildren.

Acknowledgements

My children, Paul, Peter, John, and Deborah have all encouraged me to write this book. My sons John, Paul, and Peter edited my book and made many good suggestions. They have all offered many helpful suggestions. Elinor, my loving and very much-loved wife, was suffering from dementia as I wrote, but she never complained about the time I spent writing. My life has been filled with love from my parents, my siblings, my most loving and wonderful wife, my wonderful children, grandchildren, and the many friends I have had throughout my life. I thank them all, and I thank God for allowing me such love.

Chapter 1
HOW IT STARTED

Whatever success I have had in my life, I owe to the foundation laid by my parents. They showered us with love and accepted the challenges of life without complaint. My story begins with the birth of my father and mother.

My father, Ernst, was born in Switzerland on June 19th, 1889, in a village called Werdthof, which is near the municipality of Thun. His father - my grandfather - was named Christian Burgener, and he was born November 21st, 1861, in Grindelwald, Switzerland. My father's mother was Marie Kocher and she was born July 1st, 1864, in Kappelen, near Worben, Switzerland.

My father's family in 1905 before they left Switzerland.

John E. Burgener

Christian Burgener was a successful cheese maker in Switzerland who eventually became interested in broader fields. He felt that opportunities in Switzerland were too limited. The cheese factory he had there was the back of his house. His factory was one of a multitude of little factories, but he had a broader vision. He wanted a much larger company that could produce high quality cheese for everyone, which he could not do in Switzerland. He saw Poland, Russia and Canada as places with more opportunity for himself and his children. The challenges of a new country excited him, though one wonders why he was so driven. He had a comfortable living in a beautiful country where his ancestors had lived for centuries. He went with his two sons, Ernst and Christian, to Poland, but found the opportunities there even more limited. He debated moving to Russia, but concluded that the climate was unsuitable for dairy farming. In 1905 he boarded a ship in Antwerp, Belgium, and arrived in Saint John, New Brunswick, Canada, on February 24, 1905, with his sons, Ernst and Christian, leaving his wife and three daughters in Switzerland.

The house where my father was born. This was a typical Swiss mountain house. The front of the building is living quarters and the back part is a barn or work shop. Snowfalls of up to five feet make it easier to have everything in one building

They traveled to Toronto and stayed at a hotel (which no longer exists) at Front and York Street. From there they went to Kitchener. At that time

A Broader Vision

Kitchener was known as Berlin due to a large German settlement there. After interviewing farmers in the area, he decided that the handling of milk was not up to his requirements and returned to Toronto, intending to return to Switzerland. When he got back to the hotel there was a telegram from his wife. It stated that she and the girls were tired of waiting. They were boarding a ship in Antwerp, Belgium, and would arrive in Montreal on June 6, 1905. She asked him to meet her there.

With his wife and daughters arriving in Canada, he decided to remain. Ontario had the potential of a good a dairy industry and he was hopeful that he could change the way milk was handled by his suppliers. He bought a cheese factory in Wellesley, Ontario. He upgraded it and sold it at a considerable profit about six months later and bought a larger factory in Sebringville, near Stratford, Ontario, which he operated for the rest of his life.

When my father arrived in Canada he was sixteen. He had not yet finished his education. He enrolled in correspondence courses and over several years acquired a diploma in telephone engineering. To finance these courses, he worked in a furniture factory and also spent time logging in northern Ontario. In addition to his regular job, he had a set of traps, which he serviced by making the rounds, starting at four in the morning, before he went to work. After work he would study until ten or eleven at night. His vision was to be more than a factory worker and have his own business. During this time he, along with his brother Chris, invented a system that made telephone party lines act like private lines. To accomplish this he invented the mercury switch. The mercury switch is in use today in thermostats controlling heating and cooling systems worldwide. They got a patent on the system, which included the switch. Unfortunately the lawyer they hired was not a good patent lawyer. Some years later General Electric started producing the mercury switch. He consulted a lawyer, who pointed out that his patent was weak, and GE would spend millions to defend themselves. Unless he could do likewise, he had no hope of winning.

By the time he reached his twentieth birthday he was a physical wreck and a doctor gave him six months to live. He embarked on a physical development program that included living outdoors in a tent during the summer and winter, which restored his health. After that he formed a company called Signal Systems Limited and developed a business that provided call systems in hospitals and industry. In the early 1900s telephones were rare and were just starting to be used. There was no simple means of contacting individuals. His company did so with flashing lights and sounds. It was reasonably successful. At the end of World War I he hired his brother Chris as a salesman. Chris had been a pilot in the Royal Flying Corp. He flew Handely Page bombers and survived being shot down twice, fortunately crashing behind the Allied lines. Chris kept a propeller from his last plane over his fireplace.

My father's brother, Chris, served in the Royal Flying Corp in WWI. He was shot down twice and survived.

The signal business was increasingly being served by the telephone and its derivatives. During the short depression of the early twenties my father sold out to an intercom company, Dictograph, which was based in New York. Over the years he installed Dictograph Executive Intercoms in the offices of the Prime Minister of Canada and the Premier of Ontario. Presidents of the major banks and executives of major industries in Ontario had Dictographs. In my teen years I often accompanied my father on weekend service calls. I sat in many of the executive chairs as we tested the intercoms. He remained with this company the rest of his working life.

During the Great Depression of the thirties my father retained his job, but at a greatly reduced income. By 1930 he had a wife and five children to support. Anticipating that economic conditions would get even worse, my mother and father had the insight and courage to give up their comfortable living in the beaches area of Toronto and move to where they could grow food. They purchased a two acre lot with lots of fruit trees and a small house on Indian Road in Lorne Park, which is in the Port Credit area of Mississauga, about twenty miles west of Toronto. At that time Lorne Park was a farming area and not the affluent suburb it is today. The house only had one bedroom and a kitchen/living room. Dad eventually expanded it to accommodate us. The property provided food and accommodation for our family throughout the years of the Depression. My teenage years were spent there. The skills I gained from cultivating the gardens, pruning trees, tending chickens, and construction were valuable experiences that many never get the chance to enjoy. They have served me well throughout my life.

My mother, Jane Elizabeth Flynn (Jennie) was born on December 20th, 1892, in Leigh District, Lancashire, England. She had an Irish father, John Flynn, and an English mother, Jemima Anderson. Jemima's grandfather was a Norwegian sea captain and her father was born on his ship. My mother's father had been a coal miner, but later owned and operated a store in Leeds. My mother went to school and finished high school at a convent there. Mother was the oldest of thirteen children, of which only eight survived to adulthood. At nineteen my mother got a job as a secretary working for a generous employer. He was taking his wife to see a play in London and offered to include his secretary, my mother. Mother was thrilled and accepted. Unfortunately, my grandfather considered London plays as works of the devil, and going with her boss even worse. There was a great fight and she decided to leave home. She had a broader vision than her life in England permitted. She had been intrigued by the thought of emigrating to Canada, as a new land with probably greater opportunities. She realized that she would be leaving friends and family but felt that she could lead a more interesting and useful life by doing so and decided this was the time to go. She had been earning a good income and had some savings, and she asked her sister, Aida, to accompany her. Her father repented and begged her not to go, but she looked forward to the adventure nonetheless and applied for immigration to Canada. Since she was educated and had working skills, she was readily accepted.

She and her sister Aida sailed for Canada sometime around 1913, arriving in Quebec City. Her sister, who was about 19 years old, complained that she knew little French. She felt that Canada was an undeveloped country compared with England. She did not have my mother's vision of the challenges being worth the potential advantages of living in Canada, so she returned to England. My mother was excited by the differences and decided to stay. She asked a priest if he could help her find a job. He recommended a family who were looking for domestic help. She took the job, which gave her a chance to get to know the country. After six months had passed she moved to Toronto, where a priest recommended her for a job as secretary at St. Michael's Hospital. She got the job and later became the assistant to Dr. Fener, who set up the first medical x-ray in Toronto. After World War I the remainder of her family moved to Toronto. While she was working at St. Michael's, she met my father. He was installing a system of lights and sound signals for calling doctors. Since mother was in administration, he had to consult her frequently.

Her English accent, gentleness, and willingness to help intrigued him. Also, she was one of the few who did not look down on him because of his German accent. On top of all this, she was very pretty and vivacious. He was a handsome and gentle young man who had the self-assurance to manage his own business at the age of twenty-four. They fell in love and were married in St John's Church on Kingston Road in Toronto on January 17th, 1916. They were not allowed to be married in the church, since my father was not a Catholic. They were married in the vestibule. Such attitudes have changed since Vatican II.

I was born Saturday, March 10, 1917, at 34 Leuty Avenue in the Beaches area of Toronto. It was a breech birth that nearly killed my mother, but thankfully, by the grace of God, we both survived. I don't remember anything of it myself. It seems my parents' families celebrated my birth as a great event. I was the first of my generation in both families. Father Williamson at Saint John's Church on Kingston Road baptized me John Ernest: John, after my mother's father, and Ernest after my father. Since then we have tried to establish a tradition amongst the Ernest Burgener descendants that the first-born male in the generation should carry the name Ernest. My son Paul is Paul Ernest and his son Brian is Brian Ernest. So far there are no Burgener great-grandsons.

A Broader Vision

When I try to think back, I find that my memories are connected with the places where I lived or specific events. For this reason I will describe my memories as related to specific places and events, and the following stories are therefore not strictly chronological.

Chapter 2

MY GRANDFATHER'S CHEESE FACTORY

My earliest memory was while we lived on Victoria Park Boulevard in the beaches area of Toronto. I was about four years old. I remember the pedal car I had, and I remember my two sisters, Marie and Jenny. I remember the time my uncle, who was visiting us, noticing as he was about to leave that there seemed to be some activity on the street. He asked my mother if she would like him to stay all night, since Dad was out of town on business. She said no and that she was alright. I was frightened by his comment, since I had heard someone on our back porch. We children were put to bed. Some time later there was a great crash. I jumped out of bed and ran to my parents' room. My mother was standing by the window, which was broken. She rushed downstairs and phoned the police. Apparently she was about to go to bed when a man with a gun, standing on the veranda roof outside her window, ordered her to open the window. There was a table with a flowerpot in front of the window. She picked up the flowerpot and smashed it through the window. The thief lost his balance, and fell off the roof. She called the police, who were already in the area because of other calls. The police arrived shortly and found the thief unconscious on the ground. They said a gang had been robbing the houses on the street from the early evening. They complimented her and said they now had one of the thieves and could probably get the others.

When I was about four and a half years old my grandfather became very ill and my father took over the management of the factory.

My mother with Marie, Jennie, and me, circa 1920.

My most vivid early memories are those connected with my grandfather Burgener's cheese factory and creamery near Sebringville, Ontario. Since the factory was in a farming area, there was nowhere for employees to live nearby, so there was a big house on the property designed to accommodate the owner and some of the hired help. My grandparents and the factory foreman lived there. The remainder of the house was unused except when one or more of the families visited. I remember visiting my grandparents when I was quite young.

When Dad took over managing the factory, we lived at the factory house. We remained there until my parents rented a house. While we lived in the factory house my father gave me a goat as a pet, which had the run of the property. Billy, as he was called, was very playful. He particularly liked butting my sisters up to the wall and holding them, screaming, until my mother would come to the rescue. Billy also welcomed visiting men by hooking his horn under the visitor's trouser leg. For some reason the visitors did not appreciate it. Another playful activity was running around in the factory, jumping on benches, machinery, and anything above floor level, with the staff wildly running around trying to chase him out. This activity led to Billy's demise. One day, when the health inspector was visiting the factory, Billy jumped in through an open window and in the chase that followed, Billy ended up in a vat of several hundred gallons of milk being processed into cheese. The inspector gave the factory a demerit. The milk had to be dumped, and Billy became somebody's dinner.

My parents rented a house near the factory at Seebach's Hill. My grandparents are buried in Saint John's Cemetery at Seebach's Hill. We lived in this house, probably for a year, while my father ran the factory. My brother Ernie was born there. Ernie's birth is an event that I only vaguely remember.

My grandfather's cheese factory.

The rented house was a farmhouse, which included a barn and a big circular cattle-watering trough. I believe there were cattle on the farm that used this trough, although we were not involved with them. I do remember that my grandfather's collie dog would follow Dad home and more or less forsook Grandfather. Dad had an odd experience while living here. Mother's brother Pat was coming by train to visit us, and Dad had promised to meet him at the train. On the morning that Pat was arriving, as Dad descended the stairs, he saw himself coming up the stairs. As he stopped in surprise, the vision disappeared.

A Broader Vision

Somewhat startled, he left for the station. Within a mile of the house the car hit an icy patch, skidded off the road, and rolled over. He was thrown clear and was unhurt. He felt that the apparition had made him cautious so that he was driving slowly, which probably saved his life.

As Grandfather was convalescing, my father often took me with him when he went to the factory. When Grandfather would check the maturity of the cheese in the curing room, I would accompany him. He would insert a small tube into the round of cheese, removing a cylinder of cheese. He would taste it, then give me a piece and ask for my opinion.

The factory property consisted of a hundred acres, much of which was bush. A river called the Black Creek flowed through it. Grandfather would take me fishing, showing me how to bait a hook, impressing on me the need to be patient when waiting for a fish to bite. He also taught me how to load, aim, and shoot a rifle. We shot at targets my grandfather would put on trees. Grandfather and I spent many a pleasant afternoon either hunting or fishing. I don't remember ever shooting at anything live or catching a fish. It did not matter– it was great to be with my grandfather. If he had not been sick, we would not have lived at the factory, and I would have never had the chance to know him.

My grandfather still spent time in the factory while he was recovering and would let me help, or so I thought. I remember many things about the workings of the factory, including the farmers, who came in their wagons drawn by big horses with hairy legs. I recall how they talked to the staff and to one another, joking and laughing as they emptied the big milk cans into a trough that was moved from vat to vat as each was filled. I would guess the vats held about two hundred gallons. Some liquid would be added and the milk would be heated and allowed to curdle. The curds were screened out, cut into chips, and pressed to squeeze out the whey. I remember the machinery of the factory, especially the big steam engine with its big flywheel, the piston pushing in and out, and the rotating governor; the interconnection of the belts and pulleys operated the machinery all over the factory, all from the one steam engine. I remember how the whey was pumped to the tank on stilts. There were the pig farmers who came to get the whey in their horse-drawn wagons. There were big presses that squeezed the whey from the curds and the separators that separated the cream to make butter and ice cream.

When the family returned to Toronto we continued to visit Sebringville for many years. I remember particularly the many Burgener family reunions, when all the Burgeners would spend a weekend at the factory house. The huge family dinners were prepared by the women while the men-folk discussed the affairs of the world. Being the oldest grandchild, I got to hang around with the men while the children played. With these reunions we got to know and love our cousins, uncles and aunts.

Burgener family gathering at the factory house circa 1923.
Photographed with a single lens box camera.

The trips to Sebringville were adventures in themselves. I remember one trip when we had three flat tires and only one spare. The spare tire was simply that: a spare **tire**. It was not mounted on a rim or wheel, as they are today. So to change a tire meant removing it from the rim and mounting the spare tire on the rim. This was done by using tire irons to lever the tire off the rim, and then to fit the spare onto the rim. Of course, you had to hand pump the tire once it was remounted. For the second flat we had to repair the original tire. For the third flat, we did not have enough repair materials to repair it, so one tire had to be cut up as patches to repair the other. The tires in those days had an inner tube to hold the air. If you got a rip or cut in the tire the inner tube would burst like a balloon and cause a sudden deflation of the tire, causing the car to go out of control. Modern tires have no inner tubes and do not explosively deflate. The hundred and twenty mile trip took six hours.

A Broader Vision

Another time, Grandfather had asked for help in making some factory changes. It was winter and Dad, Uncle Chris (Dad's brother), and I had started to drive when a blizzard arose with heavy snow and strong winds. The car was not a sedan. It was what one would call today a convertible with a canvas-like top that had no insulation or glass side windows. In bad weather celluloid curtains where fastened to the roof and to the body of the car with dome fasteners. These side curtains were not very tight fitting. I was in the back, with Dad and Uncle Chris in front. In the strong winds and heavy snow the side curtains were not very effective. So much snow came in that I was sitting in it almost up to my knees. I was finally moved to the front. To add to our problems, the roads were not plowed as soon as a storm began, but could be a day or so later. Dad was worried about a long steep hill we would have to climb. We did manage to get up the hill, but it was touch and go, with Uncle and I frequently jumping out to push. Finally Dad pulled off the road and put on the tire chains. This involved jacking up the back wheels to mount the chains. Then, when we ran out of the snowstorm, the dry pavement would destroy the chains in a few miles. It meant stopping again to remove them. A winter drive of a hundred or so miles was not undertaken without plenty of warm clothes, blankets, a shovel, sand, tire chains, and a tow-rope.

When I was eleven years old, Grandfather, who was a heavy pipe smoker, contracted cancer of the tongue. For the last few months of his life he lived with us while he was being treated at St. Michael's Hospital. I was very fond of my grandfather and was glad he was living with us, but I was upset that he was not well and was probably dying. When he did die, it was my first close encounter with death and it seemed such a shame that such a nice person had to die. On the way to the funeral, which was held in Sebringville, our car broke down and I remember being very upset because I thought that we would miss it. We did indeed get there; my parents rented a car to take us the rest of the way. Apparently seven passenger cars were not available, and this was a problem, since my father's seven passenger car had been depended upon to accommodate the pallbearers. Not many farmers had cars, so the pallbearers, who were all big men, had to squeeze into a five-passenger car.

Chapter 3

THE SCHOOL YEARS

LIVING IN SCARBOROUGH

The next place of interest was a house that my Dad was building. It was in Scarborough at Stop 14 on the single track streetcar system outside the city, which was called the radial cars. It was a single rail, with double rail at the halfway point - Stop 14. There were two radial cars on the route, and they could pass at that point. When we returned from the factory, my parents bought a lot there and built, with a little help, a minimum house as a base for a permanent house.

The Depression of the early 1920s - and the business competition from telephones - had reduced my father's call system business to the degree that it provided a living for his brother Chris, who ran the business, while Dad was at the cheese factory. However, the business could not support both. He was forced to sell out to an American intercom company. As a result, he retained his job in the new company, but he then had no other resources. We lived in the house in Scarborough near Stop 14 for a year.

My mother's sister, Aunt Nellie Moldy, along with her husband and three children, also bought a lot and built a house near us. Another sister, Aunt Aida, and her husband Frank Walsh, and another brother, Uncle John Flynn, also bought land nearby. They built homes as well. Unlike my parents, who moved many times as they upgraded, my aunts and uncles spent the rest of their lives in the homes they built.

While we lived in this house, there were two memorable events. The first one was the fire. At that time, the house consisted of three rooms: a kitchen - dining room, a sitting room, and a bedroom. The children slept in bunks on each side of the bedroom and my parents slept in a bed in the middle of the room. My sister Aileen was a baby and slept in a crib. A coal stove, known as a

Quebec heater, was in the sitting room beside the doorway to the bedroom. It was the only heat for the house.

Father had repaired the side curtains for his car. Side curtains were used instead of wind-up glass windows. He had given me a piece of the clear plastic to play with. This material was quite flammable. Not being aware of the danger, I had left my piece of plastic beside the stove near the door. This proved to be disastrous. The flammable plastic suddenly caught fire and exploded, spreading burning pieces all over the bedroom. Mother had put us all to bed for an afternoon nap. Suddenly there were fires all over the bedroom. In terror I yelled for Mother. She came running and found the doorway to the bedroom in flames. Running through the flames, she came into the room with her hair on fire. She grabbed a blanket and wrapped it around herself, smothering her burning hair. Grabbing up the baby Aileen, and standing in the doorway with her back to the flames, she ordered us children to run past her and out of the house. Although the blanket was smouldering, it protected her from the flames. Seeing us children safe outside the house, she went back in to fight the fire. She proceeded to pour buckets of water on the flames and succeeded in extinguishing them. Her neck, hands, and arms had burns, but none of the children had any. We had no phone, so when Father arrived home he found the house in a mess. Mother was already cleaning up. I remember Father praising Mother for her quick thinking and courage, but he also chastised her for the risk she took in fighting the fire. Fortunately the damage was not severe. After Mother's hair grew back and her burns healed, we got back to normal living.

I have many fragments of memories, such as playing with my cousin Jack Moldy, going to the Scarborough bluffs, and playing in a ravine, which had a pedestrian bridge across it. Some older boys hung me over the side of the bridge and left me hanging there. I finally had to let go. I fell to the stream below, sprained both ankles, and had to crawl home.

The other memorable event at that house was that I started school at St. John's Separate School on Kingston Road in Toronto. A mile walk took me to the radial car, Stop 14, where I took the radial car to the end of the line, then boarded a Kingston Road streetcar at Victoria Park for about a mile to St. John's. I was six and half years old. There were no school buses in those days. The first month, an older boy going to St. John's accompanied me. After that I felt I was old enough and did not need the older boy; my parents allowed me to be independent and let me travel alone. My son Paul showed the same independence on going to kindergarten. He was tall and had to pay adult fare on the bus as he was higher than a mark that was on the pole beside the driver. He soon discovered that he looked big enough that he could hitch-hike home from school and save the bus fare. Fortunately, one of our neighbors picked him up and reported his activity to us. That quickly put a stop to our five-year-old's entrepreneurial activity.

THE VICTORIA PARK AREA

The next fall, my parents had sold our property at Stop 14 to move to a house on Blantyre Avenue, closer to the school. I remember that there was an earthquake while we lived in that house. It was a semi-detached house, and my parents had asked the neighbour next door to keep an eye on us while they went to Loblaws for some groceries, which was a block away. They had also instructed me to watch over my brother and sisters since I was the oldest. All of a sudden, the house started to shake; things rattled, creaked, and cracked. My first reaction was surprise, and then fear followed by the need to get my siblings to safety. Then the door burst open - Mom and Dad came rushing in. They had been a hundred feet from the house when the earthquake struck. No damage was done. I remember my father putting on his ear phones to listen to his radio to hear if serious damage had occurred.

The homemade radio we had was operated from a storage battery and used earphones. I also remember receiving a Meccano set for Christmas, which consisted of mechanical parts that could be assembled into cars, cranes, towers, buildings, and almost anything that you could imagine. I enjoyed it and added to it for many years. In fact, I used parts of it to make gadgets many years later, when I started my own business.

Radios were a curiosity in the early twenties. I don't know if they were available commercially, but my father built his own. Neighbours came to our house to listen to the radio, particularly when Dad got a loud speaker so that several people could hear the radio at the same time. A big aerial (a wire that was many feet long) was needed to pick up the radio waves. I remember my Dad talking about his 'super heterodyne radio'. Crystal radios, which consisted of a special crystal and a so-called 'cat's whisker' would pick up radio signals that could be heard with earphones. The crystal radios were actually the forerunner of the modern transistor, which is a crystal with fixed contacts.

I can also remember telephones on which you had to twist a crank to activate it. Then an operator would ask you for the number and she would connect you. Later you could just pick up the receiver and hold it to your ear and the operator would answer. The automatic dial phone did not appear until my teens. It was very unusual to have a private line. In the cities a party line was for the use of two or three homes, but in rural areas the party line would serve up to a dozen people. Long-distance phoning was expensive and in many cases not possible because the phone companies were not inter-connected. Even as late as the 60s, some areas of USA had difficulty being connected to Canada. The availability of today's communication was not even dreamed of.

HOUSES ON LAKE ONTARIO

Our next house was on Lake Ontario at the foot of Lee Avenue in the Beaches. Many of our relatives and others criticized my parents for living on the lake shore with small children. My parents replied that there was no danger if the parents properly looked after the children and the beach was a great place for children to grow up, without traffic. Although the new house was still in St. John's Parish, we could use the streetcar to go to Corpus Christi School. To go to St. John's was a long walk uphill. I was about eight years old at this time. I acquired a set of roller skates and found that I could go to and from school faster on the skates than on the streetcar. Incidentally, children's streetcar tickets were 16 for 25 cents, and adult tickets were 4 for 25 cents. There was a mark on a post by the conductor that determined if you were a child. I was tall for my age and usually had an argument with the conductor about whether or not I qualified for the children's fare. I remember taking my first communion and riding home in my Dad's touring car (it would be called a convertible today) on a beautiful sunny day with the roof down and having a feeling of great joy.

For children, the Beaches district was a great place to live, with both the beach and Kew Gardens beside our house. In the summer we learned to swim and often played ball with Dad and Mom. In the winter our parents bought us older children skates and taught us to skate on the outdoor rink in the Gardens. The Gardens in those days had a toboggan slide and a sleigh slide where we enjoyed many an hour.

We also got the measles and were quarantined. Only the bread-winner could leave the house. Of course we got the measles one after the other, so the quarantine lasted a long time.

John E. Burgener

There had been a number of break-ins in the area and Dad often worked late or was out of town. For Mother's protection, Dad installed an alarm system that consisted of a siren on the roof and relays to turn on lights. A switch beside Mother's bed could activate the system. One night, when Dad was working late, as he was turning from Queen Street onto Lee Avenue a block from our house, the alarm went off. He heard it, along with all the neighbours and we children. I remember being terror-struck and rushing to my mother's room. Dad raced down the street convinced that she was being attacked. If not, he surmised, she would have turned the switch off. By the time he got to the house, two neighbours were already trying to get in the front door. He opened the door and, rushing upstairs, he found Mother and us children standing there, all petrified. Mother had turned the alarm switch on instead of the light switch. He turned the switch off. The next day the switch was moved.

While we lived here I was beaten up by a couple of girls who were much older than me. One restrained me while the other bashed my face against a wooden fence, resulting in a broken tooth. The nerve was exposed. It was painful; the most severe pain I can remember was when the dentist removed the nerve. I don't know whether a painkiller was used; if so it was not very effective.

As we three older children were no longer babies (although Ernie and Aileen were still quite young), Dad bought a large tent to accommodate all seven of us. Family camping was not very common those days. There were no minivans or station wagons, so Mom and Dad solved the problem by buying a used Cadillac limousine that had jump seats between the back and front seats, and had seating for seven. This was a big car - much bigger than cars in 2012. I remember Dad trying the Cadillac out on the Kingston Road highway. He was driving beyond the 35 mile an hour speed limit and a policeman on a motor cycle started to follow him. He said, "let's see if the police man can catch me," and speeded up. We lost the policeman. Using our Cadillac we went on our first family camping trip to Rice Lake. On this outing I had the excitement of catching my first fish. While swimming I was introduced to bloodsuckers, much to my horror. Over the next several years we made several camping trips to the Kawartha Lakes. The camp sites were basically open fields where you were allowed to pitch a tent. These fields were supplied with a dry toilet, but beyond that no facilities were provided. Camping at these sites was always a great and enjoyable experience for us children, but on rainy days I believed that my parents would have preferred a hotel.

A Broader Vision

For several years, even into the mid-thirties, we camped at Cranberry Lake with the Walshes and their four children (my mother's sister Aida's family), the Hogarths and their four children (my father's sister Rosa's family), and at least one other family of relatives. We would have these gatherings during the 1st of July weekend. These were great family weekends with a minimum of twelve children and six adults. The freedom and informality of these events would not have been possible at a resort or hotel, and they drew the family together. The family of my father's brother, Chris, and his grandchildren still camp together on July 1st weekend.

My parents chose the house at the foot of Lee Avenue because it was an ideal location for us children. It unfortunately was a very cold house, full of draughts and difficult to heat, so we only stayed there about a year. Again my parents chose a location that was best for their children, and so we moved to a three story house on the lake at the foot of Kippendavy Street, at Woodbine Beach. It was a very pleasant house surrounded by huge oak trees with a veranda on each floor facing the lake. There were three similar houses, and our house was the second house from the corner. The landlady occupied the first house. In the third house lived a single man. Further down the beach there were several other houses. Behind the houses were backyards with garages with a lane providing access from the side street. In front there was a sidewalk and then the sand of the beach. A beachfront park has now replaced all of these houses.

By now, it was the mid-twenties and all five of us children were no longer babies. My three sisters, my brother, and I enjoyed the beach in all seasons. It was like living in the country, even though we were in the city. I do not remember the beach ever being crowded. Even on hot summer days very few people ever swam. I can remember my father, who was a good swimmer, being the only person at the beach swimming. The beach stretched for miles with only a few houses nearby, giving us wide open spaces to play in. To the west of us along the shore was the Woodbine Race Track, a famous horse-racing track. In recent years it has been relocated to the west of Toronto. Beyond that was Ashbridges Bay, which was an inlet from the lake where fishing boats, some pleasure craft, and some old wrecks were to be found. There was also an abandoned sewage disposal plant where some teenagers played around, but we were warned by our parents to stay away.

ASHBRIDGES BAY

Ashbridges Bay was a great place to spend an afternoon. It was here that I discovered a partly submerged sailboat. After much pestering on my part, I convinced my father to come and look at it. He agreed that it did not appear to be badly damaged and could probably be repaired. His inquiries found that it had been abandoned some years earlier and no one seemed to want it. On a summer weekend two of my uncles, my Dad and I set out to salvage the boat. We managed with the use of block and tackle, much digging, pushing, and pulling to get the boat on to dry land. My Dad and I spent the next several weekends patching it. Finally, just about the time school reopened for the autumn, we got the boat into the water and it floated. Dad decided we should sail it to the front of our house so that it could be pulled up on our lot. This would make good winter storage, while also making it convenient to do further work. On the first weekend of September we set out from Ashbridges Bay with great enthusiasm. We had no sails and no motor, so our plan was to paddle it out past the weir at the entrance to the bay and then back to shore. Once near the shore, we would pull it through the shallow water for a mile or so to the front of our house.

The boat was about 20 feet long, and paddling proved to be slower than we had expected. It took about an hour of hard paddling to get the boat around the weir and back to shore. A wind had started to blow from the east, the direction we had to go. Two piers were in our way and we had to pull the boat around each of these obstacles. On the leeward side this was not too much of a problem, but on the windward side the wind and waves bashed the boat against the pier, destroying our weeks of handiwork. By the time we reached the second pier the storm had increased with big waves, so we decided to beach the boat on the leeward side of the pier until the weather was more cooperative. We pulled the boat up on the shore as far as we could. There was nothing to tie it to, so we could only hope the waves would not dislodge it. Getting up early the next morning, I rushed to look at our boat. It was gone. The storm worsened during the night and had washed the boat away. I found it, to my dismay, against the first pier, completely smashed. With my dreams of a sailing boat gone I went home and told Dad the disappointing news.

***

A Broader Vision

The Woodbine Race Track attracted some rough characters to the area. Coxwell Avenue, which was nearby, also seemed to collect rough families. Some of these people were often seen on the beach, but we were warned to stay away from them. Some would get into fights, but we did not stand and watch; we ran away. Unfortunately, some of them attended Corpus Christi School. One particular person caused trouble frequently. He would walk up to someone, and, completely unprovoked, would punch him or her in the face and then walk away. One day he walked up to me, pulled my glasses off, stamped on them, punched me in both eyes, and walked away. My parents complained to the school and the police were called, but as far as I know nothing more was done about it. Some weeks later, as my sister Marie was walking home, this bully punched her in the face. Dad found out where the bully lived and went to see his parents. When the bully's father answered the door, Dad started to explain why he was there. The bully's father told Dad to get the hell off his porch or he would beat the hell out of him. Dad decided the only way to solve this problem was to arm us. He gave Marie and I each a big heavy pencil box and said, "If this bully comes near you, don't wait for him to attack you - attack him. Hit him with the box with all your strength." The next time he approached me I started bashing him with the box. He backed off and never bothered Marie or me again. Some years later he was convicted in a murder. With current attitudes, many bullies never get hurt, and therefore it is a game. If they got hurt it would not be a pleasant game. The solution to stop a bully is to bully him.

About a block away from the beach, on the street beside our house, lived a family of four brothers. The youngest was in my class at school. He was a bully and his older brothers encouraged it. Walking to and from school afforded the opportunity for bullying. He did not bother my sisters and his bullying was mild. Not being a fighter, I tried to arrange my walking to avoid him, but was often unsuccessful. He would push me around, throw my hat or coat in a puddle, and mess up my books. Not wanting to be considered a coward, I never told my parents why I appeared to be so careless with my books and clothes, so when I got home I was again in trouble from my parents for my carelessness.

For a whole school year he pestered me. When the summer came I enjoyed some peace, as he did not frequent the same places I did. This was not to last. I spent a lot of time around Ashbridges Bay where the bully, either missing his bullying or looking for new places, started frequenting. Now he didn't just push me around, he started hitting, punching, and kicking. As usual I tried to avoid a fight. After a couple of these attacks I became annoyed. When the next attack started, I saw red. Without caring how much damage I'd do to either of us, I sailed into him with all my strength, punching, kicking, and doing anything I could do. To my absolute amazement, he turned and ran screaming. I was so mad that I didn't stop there. I attacked his older brother, who was at least two years older. He too turned and ran. That ended my problems with that family. Having been beaten up himself, it was not a game, and he was no longer interested in beating others. In fact, the family of the bully became friends of ours. Some years later this same chap (Bruce Daniels) was frequently seen on TV advertising CN Telex.

Many times after that I have encountered people who have tried pushing me around, and although I have always tried to avoid fights or quarrels, when I stood up to them, they have usually backed off. Occasionally I have been hurt, but the fighting back has always ended the pushing around.

EYES IN THE NIGHT

Another episode was the ghost that haunted this house. It was a large house, and having a few spare rooms we often had guests. The front bedroom on the third floor was very pleasant room with a porch. This was kept as the guestroom. One of our guests was my mother's father, an Irishman with all the typical Irish superstitions. He occupied the two front rooms of the three rooms on the third floor. The third room was a playroom for us children. His quarters included the third floor porch.

One morning after he had been with us for a few weeks, I came down to breakfast to hear him talking to my mother in a low but agitated voice. He seemed to be saying something about the little people had followed him from Ireland. They stopped their discussion when they noticed me, so I assumed somebody's children were coming to visit us. During the next couple of weeks I heard no more about children, so I forgot about the expected visitors.

About three weeks later I again heard my grandfather talking about the little people, but this time he was not whispering. He was emphatically stating that he was not staying in our house with those little people. When I asked, "Who are these little people that are coming to stay with us?" Grandfather answered that the little people were Leprechauns from Ireland. They were similar to fairies and he didn't like being in the same house as them, so he was leaving.

A Broader Vision

Mother argued that Leprechauns would not leave Ireland. He decided to visit another daughter.

Since Grandfather was no longer using the third floor front rooms, we children expanded our play area to include them. I was about ten years old but my youngest sister was only four years old. We now had summer weather and we often liked to play on the third floor porch. One morning when going to the porch, I could not open the front room door. Something seemed to be against it. When Dad came home from work he managed to push the door open. A heavy dresser had been pushed against the door on the inside of the room. We were all amazed. How could this heavy dresser get against the door? It could not have moved itself and there was no other entrance into the room. We began to wonder if Grandfather was right about the little people.

Other strange things began to happen. Aileen, my youngest sister, started waking up in the middle of the night screaming about big eyes. Ernie, who shared a room with me, was awakened on several occasions seeing large glowing eyes staring at him. Several times, just before dawn, Mother heard someone walking around on the third floor. When my father would investigate, there was no one there. These things happened off and on over several weeks.

Father and I never saw or heard any of these things. We insisted that Grandfather's fears of little people had awakened imaginations, so that any natural noise or light was imagined to be a ghost. Mother, when visiting Grandfather at her sisters, mentioned these happenings. He told her that he had also seen the eyes, and on two occasions he had seen the porch door open and close. He was now certain that it was not leprechauns. Instead, he thought that the house was haunted.

Every summer my cousin Pauline Walsh would spend a week or two visiting us. When she came that summer, Mother felt uneasy about letting her sleep in the front room on the third floor, our usual guest room. A bed was moved into our playroom at the back. One night Pauline came down to the second floor to the bathroom. As she started down the stairs, she noticed that the door to the third floor porch was open. While Pauline was in the bathroom, Mother heard footsteps on the third floor. Thinking one of my sisters had gone upstairs to visit with Pauline, she went up to investigate. As she ascended the stairs she heard the porch door close. Assuming my sister had heard her coming and slipped onto the porch to hide, she went to look. There was no one there.

Pauline complained the next morning that she had not slept well since the neighbor next door had spent most of the night working in his garden and singing to his flowers, "Moon, moon, shine on my pretty blue flowers." The back third floor room was the only bedroom that looked out on the backyard. Although our neighbor may have frequently spent the night so occupied, we were not aware of it. A few days later, my mother, when talking to another neighbor, was told that our next-door neighbor, who was a bit odd, often spent the whole night wandering around.

A few nights later, for the first time, Mother saw the eyes. A black shape with glowing eyes was leaning over her. She screamed, and as she did so the black shape disappeared through the door to the porch off her bedroom. Dad, jumping out of bed, rushed out onto the porch, where he saw a black shape climbing down a tree. When the shape reached the ground, it ran up the beach and disappeared. It was no ghost, it was our odd next-door neighbour. He must have worn a mask with lighted eyes. Dad also observed that each of the porches had trees with overhanging branches that would allow an agile person access to them.

Pauline's discovery and Father's observation identified our ghost. Father put good stout locks on the porch doors and we never saw the ghost again. Grandfather was still not convinced and refused to visit in that house.

***

My mother had a good voice and loved to sing as she did her daily chores. She encouraged us all to sing and got me to join the junior choir at church. It seems that I had a good voice, and was asked to join the senior choir to sing at the Latin High Mass on Sundays. I was only ten years old but I enjoyed the choir and looked forward to 11 AM Mass on Sunday.

***

NARROW ESCAPES AT THE LAKE

Since we lived on the beach, the lake was the center of our activities. In summer we built sandcastles and swam; in winter we played on the ice that accumulated along the shore. In those days, huge icebergs would form along the shore. To us children they were mountains, crevasses and caves. We spent many hours playing on them. We were warned of the dangers and in general did not take chances. Since the ice formed on the shore, if one fell in, the water was shallow. Occasionally one did get wet. As can be expected when children live so close to the water, there were some narrow escapes. One time my brother fell off a pier into water over his head. It was too deep for me and as I asked God for help and wondered what to do, I saw Ernie crawl along the bottom towards the shore, stand up where the water was shallow, and walk out. His guardian angel must have guided him.

The Burgener children circa 1928.

Another incident: for my birthday (March 10th), I got a model speedboat that was powered by a steam engine. I had to wait for warmer weather to test it out in the lake. On a late spring weekend, Dad decided that we would take the model out and run it along the side of a pier with one of us at each end to catch the model and send it back. This worked well and we soon had an audience. On one of the passes back to me, the boat appeared to be veering away from the pier. Being concerned about losing my boat, I leaned out too far and fell in. The previous summer this location had been shallow, but the ice and winter storms had deepened it. The water was now above my head. Being buoyed up by my heavy clothes, it appeared that I was standing on the bottom. Dad expected me to walk out. Instead, I was sinking. I could swim but the heavy clothes hampered me and I was having difficulty staying afloat. Fortunately the lifeguard was present as he was on duty on weekends. He had been watching the boat and realized my situation. I believe I was starting to get control when suddenly something hit me in the back and I went under. The next thing I remembered was that I was on my back being towed ashore. The lifeguard came into our house to phone for a relief guard while he got dry clothes. The newspapers ran an article on the foolishness of some adults who endanger their children. As well, Mother was angry with Dad. It was a great boat that I kept and played with for many years.

THE BARN

Mother continued to love moving. We would no sooner get settled in a house than she would start talking about moving. Somehow she would always find a better place. Four or five years was the longest I recall staying in any house. Probably the nicest house we lived in, during my preteen years, was the next house on Balsam Ave., which is still in the Beaches. It was a large old house with a small barn at the back of the property. The barn had two horse stalls, space for a carriage, and a hayloft with a swing-out crane to lift hay into the barn loft. It also had a couple of rooms, which must have been the groom's quarters. We did not have horses or carriages, but we did use it as a garage.

The barn was also a great play area to re-enact what we saw at the movies, and we played at Cops and Robbers or Cowboys and Indians. That is what we saw for ten cents at Saturday matinee movies, which always included a serial show that continued from week to week. It always ended with the hero falling off a cliff or being shot. The next week you would see that he was saved at the last second. Originally we would hear the gun shots or car crashes, but there was no talking. Later, talkies became universal. By the thirties sound movies had come into their own. Since there was no TV, it was only at the movies that could you see what was happening in the world. The movie always started with movie news. It was amazing to see action from around the world. The disasters were written up in the newspapers, but if you wanted to see the actual occurrence, you went to the movies.

At the back of the barn was a garden hidden from the house. One of my friends, bringing a package of cigarettes, suggested that no one would ever know if we smoked there. Of course my mother could smell the smoke as soon as I entered the house. She accused me of smoking and was quite annoyed at me. When Dad came home she immediately told him. I anticipated some punishment, but to my surprise Dad reacted entirely differently. He said that if I wanted to smoke that was okay with him. However, I should smoke openly and like a man. He suggested that we go and sit in the living room and both have a cigar. Feeling pretty big, I lit up my cigar and started puffing along with Dad. After a few puffs I began to feel a little queasy, but there was no way this was going to stop me. However, after not many more puffs, I became quite sick and had to quit. That took the glamour out of smoking. However, I did smoke a pipe for a while after graduation from university and did smoke an occasional cigar; still, I never became a smoker.

THE TRAILER

Since we went camping most summers, Father decided that, with the five children, it would be more convenient if we could set everything up at home and then arrive at our destination ready to camp. He visualized that a better but unusual way to go camping was to build a caravan to be pulled by car. There were horse-drawn caravans, but few (if any) were drawn by motor. The caravan or trailer, as it would now be called, was to be set up with running water from a water tank at ceiling level. It had a sink with a drain that led to under the trailer, a built-in gasoline stove, an ice box, a foldout dining table, and beds for seven - all the conveniences of home. As a base to build the trailer on, Dad bought a Buick, which had been damaged in an accident, but the frame was in good shape. Dad and I stripped the car down to its frame. My Uncle Frank had a similar Buick, and, deciding that the engine in our Buick was in better condition than his, we replaced his engine with ours. The exchange was made feasible by the foldout crane on the barn. His engine was sold to an auto wrecker for ten dollars. The remainder of the parts from the stripped-down car were sold to the junk dealers that roamed the streets in their horse-drawn wagons. The junk dealers would shout something that sounded like "rags and bones". I remember several dickering with my mother over the prices they would pay. We did not have blue boxes, government controlled recycling, or environmentalists; nevertheless, junk was disposed of.

Back to the trailer: a wooden skeleton was built onto the stripped-down car frame and was covered by sheet steel. The right side of the trailer folded down with a canvas top and had a double bed spring and mattress attached for Mom and Dad's bed. It also held two fold-up camp cots. There was sleeping accommodation for the other three at the rear. The kitchen was at the front and the center part was dining and sitting. Electric lights were included, which ran from a battery, charged from the car. Not as deluxe as a modern travel trailer, but a lot better than a tent on a rainy day.

It had one weakness. Since it was a four-wheeled trailer, it had to be steered as well as towed. Dad had worked out a system to control the steering using the tow bar. On trial runs it worked well. We started out on our first trailer holiday. By the time we reached Oshawa (20 miles away), the steering had broken and the trailer was swaying wildly from side to side. Other cars were staying away from us. Dad was afraid it would break loose and was crawling along. At last we reached a service station and pulled in. We spent our first night in our trailer at a service station in Oshawa. The next day Dad found a mechanic, who not only repaired the hitch, but also improved it.

This holiday was not meant to be an easy one. Uncle Peter Flynn (Mother's brother) had joined us at Oshawa on our way to the Kawartha Lakes. A few miles from Peterborough, Uncle Peter's car broke down. We spent the second night in a field by the highway while Dad and Uncle worked on his car. The next day we went on and stayed at several different lakes during our two week holiday. The trailer was used on two more holidays and then the Great Depression of the thirties hit. The second holiday was a trip to Pennsylvania, USA, to visit my mother's father, who had purchased a farm there. At the American border we were detained and had to go before a judge. I don't know why, but my father was taken into custody while we stayed in our trailer wondering and worrying. Whatever the reason, when he and my mother were brought before a judge, the judge condemned the authorities for holding us up and apologized to Mom and Dad. We were allowed to continue on our journey. It may have been because the trailer was not licensed. In later years, as trailers became more available, licenses were required in Canada. For the next several years Dad was too busy improving our house and feeding us to think about traveling.

DELIVERY SERVICES

    Horse-drawn milk wagons delivered fresh milk to our home every morning. Milk was not homogenized, so the cream separated and was at the top of the bottle. In the winter the milk would freeze and expand out of the bottle so that the cream would be half an inch or more above the bottle with the bottle cap sitting on top. The bread-man delivered bread and pastries every other day from a horse-drawn bread wagon. The fuel those days was coal. The coal-man delivered the coal from his horse-drawn wagon. He carried the big bags of coal on his shoulder to your coal shoot or into your basement. You counted the number of bags to make sure you were getting what you were paying for. There were no electric refrigerators those days, so the ice-man delivered a block of ice to your ice box from his horse-drawn ice wagon. Boys liked to ride on the back of the ice-man's wagon to get pieces of ice to suck on. The Eaton's man and the Simpson's man delivered the merchandise you bought with horse-drawn wagons. Some of the delivery men would hire high school students to help them make their deliveries, so they could cover larger territories. The horses have gone, and so have these services and jobs. The Eaton's man was the first to use a truck.

Chapter 4

THE 1930S – FARMING TO SURVIVE THE DEPRESSION

In 1930 Father recognized that times were going to be really hard. To ensure that they could adequately feed their family, my parents decided to acquire some land where they could grow sufficient food to feed themselves and their five children. In the spring of 1931 my parents bought a two-roomed house with a stone and mortar basement reached by a trap door in the floor. It was on a two acre plot and had sixty fruit trees: apples, pears, plums, and cherries. This property was on Indian Road in Lorne Park. There were no paved roads, no million-dollar houses, only farms. During the summer of 1931, Dad, along with some hired help, added three bedrooms and extended the two original rooms, making it suitable for our family. In September we moved into our new house, which was occupied by our family off and on for more than thirty years. During the Depression the land met my parents' objectives. We grew all our vegetables including luxuries like asparagus. The first year we planted two sacks of potatoes so that we would have enough for a year. To our surprise we harvested sixteen sacks, enough for several years. We had all the fruit we could eat including apples, pears, plums, cherries, strawberries, raspberries, and thimbleberries. Chickens provided meat and eggs. The house provided comfortable accommodation. If my father had lost his job, as so many others did, we could have lived on our small farm.

When we moved into our new house it was a big step down from our pleasant house on Balsam Avenue. It was basic, consisting of a living room, a kitchen and three bedrooms. My parents had a bedroom, my brother Ernie and I shared a bedroom, and Marie, Jennie, and Aileen shared the other. Water was from a well and had to be hand pumped at the wellhead. We had no bathroom so we had to use outdoor plumbing. Baths were taken in the kitchen in a washtub. The trap door in the floor of the kitchen was the entrance to the basement. In the modified house one of the original rooms served as the living room and the other with the trap door was the kitchen and dining room. This basement later served as our cold room for storage of fruit and vegetables. During our first winter Mother fell down this stairway, and although badly bruised and shaken, she was not seriously hurt. Dad decided that a basement with a proper entrance was essential and he started that winter to excavate under the remainder of the house. This was done by hand digging. By spring enough was excavated that a proper stairway and a furnace could be installed.

One of the first improvements was a water pumping system so that we could have running water in the house. Over the next few years Dad kept improving the house. He added a large living room, a dining room, and a bathroom. The original rooms became a den and a modern kitchen. It became a very comfortable house.

While my father was improving the house, my mother was doing her part. She never complained about the mess that came with continual construction. Instead, she kept it clean. She canned the food and by late fall she would have 500 quarts of preserved fruits, vegetables and chicken meat, some of which she would give to relatives who were having hard times. She would pack carrots, turnips, and other root vegetables in barrels of sand. Apples were put out on shelves and turned every week. Berries were made into jams. She made ketchup from our tomatoes. Once a month she would make root beer and bottle it for us to drink. Of course she also made good dinners from our home grown foods and looked after five children. She did her part in assuring that the Depression would neither hurt her family nor the relatives who needed help.

In the early thirties we could certainly have been classed as living in poverty. We never considered ourselves as poor. We recognized that our standard of living at the time was low, but we were happy and content and we were taking action to improve our standard of living. We knew others who were complaining about their poverty, even though they were better off than us and were doing nothing to alleviate it. In North America, to a great extent, poverty is a state of mind.

As a result of our low standard of living, I learned a great deal about carpentry, plumbing, electrical wiring, cement work, gardening, raising chickens, pruning trees and many other skills, including preserving food. I believe our low standard of living, if you may call it that, was of tremendous advantage to me. Dad fortunately did not lose his job, but earned much less than he felt we needed. He took on other part-time activities to supplement his reduced income. One of these jobs was servicing clocks in office buildings, churches, and institutions like hospitals and city halls. There were no electric clocks as we have today. The clocks in an institution were controlled by a main pendulum that operated from a battery. I often accompanied him on these service calls. When the problem was not too complicated he would let me correct it. He maintained this activity for many years after the Depression, servicing many of Ontario's public clocks including the old city hall in Toronto and the clock in the center of Niagara-on-the-Lake. Another activity was installing lightning protection. The protection was accomplished by mounting a vertical rod at the highest point on the building and a copper conductor to ground. This allowed the static charge to leak off before it built up a high enough potential to strike. He installed this system in many barns and buildings, including the Toronto City Hall. With this extra work my parents were able to actually increase their savings during the Depression.

PROBLEMS WITH THE SCHOOL.

The autumn we moved to Indian road I was in grade eight at Corpus Christi School in the Beaches area. Marie was in grade seven, Jennie in grade six, Ernie in grade four and Aileen in grade three. When we moved we naturally went to Lorne Park Public School. At that time it was a four-roomed school. The principal, Miss Smith, was also the teacher for grades seven and eight. She informed my parents that separate schools were so inferior that we would all have to go back at least one grade, and probably two grades. My parents put up an argument and the principal reluctantly agreed that she would try out those in the lower grades and see if they could meet her standards. However, there was no way that she was going to have her school disgraced by allowing me to try the departmental examination. To go to high school one had to pass the departmental examination known as the Entrance Examination. Dad went to the school board. They flatly stated that she was right: separate schools had very low standards. They further pointed out that she had been teaching in the

A Broader Vision

Lorne Park area for over forty years and was obviously very competent. One of the board members boasted she had taught him. On another occasion he admitted he could barely read or write. Dad next contacted the Department of Education and was informed that it was up to the school board.

I certainly did not like the prospect of spending an extra year in school because of her bigotry. Even worse, she was completely out of date in her choice of instructional material. The arithmetic she forced on us was not of the current century and her grammar was terrible. The other teachers were more up-to-date in their teaching methods and material, and they ignored her. Only Marie (in grade seven) and I were affected. Since I had an immediate problem, it was decided that I had to go back to Corpus Christi School. It was arranged with Corpus Christi that I would stay in Lorne Park until after Easter. The principal at Corpus Christi arranged to send me lessons so that I would not be behind. After Easter I went to live with my good friend Conrad Myers on Kenilworth Avenue until the end of the school year. I passed the departmental entrance examinations with honours.

The next school year in 1932, Marie and Jennie were now at Miss Smith's mercy. Dad had started immediately to retire Miss Smith by holding meetings and voting out the members of the school board. It took three years to have Miss Smith retired. She was seventy six at the time. She had started teaching in 1880. Instead of accepting the circumstances of the local school, my parents decided that the solution for Marie and Jennie was to send all the children to a separate school in Toronto. There were none near Lorne Park at the time. Since I had started going to St. Michael's College School in Toronto at Bay and St. Joseph Streets, they arranged for the others to go to St. Basil's School, which was in the same area. Dad drove us to school and home every day until an apartment was found and rented near St. Basil's School. We moved into the city until the end of the school year. We children were certainly fortunate in having such resourceful and concerned parents

When we moved into the city apartment we took our cat Topsy with us. Topsy was accustomed to much more freedom than could be allowed in an apartment. Whenever she got the chance to escape, she did. At the end of the school year we moved back to Lorne Park and Topsy was missing. My brother Ernie was especially upset, but we had to move and could not delay in order to find Topsy. A month later we heard a cat at the door. When we opened the door, Topsy ran in and started brushing its back against Ernie's leg. Ernie picked her up and hugged her with great joy. I do not know how she found her way from downtown Toronto to Lorne Park, but she did.

The following year I had my driver's license so I drove us all to school. By the end of that school year (which was my second year at St Mike's), Marie and Jennie were through eighth grade. By the time Ernie got into the seventh grade, Lorne Park School had a new principal.

I have many memories of my teenage years spent in the Lorne Park house. Indian Road was a nice place to live with lots of bush to play in, many pastures, several ponds, the Credit River, and the lake. The local postman with his family lived on Indian Road and his son Jim Lee became a good friend. Also, the Frasers lived on Indian road near us and Roy Fraser became a good friend. During my first summer I managed to buy a used bicycle from earnings made by picking fruit. This greatly expanded my horizons. Although working in our gardens required considerable time and effort, I had lots of time for other activities. One of these activities was building a model airplane. I spent many hours making wing ribs and body frames out of balsa wood. After the frames were assembled, they were covered with a parchment-like paper that was flexible and strong. After several months of working on it I mounted the little alcohol engine and Dad and I sent it on its maiden flight. It was not radio controlled so we flew it along Indian Road. It flew beautifully and landed a few hundred feet down the road. Both Dad and I were elated. I flew it a few more times, but the last time a gust of wind blew it off course into a tree by the side of the road and it fell to the ground a wreck. It never was repaired.

SWIMMING

In hot weather farming was dusty and sweaty, so I often rode my bicycle to the lake or the Credit River for a swim instead of a bath. In those days the Canadian National Exhibition held a marathon swim in Lake Ontario in front of the Exhibition Park. Originally it was a triangle, seven miles along the shore, seven miles out and seven miles back - a twenty-one mile swim. It was later reduced to ten miles, in several laps, in front of Exhibition Park. Johnny Walker, a former marathon winner, had a marathon swimmer's training camp at the mouth of the Credit River. My friends Roy Fraser, Jim Lee and I spent some of our spare time hanging around this camp. The camp opened in early June (the lake was too cold, but the Credit River was endurable), and the swimmers would start practicing. They would swim from the mouth of the river up to where the Queen Elizabeth Highway Bridge is now. Then they would swim back, sometimes with us trailing along behind them. We did not become marathon swimmers, but we did improve our swimming. Fred Glen, a Lorne Park young man, whom we hung around with occasionally, did train and enter the marathon for a couple years. The second year he came in tenth out of about thirty. We thought that was pretty good.

All three of us often would cool off and wash off from our farm work by riding our bicycles to the beach at Lorne Park for a swim when the weather was warm. When Lake Ontario was not too cold, we would swim to the lighthouse at Port Credit, climb upon the crib, and rest before returning. On one such swim Roy and I almost didn't make it. While we rested, a strong offshore breeze sprang up. As we swam back we realized that the offshore surface current was preventing us from making much headway towards the beach. It took us more than an hour to finally make shore at the point of land that is now occupied by the Clarkson oil refinery, which is about five miles from the light house.

The Credit River offered warmer water and several good places to swim. The mouth of the river was warmer than the lake but had a strong current that could easily drag an unsuspecting swimmer into the frigid lake water. During my teenage years two swimmers drowned at the mouth of the river. My uncle Frank Walsh saved a third person. Someone pulled a teenager out of the Credit River, and Frank - who was trained in artificial respiration - worked on him and revived him. On another occasion a friend of mine panicked when he discovered the current was dragging him out into the lake. Fortunately, I was nearby and got him to hang on to my shoulder while we swam for shore.

Another good swimming hole on the Credit River was just south of the present QEW Bridge. It had a diving board, and at this location my brother Ernie learned to swim. He would dive into the water and depend on the other swimmers to tow him to shore. After a few dives he learned to swim. We often rode our bikes up to the Huttonville dam to swim, where the river was even warmer. When cars became available to us, a gang of us often spent a pleasant afternoon there.

Roy had a sister named Thelma whom I thought was very pretty. I was always in awe of her and I liked to be in her presence. She had lots of attention from hockey, baseball and football players, so I asked myself, **Why would she be interested in me?** With my poor eyesight I could not see the puck or catch a ball, so I did not get involved in these sports. There were girls that I met at St.

Mary's Church but I always assumed that they were not interested in me - and even if they were, I did not know what to do about it. There was one girl that I had known for several years: she was a daughter of friends of my parents, and she started visiting whenever her parents visited. She was a nice person and I was comfortable with her. Her father did not like me (for some unknown reason), and stopped visiting my parents. As a result, she had no reason to visit. I suspect her father disliked any male who showed an interest in her, because as far as I know she never married. The only girl I was completely at ease with was my cousin Pauline Walsh. In her case, though, there was none of this falling in love business. When I think back, I realize that I was a good catch. I went to a private boy's school and had a car. Very few teenage boys had a car those days. However, not knowing what to do about girls meant I had more time to pursue the things I was good at.

LIVING ON INDIAN ROAD.

The house on Indian Road by 1935.

The large tent Dad had bought several years before for our camping trips now became useful again. Dad set it up near the house and Ernie and I slept there most of the summer. To us this was like camping. Every summer Conrad Myers (a friend from first grade), would spend a couple of weeks with us, and of course we slept in the tent where we could talk all night without bothering anyone. With the call of the whippoorwills, hoot of the owls, and barking of dogs, it seemed as if we were far from civilization. When younger cousins visited, we told them the calls were wild Indians. Frank and Aida Walsh and their four children would usually visit us for a week or two in the summer. The parents used the bedroom that I shared with Ernie while all of us cousins slept in the tent. Pauline, their eldest, was my favourite cousin, and every summer she would spend several weeks with us. Pearl (their other daughter) was younger and got a severe case of poison ivy every time she came. She only visited us when the whole family did and was limited in what she could do because of the poison ivy.

One advantage of having spent seven months at Lorne Park School was that I got to know the students of my age in the area and often joined some of them in outdoor activities. Winters were spent going to school. On the weekends and school holidays we skated on the many frozen ponds and skied and tobogganed on the hills. As we grew older we had skating parties on the Fox Estate pond. A fire would be built in the center of the frozen pond, and we would skate and sit on logs around the fire, chatting and singing. Several New Year's Eves were celebrated doing this. As we made our way home through the bush after one of these skating parties, my brother Ernie ran a twig into his eye. He stood there with the twig attached to the branch and sticking into his eye. We were horrified and stood there certain that he was blinded. Carefully cutting the twig from the branch with my pocket knife, we led him home with the piece of twig sticking out of his eye. My parents took him to a doctor who removed it. Fortunately the twig had gone into the side of the eye and had not punctured the eyeball. He had a sore eye, but no permanent damage. In those days you went directly to your own doctor in emergencies at any time of the day or night for personal treatment - not the hospital emergency as is done today. The doctors were true professionals.

The Mississauga Golf Course had some good hills for skiing. My original skis were handmade by Dad. Coming from the mountain area of Switzerland, he was familiar with skiing. Skis were not available in Toronto in the early 1900s, so he simply made his own. Dad introduced skiing to the Toronto area by skiing on the toboggan runs in High Park. Dad was an avid ice boat sailor in his bachelor days. The Toronto Bay did not have ferries running all winter and would freeze over, allowing the entire bay to be used for ice boat races.

Skis were still not readily available in the early thirties. Dad suggested that it would be good experience if I made skis for my brother, my sisters, and myself. To encourage this, he bought five pairs of hickory 2X4s. Under his guidance I crafted five pairs of skis by hand. They served us for many years of skiing. Mine finally wore out, but there is still one of the other pairs in the family.

In the early spring, when the sap stared to run, we children would enthusiastically tap the maple trees on our property and the surrounding bush for maple syrup. Mother would keep a large pan on the kitchen stove to pour the maple syrup into as we collected it. We would end up with a few quarts of delicious syrup and some maple sugar. As the spring progressed, I (with some help from my sisters) would become busy with pruning the fruit trees, preparing the garden and hatching eggs. We always had lots to do; we were never bored. When working the gardens, we often found arrowheads. We were, after all, living on Indian Road.

Indian Road was a mud road in those early days. In the spring it was almost impassable and several times we got stuck in the mud at the dip in the road just before what is now Tecumseh Park Rd. When this occurred we would have to get Cecil Denison to pull us out with his team of horses. The road through the valley, which was just east of our house, went down to the bottom, and every heavy rain would wash it out. In later years the township put in a culvert and raised the road level.

Storms seemed to be more severe with lots of wild lightning. Our house was struck by lightning in one of these storms and a huge spark jumped from my metal bed to the hot water radiator at the foot of my bed. I think I rose vertically out of the bed in fright. The bed lamp and its cord were fried; the automatic water pump started running and stopped when the water pressure got so high the motor burned out; the hand pump on the well became electrified; the hydro service panel suffered; but no other damage was done.

On another occasion a violent storm blew down the hydro poles and the live wires were about a foot from the ground across the front of our lot. We could not leave our property. The wires were live and this meant certain death to anyone who touched them. My father phoned the hydro department, but the line was continuously busy. Eventually Dad took a branch that had blown down from one of our trees, threw it across the wires, forcing them down to the ground. As a result, the wires shorted and caused a fuse to blow, turning the power off. He then drove us children over the wires to school in his car and then he went to work.

As mentioned before, we had chickens, and of course a chicken's yard, which was fenced in with chicken wire. Dad, who loved animals, bought each one of us children a rabbit. He housed them in cages in the chicken yard. We children would take them out and play with them. Since the chicken yard was well fenced, we could see no reason to leave them caged and so we allowed them the run of the chicken yard. However, being rabbits, they started digging. We ended up with a real rabbit warren under the chicken yard. This meant that the rabbits were not that readily available to us children, but we still got to play with them. Now cute baby rabbits appeared and there were many of them. Although the chicken wire fence was dug into the ground about a foot, the rabbits soon dug below it. I believe we populated the Lorne Park area with rabbits.

Another time, as Dad and I walked home from the Lorne Park station through the farmer's fields, we saw a crow with an obviously broken wing. Dad attempted to pick it up, but it tried to run away. Dad caught it and carried it home. Dad then bound up its wing and gave it water and some food, which it consumed. He kept it in a box for some days until it appeared to be better, then put it with the chickens. With a broken wing it could not fly. At first the chickens would stay away from the crow, but later they accepted it as one of them. The crow was friendly to us and seemed to try to talk to us. It would always go to Dad when he walked into the chicken's yard. However, come spring (and chick-raising time), Mom observed that every day she would have one less chick. Apparently the crow was helping itself to a chick every day. Mom insisted that our need to raise chickens for food was more important than feeding a crow, so Dad found someone to take it.

✳ ✳ ✳

In the thirties stealing gasoline was a common occurrence. With a length of rubber tubing, it was easy to siphon gasoline from a car's gas tank. In fact, cars that were parked where they were not easily seen were often emptied. Someone on Indian Road emptied Dad's tank every second week. Dad said he did not object to him stealing the gas as he probably needed it, but he would be happy if the thief would leave enough gas to get to a gas station. Dad kept a two gallon can of gas as an emergency, but when the thief started emptying the extra can of gas as well, Dad finally decided to stop the gas stealing. We had an Airedale dog that was quite possessive of our property. It usually lived in the house, but it did have a doghouse. Since it was about time for the gas thief to show, Dad put the dog in the doghouse overnight. The second night the dog was in the doghouse, in the middle of the night there was some growling and barking, then a scream followed by someone running up the road followed by a growling dog. Our gasoline was never stolen again.

Chapter 5

CARS

Driving in the twenties and thirties was much different than today. There was very little motor traffic in the early twenties, but still lots of horse-drawn traffic. By the thirties motor traffic had increased, with a corresponding decrease in horse-drawn traffic. There were still a few electric cars and some Stanley Steamers that used coal oil to produce steam. The speed limit on the highways was 35 miles per hour and generally 20 miles per hour in cities, except in busy areas where the limit was 15 miles an hour. I do not remember when traffic lights started to be used, but I do remember the policemen standing in the middle of an intersection and directing the traffic. In some places there were islands in the center of the intersection for the police to stand. However, I remember one of my Dad's employees being hit by a fire truck going through a red light, and the controversy that followed. The fire truck had the right of way, but it had gone against the red light without slowing down and did not have its siren on. The fire department had to pay damages because it did not proceed with caution when crossing against a red light. There were no tractor-trailer trucks and in the twenties many of the trucks had solid rubber tires because the pneumatic tires could not stand the loads. Tires that lasted 5000 miles were unheard of.

Gasoline was dispensed from a glass bowl on a pedestal so you could see the gasoline going into you tank. However, whether you got good measure depended on your height because of parallax. During my early driving days I remember being horrified at the new price of gasoline, which was at 30 cents per imperial gallon (approx 4 litres). The police rode motorcycles and bicycles; they did not have cars. In my early days there were some paved roads, but there were no super highways. By the mid-thirties Ontario was getting paved. For much of my younger days the only major highways in Ontario I knew of were the Dundas (Highway No 5) and the Lakeshore (Highway No 2). Not till my teens did I find out where the other highways were. When accidents occurred they caused tie-ups worse than today. I remember sitting in a tie-up on the Number 2 highway in the twenties. We were coming home to our east Toronto house on Sunday evening after an afternoon visit with some friends in Oshawa. We did not arrive home until sunrise. There were no parallel roads, so we just waited.

The spring of 1932 I had finished elementary school and we were looking forward to our first summer in Lorne Park. Since I had finished elementary school I felt very grown up and wanted to drive. Dad let me drive but said I could only drive on Indian Road with him. I had noticed an old truck sitting in Bert Denison's farm behind our property and asked Mr. Denison if I could have it. He said he would be glad to get rid of it. I told Dad that I could have the truck if he would pull it out and bring it to our place. Dad said he would go and look at it and see if it was worth pulling out. We both went and Dad checked it, cranked the engine, and said it turned over, which meant the engine was not seized up and could probably be repaired. It was pulled out to our property where I could work on it. With help from my father it took me about a month of searching through dumps, wreckers, and service stations to get all the parts I needed. I did get it running. I stripped the body off leaving the front, which contained the dashboard, steering wheel, and pedals. The gas tank in those old models was under the front seat, so it acted as the driver's seat. As I was fifteen at the time, I could not get a driver's license, so I drove around the meadows and local farmers' private roads and along Indian Road where traffic of any kind was seldom seen.

My friends Roy and Jim were not to be outdone so they searched around for old cars. Jim got a Model T that was actually running from a friend of his father. Roy's father had a 1922 Chevrolet pickup truck that had caught fire. I traded Roy my Model T for his father's Chevrolet. Basically the body had been destroyed and the wiring burned, but otherwise it was unharmed. I quickly got it repaired and stripped down to the front dashboard. Now the three of us each had a hot rod. We had a lot of fun with them racing in the fields, driving along lanes, and competing for the heaviest load to tow. The Chevrolet was faster and more powerful than the Model T. Along Indian Road my Chevy could get up to 48 M.P.H. while the Model T peaked out at 39 M.P.H. This was, of course, according to our speedometers.

Stripping the body off the truck.

When I turned sixteen in March of 1933 we were living in a rented apartment in the city because of the problems with Lorne Park School. Early in the summer I wanted a driver's license. The local constable, Bert Denison, was the driver license tester. His farm was the one where I got my original Model T. I asked for a test and he set it for the next Saturday morning. He arrived at our house and the test started. My Dad and Bert sat in the back of the car and had a beer and discussed world events while I drove around for half an hour. I doubt that Mr. Denison paid any attention to my driving. I passed and got my license.

That fall Dad bought me a 1927 Ford Model T to drive my siblings and myself to school in Toronto. That ended my hot-rodding, so the next summer I converted the old Chevy into a tractor. I replaced the differential and rear wheels with an old truck rear end that had large wheels. I bought a Star transmission from an auto wrecker and put it between the Chevy transmission and the differential. In this way the old Chevy had a low - low gear. It made a very powerful tractor. One of my brothers-in-law became confused with the double gear shift while playing with it. He backed the tractor into the brick wall of the garage and had started to push the wall in before he realized what he was doing and quickly turned the engine off.

My hot rod converted to a tractor.

The Ford Model T Dad bought for us to go to school was not up to the daily grind of driving to school in Toronto. Something was always breaking down. Dad then bought a 1927 Chevrolet for me for $125. This was a real car. It had a standard clutch and gearshift, instead of the Model T's pedal shift. This car served me for more than nine years.

AUTOMOBILES IN THE TWENTIES AND EARLY THIRTIES

Automobiles were not as rugged in those days as they are today. Every autumn I had to do a major overhaul on my Chevrolet to keep it running. One of its weaknesses was the rear axle. It would snap without warning and leave me stuck somewhere, needing a tow. To replace it meant jacking up the back of the car, removing the entire rear end, including the wheels, the axles, the differential, and the springs. Then I had to disassemble the differential, replace the axle, and reassemble it all. I got so good at it that I could replace an axle in less then an hour. Fortunately I always kept a spare one on hand. On one occasion I was on my way to a date when the axle broke just as I was leaving the driveway. I was only a half-hour late for the date.

With the frequent repairs I also upgraded the car. I finally replaced the rear end with a later model, which had a higher ratio and was more durable. My Uncle, Jim Hogarth, was a teacher of motor mechanics at Danforth Technical School, so I arranged with him to loan my car to the school for training of students. In this way I had the cylinders rebored to a larger diameter, the iron pistons replaced with aluminum pistons, and the carburetor replaced with a down draft unit (used on later cars), instead of the up draft in use those days. These changes increased the engine power considerably. To compensate, an extra leaf was added to each spring to stiffen the suspension. The top speed of the car was increased from 55 mph to 85 mph. Unfortunately this also increased the gasoline consumption, and gasoline had gone up to 30 cents an imperial gallon. To overcome this I modified the carburetor so that I could open a valve in the intake manifold to let in more air. Once the car reached cruising speed I could adjust the extra air intake so that the car maintained its speed, but had no extra power. I could get up to about 35 miles per gallon on the highway.

This car served me up to my third year in university. It taught me a great deal about automobiles. My brother Ernie learned to drive with it and on several occasions it acted as the family car. One day while driving home from University along College Street, a car suddenly cut in front of me and forced me to stop. Two men jumped out and came towards me. Anticipating an attack I grabbed the crank I always kept beside the front seat and raised it to warn the attackers I was prepared to fight. They stopped and the closest one pulled out a wallet and showed me. He was a plain-clothed policeman and was arresting me for stealing the car. I protested that I owned the car, and showed the ownership card. He said since most people keep the ownership card in the glove compartment so that was no proof. They made me get in the police car and the other policeman drove my car as we went to the nearby police station. They did not put me in a cell but made me sit there while they did some phoning, then asked me some questions about where I lived and what I was doing on College Street. They said a car like mine had been reported stolen. Since there were very few cars like mine still on the roads, they had assumed that my car was the stolen one. When they realized their error, they apologized and let me go. My father was very annoyed and wanted to sue the police for false arrest. I said they had not mistreated me and I felt if we sued them then they would be out to get me.

Unfortunately, the hand brake never worked well. One day, while driving along Kingston Road in the Beaches area, I was stopped by a policeman. On testing the brakes, the hand brake failed. I was given 48 hours to report with the brake repaired or face a fine of $25. The fine was a lot of money and the pressure of university did not allow time to repair the brake. I handed in my license plates and sold the car to an auto wrecker for $20. The experience gained from this automobile has served me in many ways. Besides learning a great deal about the mechanics of automobiles, I acquired the confidence to deal with any mechanical device and found this confidence to be a great help at university and throughout life. I also learned to be a good driver. I drove for more than 75 years covering more than a million and a half miles without causing an accident. I have been in accidents in which someone else ran into my car, but I have been able to avoid many other possible accidents. I have on several occasions driven with others where I have seen an impending accident and compelled the driver to react. On one occasion we were going up a hill when two cars - one passing the other - came over the top. The driver simply drove towards them. A head-on collision was inevitable. I grabbed the steering wheel and swung us into the ditch. We missed a head-on by inches. Being in the ditch was a lot better than a head-on collision at highway speeds.

I don't know what year the Model T towed out of the farmers field was - I would guess about a 1921 model. There was little change in Ford in those early years up until 1929 when Ford produced the Model A. This was Ford's first real car with a gearshift and foot pedal accelerator. The 1927 Model T Ford that Dad bought for me in 1933 was little different than the one I towed from Denison's farm. General Motors and Chrysler, along with smaller manufacturers, were producing real cars even before the twenties. My '27 Chevrolet, certainly after the upgrade, was close to average cars today in performance. Cars like Cadillac, Chrysler Imperial, and Pierce Arrow were very similar to cars today. The advances are probably more improvements like power steering. It makes it easier to steer, especially when standing or moving slow (such as when the driver is parking). Of course they did not have the safety items such as seat belts, shatter-proof glass, or anti-skid devices.

A Broader Vision

Four-wheel brakes were only on expensive cars. Chevrolet added them in 1928, as did Ford in 1929. They could stop faster and it was mandatory to carry a sign indicating that the car was so equipped. I do not remember when hydraulic brakes came into use (which greatly improved braking), because it was difficult to equalize the mechanical brakes. Automatic transmissions and car radios became available in the forties, and soon after air conditioning was available, but few bought them. I felt as safe in rough driving conditions in our 1935 La Salle as I did in the average modern cars. However, I enjoyed driving performance cars ever since I upgraded my '27 Chevrolet. During the war cars of any type were basically unavailable. When I started my business I could not afford them.

In 1963 I bought a Chevrolet sport model with an eight cylinder engine. I enjoyed driving that car. In fact, I did what my father had done back in the twenties. Driving out of Florida on a back road to avoid traffic and police, I was cruising at 95 to 100 miles per hour when I spotted a vehicle some distance back pacing me. I figured that if it was pacing me it must be a police car. I was about 15 miles from the Georgia border and decided I would race it. I crossed the border before he got to me, and I of course immediately slowed down because I expected the Georgia police were informed that I was coming.

In 1968 I bought my first Oldsmobile Toronado, a performance car. I drove Toronados until they downsized and downgraded it in 1985. By then I was approaching seventy and decided to slow down a bit, so I bought Oldsmobile '98s. In my driving days I was a hard driver, on occasions driving from Toronto to Chicago to do a day's business and return the same day. This was a distance of 450 miles each way. In those days the speed limit on the Interstates was 80 miles per hour (130 km/h).

On one occasion, just before Christmas, I started for home from Montreal at about 8 PM, and when I reached Ontario I decided to speed up. The speed limit on the 401 at the time was 70 miles per hour. At the speed limit it would be well after midnight when I got home. The traffic was light so I speeded up and was traveling between 100 and 110 miles per hour. I was doing this for some time while watching for someone to pace me. I finally saw a car pacing me some distance back. I passed a truck and pulled in front and slowed down to 80 miles an hour. Not long after a police car was behind me and pulled me over. The rule at the time was that a police car had to follow you for a quarter mile to charge you. He charged me with ten miles over the speed limit and gave me the ticket. He then said, "Okay, you got the ticket - how fast were you going? I followed you at speeds up to 120 miles an hour for ten miles and could not gain on you."

I replied, "It must have been someone else as I was going about 80."

He said, "It was you - come on, how fast were you going?"

"About 80."

"You liar! Get going," he said.

I held the speed down the rest of the way home.

On an empty highway in Nevada where there was no speed limit I pushed a Toronado up to 160 miles an hour (265 km/h) and it still had acceleration left. The tires apparently could not take it and started leaking. It appeared that the centrifugal force of the high speed caused the fabric to separate. I have driven on European highways where these speeds were not exceptional.

Chapter 6

HIGH SCHOOL YEARS

After second year at St. Mike's I occasionally drove, but most of the time I took the commuter train from Lorne Park station. This station was eliminated when the Go Train started. Dad did the same. As the train home did not leave Union station until 5:20 PM, I had two hours to kill every afternoon. Often I would go to the detention room and study, usually to the consternation of the detention master since he did not have my name on his list. Other afternoons I would walk down to Dad's office at Adelaide and Bay Street.

When the weather was good there was a man without legs who sat on a board with castors selling pencils at that corner. I would often stop and talk to him. He had lost both legs in an accident and was interesting to talk to. Of course I felt sorry for his situation, but he said he did this because it gave him a chance to be out and be with people. He also gave stock market suggestions to those who talked to him. One day he was not there and my father said he had died. The write-up in the newspaper pointed out that he had been a very good at investing and left a fortune when he died.

At my father's office I could find an empty desk and do my homework, or I could go to the repair shop and watch the technicians do their work. My father was always carrying on some experimental program. One program I remember was his attempt to record sound magnetically on iron wire. He did succeed but it was very poor quality. Magnetic tape was not available at the time. I believe now that if he had moved the wire fast enough he would have succeeded. I also remember my Dad complaining about what he called "squawker boxes" cutting into his business. These were two-way electronic intercoms that you pressed to talk and released to listen. They were cheap and non-specific, whereas his intercoms were connected directly to the person called and offered high quality sound. Additionally, they were housed in walnut or quarter sawn oak or other types of wood.

In the same building that Dad had his office there were some mining exploration company offices. One of these was a silver mine prospect. Apparently the project was not a success and closed down. They threw out all their silver containing samples and Dad retrieved them. Some of these samples had veins of silver two inches thick. Dad put the rocks in our coal furnace and a tray in the ash pit to collect the molten silver. He collected about twenty pounds of it. Dad then silver-plated everything he could handle - even electric light fixtures. Our house was silver-plated.

* * *

St. Mike's was a private school for boys. We had to wear a suit and tie or a blazer to class. It was essentially a boarding school, and to keep the boarders busy, we had to go to school on Saturday morning. To compensate, there were no classes on Wednesday afternoon. Wednesday afternoons were often spent in the Royal Ontario Museum, only a few blocks from the school. I enjoyed these afternoons and learned a lot about archaeology and geology. On the Wednesdays that I did not visit the museum I caught a passenger train bound for Chicago. It was a train of many coaches, pulled by a huge steam engine that left Union Station in Toronto at 1:30 PM. The train was a through train with only a few stops. However, it was allowed to stop in Port Credit (a so - called whistle stop) to pick up passengers only, not to let them off. Since it was a whistle stop, the train had to slow down in case it had to stop to pick up passengers. The conductor slowed it down enough for me to jump off. I then walked the remaining three miles home. On Saturdays I always took this train and walked home from Port Credit. With all this commuting throughout high school, I did a lot of walking. I rarely used the streetcar to go from St. Joseph Street to the station. Instead I took about a two and a half mile walk, then a mile and a half each way from home to Lorne Park station. All this walking probably contributed to the good health I enjoyed in my high school days. I had no serious sickness and rarely had a cold.

HIGH SCHOOL JOKERS

St. Mike's, like any other school, had its bullies and jokers. One bully was a boarder and liked to bother the day students, like me. The rule at St. Mike's was that if you were caught fighting, you had to put on the gloves, get in the ring, and fight it out. I ended up in the ring with this chap, and although I did defend myself, I did not like boxing. At that time Jujitsu was in vogue and my friend Roy Fraser and I decided to learn it. We became quite proficient at it and could toss one another around. There was a joker in my class who liked tossing books out windows and making a joke out of the detention the student got for not having his homework completed. He did this to me. But the joke that really angered me was when he released the brake on my car, letting it coast down the driveway onto the street. Fortunately it did not cause an accident.

After the next class he stood up and taunted me. I pushed at him and he did what I wanted: he punched at me. I grabbed his arm and twisted and he ended up on his back over a desk. I was afraid I had broken his back. He got up went to his seat and went home after the next class. Each day I expected the police to come and arrest me. He finally came back to class after three days but said nothing, and the police did not come. No one messed with me after that.

St. Michael's school was attached to St. Basil's church, where there was a noonday Mass every day. It was convenient for students to attend. I often did so, and although I was not a brilliant student, I believe that my success in high school (usually being in the top ten of the class) was aided by these Masses, along with a lot of studying. Languages, particularly Latin, were my weaknesses. Mathematics and science were my strengths. Trigonometry I enjoyed so much that in the first two months of the three semester course, I had studied the whole course on my own. The teacher became aware of this and had me spend his classes tutoring those who were having difficulty. Physics was another love. Again, I studied all the texts being used and ended up helping the teacher with the experiments. With all this studying, and the time spent on commuting, I had very little time for social life during the school year.

St. Michael's College was a private school run by the Basilian Fathers, and as such, one had to pay tuition. My parents suggested that I attend St. Michael's but said I would have to pay the tuition myself. At that time tuition was 150 dollars a year. This was a month's pay for many. I earned the tuition by the allowances my parents gave me for working on our small farm. Fortunately my father had a job throughout the Depression. A lot of the physical work fell to me: pruning trees in the spring, planting and cultivating vegetables, looking after the chickens, and harvesting our produce and fruit. As well there was work to be done on the house, for example the excavation (by hand) of the basement.

When I turned sixteen and had a car, I started selling our surplus fruit by peddling it door-to-door in the city. My brother Ernie and I would pack the fruit into baskets, load the baskets into my car, and fill up a two-wheeled trailer pulled by the car. We would then go to West Toronto and knock on doors. My brother Ernie was a cute ten-year-old with a very charming smile and he did better than I. We sold our apples at 25 cents for a six quart basket. This was about 10 cents less than the stores. What we had not sold by the end of the day we would offer the local stores, selling them our baskets at ten cents, plus we would offer our windfalls at fifty cents a bushel. For most of August and part of September we would do this twice a week. After my second year at St. Mike's I had no difficulty meeting my financial obligations, and both Ernie and I had some spending money.

Packing apples to sell in the city.

THE SOCIAL FORUM

There was much poverty during my high school days due to the Depression. At St. Mike's we were encouraged to help the poor by personal sacrifice. On a side street near Spadina Avenue and Queen Street, a place called Madonna House had been opened to help the poor in the district. This was founded by a Russian Baroness (Baroness De Hueck) who had escaped from the Communists. A number of students from St. Mike's, including myself, went there to help distribute food and offer any other help. Since I lived in the country, I arranged with neighbouring farmers to send a truck to bring out a group of the poor in the area to Lorne Park to pick vegetables like potatoes, carrots, beets, turnips; vegetables that keep. Two men showed up. The driver decided it was not worthwhile for two people but instead offered to deliver vegetables to the two that had shown up. Poverty is often self-inflicted.

Besides poverty, the 1930s were a period of social unrest. Communism was believed by many people to be the answer. Toronto had a Communist mayor, Tim Buck. There were May Day parades throughout Toronto with thousands of participants singing "The Communist International". Frequent rallies in Queen's Park beside the Ontario Parliament buildings were held denouncing the government. Communism was promoted by the limited vision of the media, the labour unions, the schools, the universities, the intellectuals, and a well-organized and Russian-financed Communist party in Ottawa.

Today the horrors of Communism are well known, but in the thirties it was the saviour of the world. Few people recognized its true nature. Communism states that the only thing that survives is the State. Therefore the individual has value only if useful to the State. If not useful or an impediment to the State, they should be eliminated. We have seen the consequences of Communism. Nevertheless, the intellectuals of the thirties praised it. One wonders how the so-called intellectuals were so easily fooled and showed such lack of intellectual vision. Of course the same lack of vision is being shown today in climate control, carbon tax, and many other areas promoted by shallow thinkers or those with an agenda. In the thirties, and even today, few are wise enough to realize what they are advocating.

Olga Laplant who managed Madonna House did recognize the shallow thinking. She introduced me to the Social Forum, an organization that was advocating Christian social teachings as a contrast to Communism. It had been started by a Father Sullivan at Ottawa University. A monthly paper was published interpreting Catholic social teaching to current events. The organization consisted of members who wrote articles for the paper, organized its distribution, held meetings, gave talks, tried to counter Communist propaganda, and worked to influence young people to live as Christians.

What social life I had time for throughout high school and university centred on this society. The main centres of activity were Ottawa, Montreal, and Toronto, where large groups were involved. We even had annual conventions where several hundred people would attend. One of the activities of the members was to sell the paper after Sunday services on the steps of the churches. Most pastors permitted this, although some refused. The paper was also mailed to many individuals and smaller groups across the country. In later years I met several people from other parts of Canada who were familiar with the Social Forum. We distributed the paper at meetings such as May Day Communist rallies and parades, meetings held by radical and Communist groups, and wherever we felt that Christian social teachings should be heard. By some odd mistake, three of us were invited to an anarchist meeting in Toronto. The meeting was called to order and the chairman started discussing weapons caches in the Toronto area. Suddenly one of those present stood up and asked for our identification. We presented our invitations, which probably saved our hides, but the meeting broke up with everyone shouting and blaming the other while we beat a hasty retreat. We at least ruined their meeting and possibly damaged their trust in each other and the effectiveness of their organization. We often found ourselves in such difficult positions, but fortunately, though often threatened, no one ever got hurt.

We also encouraged the spiritual life of our members. We got the bishop's approval for dialogue Masses, in which the congregation joined the priest in saying the Mass. It was said in Latin but was the forerunner of the modern vernacular Mass. Our greatest recognition came when the Pope appointed a new Apostolic Delegate to Canada. His first official act in Canada was to recognize the Social Forum by inviting the members to a private meeting in each of the three cities. In Toronto we were invited to the bishop's palace to meet the Apostolic Delegate. About fifty of us were met at the door by a priest and shown into a conference room where the Apostolic Delegate was waiting for us. He said that our work was known in the Vatican. He praised us and gave us a special blessing from the Pope. It is possible that groups like ours saved Canada from becoming a Communist state.

A Broader Vision

This group, as I mentioned earlier, formed the basis of my social life. After selling papers on Sunday the members would meet at a snack bar and have coffee. We had numerous social gatherings and outings. Many of the members found their spouses in the group, while others became priests. As I will explain later, I met Elinor O'Neill there, who became my wife. World War II brought an end to the Social Forum and as far as I know nothing has replaced it.

Chapter 7

AFTER HIGH SCHOOL AND MY JET ENGINE

I graduated with honours from St. Michael's College High School in the spring of 1936. I had hoped, though not very confidently, that I would win a scholarship. However, I didn't, so I felt that I probably was not university material. I certainly did not have the financial resources. I had found chemistry and physics in school interesting, so I looked for a job in such places. Fortunately my father had business dealings with the J.F. Hartz Co., a drug manufacturer on Grenville Street in Toronto. I got a job as a shipping and receiving clerk there. It was heavy work and forklifts were not available. When I started I could barely drag a two hundred and twenty pound (a hundred kilogram) bag of chemicals. After a few months I had no difficulty in heaving such a bag on my shoulders. This job not only built my muscles, but also convinced me that without a higher education, this was the way I would spend my life. I felt that with the help of God I could do more with my life. The chemists and engineers in this plant had much more interesting jobs. I decided to save every penny I could so I could apply to go to the University of Toronto the following fall.

The summer while I was at Hartz, my sisters Jennie and Marie and I were all in our late teens. My sisters, being concerned that choices for potential husbands were too limited in Lorne Park, wanted to move into the city. My parents, always doing the best for their children, decided to do so. They rented a unique one-hundred-year-old house at 79 Edgewood Avenue. It had a big veranda at the front and a large sunroom on the side. It had a front stairway from the entrance foyer. It also had a stairway from the kitchen, which connected to two rooms at the back of the house, probably servant's quarters. The house was on a large property with huge old trees, including a barn, which we used as a two car garage. We lived there throughout my university days.

My mother, probably concerned about the evils of the city for teenagers, made a rule that we all had to be home and in bed at 10 PM. To make sure that this rule was enforced, she did not allow us to have a key. If you came home after 10 PM, you had to ring the doorbell and face Mom with an explanation for being late. On one occasion I was playing poker with some friends and the game did not finish till after midnight. I decided I was not going to ring the doorbell and face my mother. The bedroom that Ernie and I shared had the roof of the sunroom outside our bedroom window. I decided I would climb on the roof and enter my bedroom through the window. I had no difficulty getting on the roof, but I could not open the window from outside. I knocked on the window to awaken Ernie. Ernie awoke, but seeing someone at the window assumed it was a burglar, he let out a shout. My father came running into the room and turned on the light. Seeing a man on the roof he called for Mother to call the police. She did. The neighbour next door awakened and saw someone standing on our roof. He also called the police. By the time my father recognized me, the police were already coming with the siren screaming. My attempt to quietly sneak in woke the whole neighbourhood. As a result, my father insisted that my mother's rule of not allowing us a key had to change, and Jennie, Marie and I got a key. However, the 10 PM curfew still applied.

Once I invited Elinor to spend a weekend at our house just before I left for Arvida. Elinor, whose family never went to bed before midnight, was dumfounded when my mother insisted it was 10 PM and bedtime. My brother Ernie (who joined the Army when he was eighteen) would come home on a leave, usually arriving in Toronto after 10 PM. He would go to Elinor's house where he knew someone would be awake.

MY JET ENGINE

The summer I was working at Hartz (when we moved to Edgewood), I became interested in marine engines. I wondered why the water itself could not be used instead of a piston in an engine. It appeared to me that an engine could be built such that the burning gasoline could react directly on the water instead of pistons, crankshafts, drive shafts, etc. To test this I designed and built an engine, which consisted of a pipe with a right angle bend in it, to be immersed in water with the horizontal part under water and the top of the vertical part out of water. The top of the pipe had a valve system for inlet and outlet gasses and a spark plug. Connected to the inlet valve was a manifold with a bellows controlled by a small electric motor, which also controlled the valves and spark plug. The air gasoline mixture was injected into the head by the bellows and the spark ignited the explosion mixture. The arrangement was not satisfactory. If the gasoline did not ignite immediately, it floated on the water. When ignition did occur, the gasoline on the water would ignite, and then the air gasoline mixture in the bellows would explode. This resulted in a few minor fires in the basement, which my mother never heard about.

I rebuilt it so that the air was injected into the head first, then the gasoline. This worked better, with ignition occurring each time. At this point I was operating it on one ignition at a time with a minimal charge. It seemed to be working so I mounted it in a vise on the workbench to try a continuous run in air on a one second cycle, with a full charge of gasoline. I started it up. Ignition occurred immediately and a flame about two feet long shot out of the lower end, followed by another and another. Each time the bench gave a shudder. I reached to turn it off, but the engine broke out of the vise and slid along the bench, spilling gasoline all over. A second later there were fires all over the place, including on me. I dashed over to the laundry tubs, where as a precaution I had attached a hose. I sprayed myself, then the fires around the bench. Fortunately, except for my burned clothing, no serious damage resulted. Mother was entertaining her bridge party at the time and complained of the noise and smell of gasoline, but knew nothing of the fire. Dad discovered what had happened and recommended that testing be curtailed. Together we did a few more tests in air and water and decided that it had real possibilities. To establish priority we went to a lawyer and took out a caveat as a first step to a patent. This was during the year before I started at the University of Toronto. Starting university, I then became too busy to pursue it. I actually had made a jet engine. I would have pursued it had I not gone to university, and no doubt would have become a multi-millionaire. As I have often observed, a university degree can make you rich, but it can also prevent you from becoming rich. Many graduates stick to their specialty, even though the opportunity and capability is there for more lucrative activities.

OTHER INTERESTING EVENTS

We did not abandon the Lorne Park property, but spent much of the summers there, enjoying the country atmosphere. We did prune and spray the fruit trees, but did not cultivate vegetables or raise chickens. Ernie and I often enjoyed the peacefulness of a winter weekend in Lorne Park. We did, however, have a break-in one winter. The most valuable thing stolen, from my point of view, was the .22 calibre rifle my grandfather had given me. It was a Swiss rifle that he had as a young man. The next summer I saw the thief with my rifle and accused him. His response was to slip a bullet into the breech, point at me, and challenge me to try and take it. I wanted to go to the police but Dad pointed out that he was from a rough family and would probably burn our house down if I did so. However, Dad posted signs on our house that stated the house had been wired with high voltage electricity and any unauthorized entry was dangerous and was at their risk. We had no more break-ins.

Doug Bond, a student at St. Mike's, became a very good friend and we enjoyed many things in common. However, he lived in the city and I lived in Lorne Park. When we moved to Edgewood Avenue, I discovered that he lived a block away. That was a pleasant discovery and we were able to enjoy one another and his family. His brother, Al, belonged to the Corpus Christi Church Tennis Club. My sister Marie also played tennis, and got to know Al and often played with him. They fell in love and became husband and wife. My sister Jennie met her husband, Jim O'Neill, and my sister Aileen met her husband, Alfred Williams, while in this house. Apparently moving from Lorne Park accomplished my sisters' goals.

The large room on the second floor of the house, accessible only by the back stairs, became my study. Between my second and third year at U of T, I had not found a summer job. I had taken on several projects to earn the money needed. I had sold a hearing aid exhibitor at the Canadian National Exhibition (which was held in Toronto in late August) a model of how sound affected the ear and started to build it in my back room study. At the same time my sisters, who often took advantage of the large living room, dining room, and sunroom combination of this house, were having a party. It seems that some of the guests at the party asked where I was and were told I was "working on my ear". My sister Jennie's boyfriend and his sister Elinor were at the party. Elinor wanted to know what I was doing with my ear. Jennie brought her up to my back room study where I was building the CNE exhibit. Elinor, with her beautiful light red hair, was dressed beautifully and looked stunning. Although I knew her at Social Forum meetings, she had been just one of the girls. Seeing her that day changed my point of view.

Elinor O'Neill in her twenties.

A month later at a Social Forum party I invited Elinor to be my date. She accepted and I had the most enjoyable time I ever had at any previous party. She was a delight to be with.

THE UNIVERSITY YEARS

The years at U of T were busy ones. The courses I enrolled in - mathematics and physics - were considered the most difficult courses offered by the university. When registering I had to be interviewed by the Dean of Mathematics. After looking over my high school record, he commented that of the fifty odd registrants, only two others and myself had not won scholarships. He felt that the course was too difficult for me and said that I should take a lesser course. Before deciding on the course, I had done a lot of thinking and a lot of praying, and was convinced that I should take this course. I had a different vision than the professor of what I could do with God's help. His comment did not lessen my decision. I replied that I had every intention of taking the course and graduating from it. His reply was that he admired my determination but that he thought I was a fool. Twenty eight students passed into second year and I was one of them. So was one of the other non-scholarship students. Of those twenty eight, only fourteen graduated. Five graduated in straight physics, myself and one other in physics and chemistry, one in mathematics, and one in astronomy; five accepted a commission in the Navy and took their fourth year in naval electronics. Two of those fourteen were non-scholarship. It was a tough course.

In first year the method of marking examinations made you appear worse than you were. The exams were set so that no one could finish them. The one who got the highest mark got 100%, and everyone was graded against this mark. There was always one who was way ahead of everyone else, hence most got very low marks. In the first year Christmas exams I averaged 28%. I was devastated. When I started comparing with others, I discovered that I was about average. The professors didn't make this known until later in the year. This trick did discourage several students and many of them transferred to other courses.

We had a great deal of freedom with no requirement to attend classes or labs. It was up to the student. After first year we had the same freedom in the department libraries and labs as graduate students. Thus it was possible to put in extra lab or library time. In fact, it was expected. It was not unusual to see math and physics students leaving the physics building at 10 PM when the building closed. In organic chemistry, if you didn't show up in the lab on Saturday morning by 8 AM (which was not a regularly scheduled lab), you could expect a black mark. The final mark was based mainly on assignments with examinations only making up a small part of the total. The assignments were onerous. For example, in applied mathematics we had ten problems a month to solve and it took the whole month to solve them. Each department did the same.

The room under the balcony to the Great Hall in Hart House was the unofficial room for math and physics students to meet and help one another with their problem solving. Little time was left for anything but studying and some praying. Nevertheless, I enjoyed my courses and felt satisfied with what

I was learning. Second and third years were the most difficult for me. In those years we took not only all the physics and mathematics courses but also all the honour chemistry courses. As a result we had forty hours a week scheduled in labs and lectures. At the beginning of second year there were twelve physics and chemistry students. At the beginning of third there were three, one of whom was a repeater. Third year was similarly tough, with many of our lectures in the professor's office. The demonstrators and professors implied that only one would make it to fourth year. Fortunately, two made it. The repeater didn't. Fourth year I chose the physics option, which meant I got less chemistry but more physics. This was my easiest year. There was much less pressure, with more time given for assignments, and the courses seemed easier.

One course in mathematics was tough. It was a course in advanced algebra. There were eight undergraduates and fifteen post-grads in the course. Except for this course, fourth year seemed so easy that I worried that I was taking it so easy that I might fail.

Shortly after Christmas companies started looking for graduates. I had decided to do post-graduate work in solid-state physics, the new electronics field that was just opening up. I arranged with the physics department to be a demonstrator, for which I would be paid, so the prospective employers were of no interest to me. At this point a Mr. Rammer, from the Aluminum Company of Canada, approached the physics department in search of a graduate in physics who had a good background in chemistry. Dr. Burton, who was the head of the department, approached me and suggested that I see Mr. Rimmer, if only as a courtesy. He knew that I planned to do post-graduate work. I went to see Mr. Rimmer at the Royal York Hotel and had a pleasant chat, but I informed him that I planned to continue my studies. I forgot about Mr. Rimmer, but not for long: three days later, in a morning lecture, Dr. Burton stated that any student who turned down a job that was essential to Canada's war effort would not be allowed to do post-graduate work in the physics department. We students wondered what that was all about. I found out in the next lecture. Dr. Burton's secretary interrupted it to say that I had an urgent phone call in her office. Anticipating that my parents or siblings were in trouble, I answered the phone in fear. When I answered, it was Mr. Rimmer offering me a job to start immediately. I was taken aback and pointed out that first, there was still two months before the end of the school year and I intended to graduate. Additionally, I had already arranged to do post-graduate work and therefore would not be

A Broader Vision

available. He replied that graduation was not a problem, as I had a good record; special examinations would be arranged so that I could get my degree. As for post-graduate work, he assured me that the experience I would gain in this job would open many post-graduate doors at the end of the war. Furthermore, I was desperately needed and would be doing a great service to Canada. He then suggested I think it over and let him know in two days. I was astounded.

When I got off the phone, Dr. Burton said that due to the war they had decided not to accept new post-graduate students, since graduates were needed in the armed forces and war industries. Moreover, I was the only graduate in the U of T - and possibly in Canada - that fit Mr. Rimmer's unique requirements. After discussion with my parents, I concluded that further studying at Toronto was not possible and it was too late to apply to other universities. The alternatives were a war job or the armed forces. As Dr. Burton said, if I uniquely fit the Aluminum Company of Canada's needs, I would be more useful if I took their job, rather than go into the armed services where I would be just another graduate. My father's company was a war priority company since he was involved with communications and he offered me a job working for him. Although he offered $250 a month against the Aluminum Company's offer of $125 a month, I felt that the need at Alcan was greater, and that the experience would probably be greater. As I later found out, I would have been refused by the armed forces and drafted by Alcan, since Alcan had the highest priority.

The university did arrange special examinations. They were all oral except two: one in mathematics and the other in physics. In mathematics I had to solve a differential equation. For the physics class, the professor asked me to summarize the year's work in ten words or less and gave me fifteen minutes to do it. If I was able to do that, he reasoned that I understood the essence of the course. I wrote ten words and took fourteen minutes to do so. He commented that I could have done it in seven words. That was the shortest and toughest exam I ever had, and thanked God for inspiring me to choose the right words. I got my degree with second class honours. If I had continued to the end I might have got first class honours, but on the other hand, I might have failed.

Graduation Photo - 1941 Mathematics, Physics, and Chemistry

EXTRA-CURRICULAR ACTIVITIES

During my years at university I lived at home and my parents provided room and board along with other incidentals, but I had to cover my school expenses. Between first and second year I spent a month as a bellhop at the Royal Canadian Yacht Club on Toronto Island. The salary was $30 a month with no tips. I quit. More money could be earned by selling fruit from our Lorne Park orchard. At the end of the summer I did not have enough for tuition. I went to see Father Basil Sullivan, Registrar of St. Michael's College, and pointed out that I would have to postpone university for a year to earn more money. He said that I had done very well in first year and he wanted me to continue. He said that I should keep whatever money I had for expenses during the year and he would look after the university fees. Due to the generosity of St. Mike's, I

A Broader Vision

continued my studies. I have contributed to St. Mike's all my working life in order to help other students.

The next summer I did get several jobs. I spent six weeks as a truck driver for New Method Laundry, filling in for drivers on vacation. I peddled fruit grown on our Lorne Park property door-to-door in Toronto and cleaned up a warehouse after a fire, as well as any odd job I could find. As mentioned earlier, I sold a hearing aid exhibiter at the Canadian National Exhibition an idea for his display, a working model of an ear, which he bought. I made enough to cover my fees and expenses. Between third and fourth years I got a contract to build public address amplifiers, for which I had a net profit of $7.00 per unit. I could finish one in a day and therefore earned $42 a week. I was rich, never having previously done better than $20 a week. Furthermore, I was able to continue to make them during the school year, earning $14 a week.

With money in my pocket and being free of concern about finding odd jobs, I spent more time in social activities. Although I participated in Social Forum activities, I rarely took out any of the girls. However, in the spring of 1940, Elinor, who was a member of the Social Forum, had her tonsils removed at the Toronto General Hospital. I felt it my duty to visit her, since it was so close to the university. I found it a very pleasant duty, apparently over staying my visit and causing a relapse, so that she had to stay an extra day. That same winter Elinor injured her knee in a toboggan accident, landing in the Toronto General Hospital again, for ten days this time. Needless to say, it was my duty to visit her, which I did every day. I was also more aware of her charms as a result of her summer visit as I worked on my "ear" project. Elinor was easy to be with and my visits were the highlight of my day.

That year one of the Social Forum members had a New Year's Eve party to which I took Elinor on crutches. After the party we all went to a 5 am Mass at the cathedral. Elinor was on crutches in an evening dress and didn't have a hat and, since women always wore hats in church those days, she wore my fedora. I remember how proud I was to escort this lovely, plucky girl into church. From then on Elinor was my special girl. On many occasions I remember visiting her and massaging her bent knee. She remained on crutches for many months; the only treatment was massaging and exercising. Although I was not the only one massaging her knee, I made sure that I got my share.

As I mentioned earlier, after second year I had both more money and more time available, and therefore had more of a social life. My friend Doug Bond (who lived on Edgewood) and I bought a canoe the summer between second and third year. The Sunnyside Amusement Park on the lake on the west side of Toronto closed down and they sold their canoes. The canoes were known as Sunnyside Cruisers. They were beautifully made cedar-strip canoes, but the builder did not know how one should be built. They were round bottomed instead of flat bottomed. The bottom of a canoe should be wider than the top. A canoe should displace more water when tilted, thus giving it stability. The Sunnyside Cruisers with the round bottom were very unstable and several times we ended up in the water. One beautiful summer evening my sister Aileen and her boyfriend borrowed the canoe for an evening paddle. I warned Alfred about the lack of stability. The lake was very calm and they enjoyed the leisurely canoeing till after dark. They were turning around to head for home when the canoe rolled over. They were a considerable distance from shore. Alfred could easily swim to shore, but he did not want to leave Aileen. He suggested that Aileen shout for help since a female voice would carry further, but she said she felt silly doing that and suggested they push the canoe to shore. After half an hour of pushing they still had a long way to go. Aileen finally started shouting for help. Fortunately a man living in a house on the shore went out on his second story balcony to enjoy the summer evening. He heard the cry for help and phoned the police. Shortly thereafter a police boat with search lights found them. They were in the water for almost an hour. Luckily it was late summer and the lake was warm. After that, Doug and I would not let anyone else use our canoe. To stabilize it we built an outrigger.

On another occasion my brother Ernie and I paddled to a corn roast at Scarborough Bluffs, which was about a six mile paddle. While we enjoyed the corn roast, a strong wind came up and the lake became very rough. When we started for home, the canoe was swamped within a few feet from the beach. With its lack of stability there was no hope of pushing it out beyond the breakers and then getting in. We had to pull the canoe along the shore. When we got to the Victoria Park Water Works, we pulled the canoe up as far as we could on the beach and walked home. We picked it up the next day and brought it home by car. Lake Ontario is **not** a good canoeing lake.

During this time I dated several other girls but always came to the conclusion that I preferred to be with Elinor. Only one other girl had really interested me: Mary Anderson. I first met Mary at the Social Forum office on Scott Street, Toronto, while I was working at Hartz. I thought she was the most beautiful girl

A Broader Vision

I had ever seen. I decided there and then that she would be my girl. Although I dated her several times and of course saw her at SF activities, she always seemed disinterested. At any rate, I had become more involved with university and had little time for such frivolities. In my fourth year I tried to renew my relationship with Mary, but although she showed more interest, I always came to the same conclusion: I preferred to be with Elinor.

Chapter 8

THE LAB AT ALCAN, ARVIDA

When I departed from Union Station on March 30th, 1941, twenty days after my 24th birthday, I knew that a chapter of my life had closed and that a new one was opening. As I traveled through the night to Montreal (in a berth, which was an experience new to me), I was excited by what lay before me. I was sad to leave home and friends and was concerned about my abilities. Mr. Rimmer had said that I would be involved in the application of physical and chemical methods to production control. I did not know what that meant. I said five decades of the rosary and left it up to God.

The next morning in Montreal at the head office of The Aluminum Company of Canada, I filled in a bunch of forms and had a medical examination. I was taken out to lunch with three other recruits and then left on my own to catch the 8:00 PM train for Arvida. Having been to Montreal a couple of times, I knew my way around to some extent. I spent the afternoon wandering around, including a visit to Ste. Jacques, where I prayed that what I was doing and would continue to do in this new chapter of my life would be the Will of God. After eating supper in a small St. Catherine Street restaurant, I boarded the train for Arvida. It was a twelve hour ride through the wilds of northern Quebec up to Lac Ste. Jean and down the Saguenay to Arvida. I was to make this trip many times in the next few years. In winter this was the only way in or out unless one had a high enough priority to fly on the few flights servicing the area.

A Broader Vision

April 1st 1941. The day I arrived in Arvida.

On arrival in Arvida I had been instructed to go to the Saguenay Inn, where I was advised that I would be sharing a house on Radin Road with some other new arrivals until space became available in the Inn. I would have my meals at the Inn. There was a charge of $30 a month for room and board. After breakfast, which was served in a beautifully decorated dining room with a whole wall of windows overlooking the Saguenay valley, I went to 10 Radin Road. Here I was assigned a bedroom on the second floor of the three bedroom house. After settling in I walked to the laboratory building, outside the plant gates, and asked for the spectrographic laboratory. I was directed to the basement, where I met my boss: Wiley Taylor. He was about 35 years of age and was in charge of routine testing of pot metal using a spectrograph. The readiness of an electrolytic reduction pot to be tapped was checked by semi-quantitative spectrographic analysis. The technique used in the spec lab was the state of the art at the time. Using a logarithmic rotating sector in front of the entrance slit produced a spectrum line, whose length was proportional to the concentration of the element that produced the line in the spectrum. The first couple of weeks were interesting, but by then I knew all there was to know in this lab. With nothing to do but routine testing, which any technician could learn to do in a week, I became annoyed that I had been dragged out of school and prevented from doing post-graduate work for this. Expressing my dissatisfaction to Wiley, he gave me some general semi-quantitative spectrographic work to do on some special samples. I had studied Gerlac and Switzer's work on semi-quantitative methods at U of T, so this amused me for another couple of weeks, but again I felt that I was wasting my time.

After about six weeks I went to see Mr. Rimmer. I explained that I was occupied with technician jobs and if Alcan had nothing more important for me to do, I was resigning and applying to the Navy. As a graduate in physics, who had completed the officer's training course at U of T, I knew I could get a commission as a technical officer. He replied that the rearrangement of technical staff was taking longer than expected and that shortly I would be transferred to a new department. He further stated that the Navy would not take me from Alcan and that other technical people had tried and been refused. I later had this confirmed when one of my contemporaries, who, unhappy with his position, applied to the Navy and was offered a commission. As soon as he tendered his resignation to Alcan, he got a telegram cancelling his commission. About two weeks later I had contacted the Navy, but before I heard back, Mr. Rimmer called me in. He informed me that I was being transferred to a new department (known as the General Technical Department of the Aluminum Company of Canada) and would be on the Montreal head office payroll, as this department was independent of any plant. Further, I would be working with Ross Callon to develop spectrochemical and other physical methods of production control, with the immediate objective of replacing existing time consuming chemical methods. He commented that the plant was expanding so rapidly that existing methods of quality control could not handle it. Therefore it was urgent. Needless to say I was elated. I never heard back from the Navy. Probably the Navy informed Alcan, which resulted in speeding up the rearrangement.

TECHNICAL PROGRESS

Ross, who had graduated with his master's degree in physics from McMaster University the year before and had joined the company at that time, was already working on setting up an expanded spectrochemical lab. With my chemical background, plus the experience in spectroscopy for which U of T was famous, I was expected to complement his efforts. I accepted this challenge with vigour. In a matter of weeks we had our plans laid, equipment ordered, work orders were approved for building changes and special equipment was to be made by the instrument shop. We were given the highest of priorities, even to the extent of having a spectrograph flown across the Atlantic from England. In six weeks we had our new spectrograph set up and quantitative method development begun.

Our first job was to use the spectrograph to perform the analyses the chemical labs were currently doing. After a few weeks of work (with much overtime) Ross and I felt ready to start running samples in parallel with the chemical lab. We were amazed at how well our procedures worked. In fact, we demonstrated that the chemical procedure was producing erroneous values for silicon. This did not go well with the chemical lab, resulting in much discussion, extra testing and many heated arguments. After about a month of parallel operation, Mr. Rimmer ordered that we would be responsible for the analyses of three of the pot lines. We had to go on three shifts since the pots were tapped on a 24 hour basis. Ross, one technician and I handled all the work that would have required twelve chemical technicians, and we reported the information two hours after receipt of samples, as compared with eight hours from the chemical lab. After a month of this we had full approval to set up whatever was needed to take over all metal analyses. We were one of the most favoured departments in the company; anything we needed or wanted, we got. We ordered two more complete spectrographic setups from Hilger in England and one from ARL in California, all on high priority. By the spring of 1942, less than twelve months after I arrived, our routine spectrographic lab was daily analyzing over 2000 samples and reporting 10,000 determinations on a turnaround of 30 minutes with a staff of twenty one technicians and four supervisors. It was estimated that it would have otherwise required three hundred and fifty chemical technicians, plus the facilities for them to work and the turnaround would have been eight hours.

There were other benefits as well. The plant, besides producing pure metal, also produced certain alloys, particularly a high manganese alloy. They had been plagued by contamination in the pure metal by alloys. Running the samples spectrographically, it was easy to check for metals other than those being routinely analyzed. We had on several occasions noticed that a run of samples would all have the same concentrations. This was improbable, but possible if all the pots had exactly the same treatment. However, on checking the trace impurities we found that these suspect samples had identical concentrations. By the very nature of the process, this was impossible. We suspected that the sample-takers were goofing off by taking a series of samples from the same pot, then labelling them as if they came from the pots that were supposed to be sampled. We advised the plant supervisors, but nothing came of it. We suspected the supervisor knew it. Not only did this defeat the purpose of control, but also it could cause mix-ups in the blending. We again mentioned our suspicions to the pot room foreman and were told to "F" off, as he didn't need any analysis; he knew when pots were ready to tap.

On the midnight to 8:00 AM shift a few weeks later I spotted a run of ten samples, presumably from pure metal pots that all contained 3% manganese. They all had identical analyses. If samples were off grade, we were to call the foreman and report it so that immediate action could be taken. I phoned the pot room foreman and explained that there seemed to be a sample mix-up. I suggested that he should not tap those pots until they were all resampled under his supervision. He replied that no stupid chemist was going to tell him how to run the pot rooms and hung up. Not only were the samples wrong, obviously he had a mix-up in the designation of the pots, as the samples had come from supposedly pure metal pots. Normally the results were phoned in if off-grade and then hand delivered by a mailroom employee every four hours to the various departments. Anticipating trouble, I marked the reports "Urgent" and had one of my staff deliver the reports.

We also analyzed the blended metal and later in the shift the blended metal showed manganese contamination. Due to the fast spectrographic analyses, the blending furnaces had been converted to continuous pouring. Unless the blending was stopped, the manganese contamination would take some time to clear and a lot of metal would be contaminated. I phoned the blending furnace foreman and warned him of the contamination. He replied that he had not received any metal from a manganese pot and since it was spectrographic analyses he didn't believe it. At that point it was about 3:30 AM. Deciding I had better have some backup, I called Ross Callon. He arrived about 4 AM, confirmed my work and on phoning the blending furnace foreman, he got the same answer. That night and the early part of the next day over three hundred thousand pounds of metal were contaminated.

The next morning, after the analytical results on the ingot metal were reported, all hell broke loose. We got a call from Mr. Rimmer that 300,000 lbs were off grade and wanted to know why we had not issued a stop order. We explained how we had been ignored. Needless to say, the foremen claimed we had not contacted them. Fortunately I had backup: the written reports, which I had personally made sure were delivered during the night, were on the desks of the foremen. Under chemical control where the metal was blended on a batch basis and no analytical reports would be available for 8 hours, this kind of problem never arose. If a mix-up occurred, it meant that a batch of about 10,000 lbs. maximum was spoiled. Furthermore, the chemical department only reported their results and basically had no contact with the plant. Ross and I had pointed out that with continuous pouring we needed authority to stop production. No such authority had been given. A major shake-up resulted in the pot and furnace rooms, resulting in the responsibility of sample taking and the authority to issue a stop order to the pot rooms and the blending furnaces being given to the labs. From then on, no one in Arvida questioned spectrographic analysis.

Because of the quick turnaround, it was possible to accurately analyze the pots before tapping and thus make sure that no off-grade metal was blended. This greatly reduced off grade melts and resulted in the shipping quality of the metal being upgraded to 99.5%. Since the quality of the metal was known before pouring, there was no need to stockpile two million pounds of ingots per day, so the ingots could be loaded into freight cars immediately. With these successes we were relieved of the routine operation, with Wiley Taylor assuming charge of the routine lab. Ross and I rated our own office and separate development laboratory. Over the next few years we developed many new physical techniques for use in the aluminum industry involving spectrographic, x-ray and direct reading spectrometric procedures. We were now concerned with not only Arvida, but all plants in Canada and other countries as well.

Life in Arvida those days was not all work. The Saguenay Inn was filled with new recruits from across Canada. The majority of them were young, as they were recent graduates; this created a youthful culture. As a result there was always something going on. The bridge club was probably as high a level of bridge as you would find anywhere in Canada. Ross, the person I worked with, was one of the top players. He won so frequently that they could not get a game going if he was playing. Ross also played poker and again was a frequent winner. He claimed that he had paid his way through university by playing cards. He was not the only card enthusiast, however. There was a group of poker players consisting mainly of construction workers, Army personnel and some people from the Inn who played poker every Friday night. This was a big game with a maximum bump of five dollars. At the beginning of the game some of the players did a lot of jockeying to sit in the right place. A good deal of money changed hands on Friday nights. There was a lesser poker game on Wednesday night at the Inn with a maximum bump of two dollars. I often played this game. One could still lose a lot of money. I never lost too much, but I never won too much either, basically winning or losing about $25 in a month. It was a good game.

The Saguenay Inn, where I lived before marriage.

Another activity was target shooting. A group of us built up a mound about four feet high and about six feet long to set up targets on. Those of us who did the target shooting became pretty good. There were very few cars, so one used the bus or one cycled. Except for the main highway, the roads were gravel, which made for hard riding. However, in the summer a group of us would often ride to Lake Kenagami (about ten miles away) to swim or fish. The Saguenay River was a great river for fishing. Ouanaiche, a landlocked salmon, was caught there. It put up a good fight and was excellent eating. One of the accountants at the plant was so expert at catching this fish that he would invite someone for an Ounanaiche dinner and then go and catch the fish.

The company built a ski jump at the back of the Inn, which was used frequently for competitions in the winter. Of course general skiing was good. There was a very active curling club to which I belonged. The camera club held meetings at the Inn once a month, and had frequent outings to take photos of the many photogenic locations in the area. I was an active member and the only one with a movie camera.

Throughout the winter there was usually a dance or some activity on Saturday night at the inn. The dances were attended by the married people in town, as well as those at the Inn who were lucky enough to get a date.

There were concerts at the Inn, at least one in each season, by the Arvida Concert Orchestra in which I played a violin. At the end of the war more outside concerts were held, one by the Trapp family singers, of the **Sound of Music** fame, who had just come to North America. Arvida was a very active place in those days.

THE OTHER PLANTS

Our next job was to set up spectrographic labs in all the Alcan reduction plants. This was spread over some time as equipment was delivered and building changes were made. Labs were set up at Shawinigan Falls, La Tugue, Beauharnois, and Isle Maligne. Ross looked after the administrative, while I looked after the technical and training. This involved a considerable amount of traveling on my part as I installed and set up laboratories in each of these plants. I was also on call if any difficulties occurred. Because of my involvement with many plants, and the need to respond quickly to trouble calls, I was issued a Whittaker Pass. It was a very powerful pass that gave unrestricted access to any plant or operation of the company, authorizing the holder to any action necessary to carry out his duties. Only 250 out of 25,000 employees had such a pass.

The next major task was to develop methods for alloy analyses so that the fabricating plants could use spectrographic analysis. We were now working with major constituents. This was more difficult. What literature existed on major constituents used complex and time-consuming techniques, which we felt were not suited to our requirements. The major limiting factors were the photographic stage of the procedures, the methods of exciting the sample and the sample taking. We were looking at a margin of error of 10% to 15% of the amount present, which was acceptable for concentrations of less than 1%, but unacceptable for major constituents. In chemical analysis, samples of a few grams are used. In spectrographic analysis, only a few milligrams are used. Sample homogeneity is critical with such small samples. Further, the arc or spark or flame used to excite the sample has to be reproducible, and the photographic film, while acceptable for photography, has a lack of reproducibility of several percent. I worked out a mathematical model of the response of the photographic emulsion and was able to compensate for some of the photographic difficulties. We did considerable research into procedures for taking reproducible samples, and established conditions for a fast solidification producing a consistent microstructure with a minimum of segregation. We succeeded in developing procedures with a two sigma coefficient of variation of 2% (which means that the results were very reproducible and accurate). The procedures were at least as accurate as routine chemical and were more reliable.

In October of 1942, a spectrographic lab was set up in the Kingston, Ontario, fabricating plant, where alloys of up to 10% were used. I moved to Kingston for three months to set up and prove my techniques. I rented a room in a private home. The family had two daughters - including one about my age who was a pretty and charming girl. Although I did a lot of overtime at the lab and went to Toronto on most weekends, I enjoyed her company on several occasions. At the lab, the chemist saw me as competition and thus a threat, even though I explained I was only temporary. Instead of cooperating (and later being in charge of the new lab), he used every roadblock he could find. To establish the new techniques it was necessary to run in parallel with the chemical lab. This he thwarted at every turn by claiming I had not analyzed the same samples. He held up results, and then blamed me for refusing to compare results. He used any trick he could think of to discredit me and the new methods.

I finally decided I had to take drastic action. The Whittaker pass gave me the authority to carry out any activity needed in the prosecution of my work. Not even the plant manager of the Kingston plant had such a pass. I went to the Technical Director of the plant, showed him my pass and told him that in order to complete my work I was taking charge of all sampling. He agreed. In this way I knew what samples went to each lab, how they were taken and how they were identified. Chemical and spectrographic results started to agree. The chemist, not being aware that I now had control of sampling, changed the identification of some of the chemical lab samples in an apparent act of desperation. Spectrographic lab values were different, the mix-up was sorted out and no damage was done. He advised the Technical Director that I had mixed up the samples to discredit him. I arranged to have the samples taken in triplicate with an observer to number the samples sequentially, with a copy of the numbering and one set of the samples sent to the technical director. When the next mix-up occurred, I was blamed again, but **this** time it was easy to determine how it happened. Unfortunately for the chemist, he was demoted and we had to find someone else to head up the lab.

One personal advantage I gained from being in Kingston was that I bought a movie camera. My Uncle Chris (my father's brother), was very interested in photography and got me interested. Even in those black and white photographic days he was experimenting in colour printing. Kodachrome was available, but colour printing was expensive. However, movie film did not have to be printed, so I bought a movie camera. As a result I have taken many colour movies of family and travels over the years. I have at least 10,000 feet of movies. When video cameras became available, I bought one of the first. It was a big camera and effectively a VCR plus a big battery. The combination weighed about 40 lbs. As the videos advanced I bought newer models and took hundreds of rolls of videos. In those days people wanted to see my movies. Today videos are so common that everyone has videos to show.

***

Early in 1943 I set up the laboratory at the Etobicoke Plant in Long Branch. This was a high alloy casting plant with alloying constituents up to 25%. Spectrographic analyses were not considered applicable to such high values. However, we had refined our techniques to handle these casting alloys. In this case we transferred a man from Arvida (Ed Warren) to head up the lab. When I presented my expense account for this trip, the accounting department objected to the $300 I gave my mother for boarding me for ten days but did not object to the $400 I had spent for two days at the Royal York hotel. I could have stayed at the hotel the twelve days at a cost of $2400 and there would have been no objection. I had previously run into what I called stupidity on the part of the accounting department: In that case I had a big argument with them about refusing to inscribe an asset numbers on costly quartz lenses that were not mounted. The asset number would have destroyed the lenses.

In addition to inter-plant traveling, I also attended a number of conferences in Boston, Buffalo, Pittsburgh and Detroit, so that it was often possible to visit home and friends. Although I made some friends in Arvida, my interests remained in the Toronto area. This was particularly so for the tall slender redhead Elinor O'Neill, whose knee I had massaged so frequently. When I left Toronto there were no commitments, but the longer I was away the more desirable she became. There were girls in Arvida and several lived at the Inn. I dated a couple, but mainly so that I could go to the dances and parties that were frequently held. At one of these parties I had volunteered to look after some of the activities and did not have a date. As the evening wore on and my duties were completed, I noticed a beautiful petite redhead dressed in a stunning white gown sitting alone. I asked her for a dance, which she accepted. We seemed to hit it off and I danced with her for the rest evening. Her name was Peggy Jack and she was a teacher who lived with her parents in Kenagami. Her escort was drunk and she wanted nothing to do with him. I offered to escort her home, but since she lived in Kenagami (about ten miles away) I had to take a taxi and she felt that was an imposition. I refused to let her go with her drunken escort and arranged with one of my friends, who was driving his girl to Kenagami, to go with them. I found her interesting and she seemed interested in me. After a couple of dates she invited me to meet her parents and seemed to be pushing for marriage. She was a very nice girl and I enjoyed being with her, but she was in too much of a hurry for me. At that point I moved to Kingston for three months, and when I returned to Arvida she was engaged to an Air Force officer. If she had still been available when I returned she might have been competition for Elinor.

Throughout the war Arvida was the center of huge construction activity, employing several thousand men, both at the plant (which doubled its size) and at the Shipshaw Power Development. The Shipshaw power development was being constructed on a wartime schedule. The original plan called for construction over five years. Instead, in thirteen months the first generator was in place, which was a tremendous effort.

A large Air Force base at Port Alfred was twenty miles away. This base was a final base for fighter pilots before they went overseas. We often saw Spitfires flying over Arvida. On more than one occasion a flight of fighters flew across the back of the Inn almost level with the dining room windows. I guess the pilots were showing off to the girls at the Inn. It was feared the Germans would try a suicide raid on the area. Twice the air raid alarm sounded, but fortunately no attack occurred. There was a large Army base in Arvida, again because of fear of a landing party from a submarine. The Saguenay River was deep and isolated enough up to twenty miles from Arvida. It was claimed that a German submarine was sunk in the Saguenay River.

A Broader Vision

This all added to the number of men in the area. As a result, there were about ten unattached men to every single woman in the district. To go to a party without a girl meant you went to a stag. Of course the girls loved it and in the summer there would be an influx of female visitors. During the first two summers I spent a lot of time on the night shift and would be around the Inn during the day. These female visitors would latch onto those like me on the night shift. The summer of 1942 I invited Elinor to spend her holidays in Arvida and arranged for her to stay with the family of the maintenance manager of the plant. I also arranged to do all my night shift work before she came. At the beginning of the summer I was on continuous night shift and of course home all day. Being the polite type, I was easily latched on to by the visitors. At the time Elinor arrived, there was a visiting redhead that apparently considered she had me on the hook.

When Elinor arrived I went on the day shift. As Elinor hung around the Inn during the day she became acquainted with this redheaded visitor, who told her what a great guy this fellow named John was and how he had shown her around. Elinor talked about her Jack. Eventually they discovered they were talking about the same guy. Elinor accepted my explanation that I was only being polite to the other young lady.

Elinor and I had an enjoyable two weeks of hiking, swimming and partying with my Arvida friends. That fall was spent in Kingston, where it was easy to get to Toronto on weekends. Needless to say, every weekend I could arrange it I went to Toronto to be with Elinor. There was a large Army base in Kingston, the Barryfield Military Camp, which was renamed CFB Kingston in 1966. The train to Toronto on weekends was standing room only, as it was crowded with service men. On many weekends my ticket did not get collected. It was so crowded that the conductor could not go through the train to collect tickets. The weekends that I could not make it to Toronto felt like a wasted weekend. I did not look forward to finishing the job and returning to Arvida. The next spring Elinor and I met in Montreal, where I gave her an engagement ring. We set our wedding date for September.

It was customary to hold a stag party for any imminent grooms who were residents of the Inn. At these stags the objective was to get the groom drunk by the time the train for Montreal left at 9:00 PM. Some of the grooms were so drunk that they had to carry them on the train. The favourite trick was to "chugalug" a beer. However, the beer was actually half vodka. One chap was still drunk when the train arrived in Montreal. His wife-to-be met him there and when she saw how drunk he was, she cancelled the wedding. This was **not** going to happen to me, I decided, so I told no one that I was engaged or about to be married. When I came back after my holiday with a wife, it was a surprise.

Chapter 9
MARRIED

On September 11th, 1943, Elinor Ruth O'Neill and I were married in Blessed Sacrament Church in North Toronto. The reception was held at the Old Mill.

After the wedding we traveled by train to Orillia, where we spent our first night at the Champlain Inn. The next day we continued by train to Huntsville and spent the rest of the week at Cedar Grove Lodge on Fairy Lake. Elinor had made the arrangements. According to the brochure, we would be staying in our private little cottage with meals in the lodge. It sounded so romantic. What the brochure did not mention was that wood stoves heated the cottages and the occupants had to tend the stove. In September the nights were cold, and even though we had our love to keep us warm, a fire was needed. The fire always burned out during the night. Getting up in the morning for breakfast was not inviting. At the end of the week we returned to Toronto to spend a few days with family and friends. Elinor was sad that she would only see her family occasionally. We boarded the morning train to Montreal, then the night train to Arvida. Before I left Arvida I had arranged for us to stay with my friends Julie and John Gurney until a company house became available. We lived with the Gurney's for six months. They were newlyweds and both were working. Elinor was left at home while everyone else went to work. After a week Elinor found this rather dull and asked me to see if she could get a job at Alcan. I enquired on her behalf, pointing out that she was a very competent secretary. She was hired immediately to work in the stenographic pool.

Married.

Elinor and I would walk to and from work together. Many nights I would be involved in something and could not leave at 5 o'clock. Elinor would wait for me to walk home together, which I always appreciated. On one of these late nights, George Mason, the technical director, came looking for a secretary to send an urgent teletype. Elinor was there and he asked if she could send the teletype, which she did. The next morning, Harry Collins (her boss) told her that Mr. Mason wanted to see her. Mr. Mason was known as a demanding boss and she wondered what she did wrong the previous evening when she sent the teletype. She entered his office timidly, but he was all smiles and said, "Mrs. Burgener, I was impressed with the way you handled my teletype, and that you had not left work at 5:00 like most people do. I would like you to be my private secretary." Thus Elinor became secretary to the technical director, the second highest paid secretary in Arvida. When the Queen of Holland visited Arvida during the war, Elinor was one of those appointed to show her around. She held this position until she left because of the imminent birth of our first child.

We celebrated our first Christmas while we lived with the Gurneys. I remember going to Midnight Mass. It was a clear cold night about minus 40° F as we walked home together, and we cuddled close to keep warm. The sky was lit with the dancing Northern Lights; it was a magnificent and colourful display. I remember the crunch of the cold snow, and as we walked my heart was filled with the beauty surrounding us and with the love of Elinor. I thanked God for such abundance. Both Julie and Elinor had never cooked a turkey, although they had bought a frozen one for Christmas dinner. They both agreed that it would take four hours to cook it. At about 2:00 PM they brought the turkey in from outside. Of course it was frozen solid and we could do nothing with it. I had not realized that the turkey was still outside and frozen. From my experience in Lorne Park days I knew the turkey had to be thawed and prepared before cooking. I put it in a wash tub of water and let it thaw. We ate our turkey dinner at 11:30 PM; it was still Christmas.

After six months of living with the Gurneys, we got our own house on Fifth Street in Arvida. It was a semi-detached, two storey, four roomed house with a basement. It was heated with a coal furnace, which had one register in the main floor at the bottom of the stairs. We had bought a chesterfield and chair in Toronto at the time of the wedding. Before I left Arvida for the wedding I bought a maple bedroom suite from the family Elinor had stayed with when she visited Arvida. We had a few other pieces of furniture, but no pots or pans, no stove, no refrigerator, and no dishes. Fortunately, the Saguenay Inn had a meal plan for $45 a month that provided lunch and dinner for staff members. We took advantage of that until we accumulated enough furniture and equipment.

Our Arvida house - the right side was ours.

Eating at the Inn proved to be an advantage socially. Other newlyweds were doing the same, and we got to know a number of newlyweds and single people that we would not otherwise have met. The Inn was also the centre of social life in Arvida, and we attended numerous functions there. One Friday night we were invited to a party a neighbour was holding, but I had an attack of appendicitis and could not attend. Saturday I had planned to go hunting with a two friends. The attack was over by Saturday, so I started to get ready. Elinor was annoyed that I was not well enough to go the party, and that the next day I was well enough for hunting. As it turned out, I should have stayed home. Saturday night we camped in the bush. It was September and the temperature dropped to several degrees below freezing. It was so cold that we were freezing in our sleeping bags. About 2:00 AM we got up and built a fire to sit around and warm up. Of course the car radiator froze and burst. One of us got a grouse but that was all. It was not a satisfying weekend. On our way home Sunday night, we would drive a few miles and then have to stop and cool the engine off. It took many hours to get the car to a place where we could get enough water to get us the rest of the way home.

A DROWNING

There was a small sandy beach on the Saguenay River, which was a short walk from the Saguenay Inn. This was a favourite swimming place for the residents of Arvida. The water was warm, but it had a current and a tide. As high tide was approached the current came to a standstill. At low tide it was not possible to swim against it. Upstream there was logging and debris floated downriver. Our friends Amby and Victor were swimming together on an afternoon in early summer 1945, and Victor disappeared. Amby looked around and dove down looking for him, but could not find him. Victor obviously drowned. Amby, very upset, came back to the Inn and reported it. The police looked for the body, but because of the current they had little hope of finding it. Victor was a good friend and we were greatly saddened by the drowning. Ten days later Amby was awakened from sleep: Victor appeared to him in his bathing suit and was sitting on the chair beside Amby's bed. Victor said he wanted to tell Amby what happened. He told Amby that he was swimming beside him and a log hit his head, and he lost consciousness and drowned. However, if Amby went to a certain spot on the river the next day, he would find his body. In the morning Amby went to the police. They went to the spot and Victor's body was there.

The company sent Amby with Victor's body to his family and to the funeral. That summer on our holidays we met some of Victor's family and offered to put any of them up if they wished to see where Victor had lived.

We bought the first electric refrigerator after the war, and had to arrange delivery.

※ ※ ※

A FULL HOUSE

Some months before Paul was born, Elinor quit work. By then we had all the necessary furniture and equipment, so we stopped eating at the Inn. At that point our good friends Amby MacNeil and Ruth Scott got married. As they had nowhere to live, they moved into our second bedroom. We had earlier invited my friend Conrad Myers to visit us. At the same time, Elinor's aunt Ab wrote and said she was coming to visit. It was a full house. Ab slept with Elinor, I slept with Conrad on a pullout couch that separated into two single beds in the kitchen, and Amby and Ruth had the second bedroom. One morning at about 7:30, a taxi stopped in front of our house. A young woman with a suitcase got out and came to the door. She was the sister of Victor, the friend of ours who had drowned in the Saguenay River earlier that summer. Although we had offered to put her up if she should wish to come to Arvida, we had heard no more from her until she arrived at our door without any warning. There was nowhere we could put her up, and so we asked the Gurney's to do so.

THE BIRTH OF OUR FIRST SON

Finally by the end of August all visitors had left and we had a few days of peace before Paul was born. At about 9:00 PM, September 9th, 1945, Elinor started to go into labour. I took her to the hospital and discovered that a fire at the Shipshaw construction camp had killed sixteen men and left many others with serious burns, so all available medical personnel were at Shipshaw. There was only one nurse in the Arvida hospital. She pointed out that she had to look after the entire hospital, therefore I would have to look after Elinor. I had no previous knowledge of childbirth and it was probably the most frightening night of my life. She suffered for many hours. With each scream I was certain that she was dying. I said the rosary many times that night. Finally, at about 4:00 AM, Elinor's screams and groans changed. I ran around the hospital to find the nurse to tell her that Elinor must be dying. She hurried into Elinor's room, looked at her, and told me, "The baby is being born - call Dr Gilbert, who is now at home, and tell him to come in." I made the call. A sleepy doctor answered and said he would be in shortly. When I got back to the room, Elinor had been moved to the delivery room. I went back to the front of the hospital and waited. Finally the doctor arrived. About an hour and a half later the doctor came out and said that it was a breech birth, but that everything was okay and that we had a boy. Paul was a big baby but I do not remember his weight.

* * *

Living in Arvida was pleasant. It was beautiful country; close to the wilderness and yet built-up. Winters were long and cold with lots of snow. Summers were short, but when they came they were appreciated. Spring seemed to happen overnight. At the end of May one could still ski, but by the middle of June the snow was gone and the flowers were starting to bloom. Autumn, on the other hand, was slow, starting in the middle of August with cold nights and cool days. The first snowfall was early in September, but the real cold and heavy snows didn't come until the end of November. In the winter skiing was the main outdoor activity, with partying indoors. In the summer the Saguenay River and the many lakes provided good swimming and fishing, and had many places for hiking and picnicking. The autumn provided excellent hunting nearby. It was a good place to live in our early marriage, but it never felt permanent; it was more like a resort, not a permanent home.

We had many visitors during our Arvida days. As mentioned earlier, Elinor's Aunt Ab and my friend Conrad Myers visited us just before Paul was born. Doris Crouse, from the office where Elinor worked before we were married, visited in '44. That summer Elinor's mother and her brother Paul met us in Quebec City. After our tour of the city we drove up to Arvida in the car I had purchased a few months earlier. Elinor's mother spent two weeks with us after Paul was born in September '45. Conrad and my brother Ernie came up for skiing in the late winter of that year. In 1946 Elinor's brother Paul returned with us from our vacation in Toronto by ship from Montreal. The same summer, my parents drove up from Toronto and spent a week with us. The summer of '47 my friend Doug Bond, my sister Aileen and her husband Alf visited us. Arvida was an interesting place to visit. The Saguenay Inn was a beautiful hotel with an excellent dining room where one could expect some interesting activity every week. The Saguenay River, a short walk from the Inn, was great for fishing and swimming. Lake St. John, a large lake with good sandy beaches, was forty miles upstream. Twenty miles down-stream was Port Alfred, where the Canada Steam Ships docked. From here, on several occasions, we took a pleasant one day cruise to Tadoussac on the St. Lawrence and would return the same day. Between Arvida and Quebec City was the Laurentide National Park, a true wilderness park. In the winter skiing was excellent.

ALULABS

Early in 1944 our development laboratory was transferred to Aluminum Laboratories Limited (Alulabs), the research organization of Aluminum Limited, the parent Company of Alcan. We continued our service to Alcan, but became more involved in other areas of the aluminum business, such as analyses of ore using X-Ray Fluorescence and various intermediate products. We also got involved with production problems, such as the cause and remedy of blistering when rolling sheets. These activities were interesting and challenging, but as the war ended the urgency and the freedom of action decreased, and I became restless. I was further annoyed when Ross Callon got the measles. The director of research of Alulabs Arvida, Harry Collins, commented that an urgent research project had to be put on hold until Ross returned. Ross had not been working on it - I had. In fact, if management looked back, Ross had been around for a year before I started with no progress, and a mere four months after I arrived we were well on the way. If I was to receive so little recognition then it appeared pointless for me to stay. Also, the prospect of spending my life in Arvida did not appeal to me. At the same time, Alcan had started selling their houses. Our neighbour, who lived in the other half of the semi-detached house, bought both houses and he became an unreasonable landlord. On requesting another house, I was advised that there were none. I then asked for a transfer to Kingston, the main laboratory for Alulabs. This appeared to give my superiors the impression that I was a dissident and hence not worthy of consideration.

Elinor and Paul with our 1933 DeSoto in the background.

A Broader Vision

During 1946 and 1947, the company was letting staff go and budgets for research were drastically reduced. I decided that if the company had so little interest in me, and if it would not transfer me or at least give me another house, it was time to look elsewhere. During my summer holiday in 1946, I contacted some companies. I got a reply from Cornel University and went talk to them. They would have hired me, but I really did not want to move to the USA. As I pondered what to do, I realized that at thirty years of age I was very well paid, and if the company considered me worth that much, then surely I could earn as much on my own. Furthermore, I had developed spectrochemistry to a new level and I was confident that there would be a market for it. The company appeared to credit our success as due to Ross' administrative skills and not my technical skills. His administrative skills were certainly needed but my technical and organizing skills had made it happen. I could see that as a manager it would appear that administrative skills were the essential factor that led to the production of aluminum. The managers hired someone like me to make the changes. Therefore progress in Alcan was not what I wanted. I had a broader vision, and it went beyond the production of aluminum.

Additionally, Mr Rimmer (who had hired me) was transferred to Montreal as an executive; he was apparently in charge of intercompany activities and was basically never home at the age when his family most needed him. If I progressed with the company I would probably face a similar fate. My father had effectively been in his own business during my upbringing and was able to do things with his family that others could not. This started me investigating the possibilities. After considerable praying, I decided that God had other plans for me. So in July of 1947 I gave three months' notice. A generous notice, as I was planning to start my own business and hoped that Alcan could be a customer.

Producing aluminum did not seem to be worthwhile enough to be the essence of my life. Money was not my object, but having a full family life was. I had enough confidence in myself that I could make my own business succeed and it would give me an opportunity to do what I wanted to do without my life being totally immersed in my job. In retrospect, my friend Amby became a senior manager and spent too much time working at the Aluminum Company. His children grew up really not knowing or caring for him. He did not like the management position, but agreed to do so because the company insisted, or he would have been fired. He died young from the stress, which I think led to his cancer, and his family had abandoned him by then. His life had been focused on the company projections and productivity, not on his family. My focus was on life, family and God, and I could not do that well in a large company.

Apparently my generous notice was misjudged as a ploy to get my own way. In the last two weeks, when it became apparent I was leaving, Dr. Hainie, director of research of Aluminum Limited, came to Arvida and offered me a two year executive training program in Switzerland, with assurance that on completion I would start as a plant general manager, with senior management to follow. I thanked him, but pointed out that they should have listened to me earlier, as I had now progressed too far to turn back. A few days later I left. If this opportunity had been offered when I first asked for a transfer, I would have probably accepted it. Fortunately they made the offer after I had time to consider all the factors. When I look back at some of my contemporaries who later became plant managers in places like India, South America, and the wilderness of British Columbia, I am satisfied I made a wise choice.

On a cold day in mid-October of 1947 we said goodbye, with some tears, to our many Arvida friends. Elinor, Paul, and I left in our 1933 DeSoto loaded to the roof with our belongings, and with the prayer that we would not run into a snowstorm. We did not, but we did come to a wash-out on the road. Fortunately a work crew was there working on it. They laid down planks for me to drive across. Elinor and Paul got out while I carefully drove across. Thankfully the rest of the trip through the park was uneventful. A new and challenging chapter in our lives had begun.

Chapter 10

THE EARLY TSL YEARS

Our drive from Arvida to Toronto was leisurely, as we had no timetable to live by. We drove through the Laurentide National Park to Malbaie, on the St. Lawrence River, and then along the north shore to Ste. Anne-de-Beaupré. Here we stopped and visited the shrine, praying for success in our new life. Even though I had given up a good job with a good future, I did not doubt that my new life would be a success, even as I prayed. We drove through Quebec City without stopping since we had recently spent a few days there with Elinor's mother and her brother Paul. Our next stop was at a small village hotel. The name of the village I do not remember, but I do remember the owner asking why we were traveling with a baby late in October with a loaded car. We told him of our plans. We had a great discussion of the advantages of small company ownership. He had given up a good job with a large company and bought this hotel. He never regretted doing it. His comments were reassuring, as in the back of my mind I was wondering if I had made a wise choice. I did have a wife and son to look after.

Our next stop was at Cap-de-la-Madeleine. Here we visited the shrine to Our Lady of the Rosary and said a rosary for success in our new life. When the shrine was built in the early 1800s, the available source of stone for the church was on the south side of the St. Lawrence River and it was difficult to obtain. The priest and congregation prayed that the river would freeze and make it easy to get the stone across. That winter the river froze and provided a bridge. It was one of the very few occasions the river has frozen at that point.

John E. Burgener

We drove through Montreal, taking the south river road to avoid traffic, and did not recognize the highway when we crossed it; we continued all the way back along the north river road. We felt that the detour cost us a day. Nonetheless, we saw both south and north Montreal. Finally getting through the city, we drove to Ottawa to visit my brother Ernie and his wife Lilyan. We spent a few days with them. Then we continued on to Lorne Park, where we were welcomed by my parents. They were glad to see us and were happy to have us living near by, but they wondered about our wisdom in giving up a good job. They were thrilled to have Paul, their first grandson, living with them, and my parents doted on him. My father spent time in his workshop with Paul, showing him all the wonders of making things. They invited us to stay with them for as long as we needed. Paul, on arriving at my parents' house, came down with chickenpox. My mother kept the drapes closed so his eyes would not be affected and had him wear gloves so he would not scratch. With all of the changes in his life, this became his first memory, allowing him to recall his life just as he turned two.

My first order of business was to go to Galt in Cambridge to visit Munroe Fraser (Fraser Hardware). While Monroe was still in Arvida, he had encouraged us to start our own business and offered to invest in it. We had arrived in Port Credit with $2000 savings and realized that we would need more. Monroe, over a couple years did put in about $5000, $4000 of which we paid back, and the remainder was paid in shares.

The next order of business was to start acquiring the equipment needed. To purchase a complete spectrographic laboratory would have cost at least $50,000. With the experience I had acquired from working on the house, making things in my father's workshop, fixing cars, and general work on our small farm, along with my experience in Arvida, I felt confident that I could build all the equipment I needed. Our plan was to spend a month or more building the equipment and simultaneously start organizing dealerships and publishing our new services. We operated from my parents' house. Elinor, acting as my business manager, sent out letters and circulars and made phone calls while I designed and built the needed equipment. My father had a large, well-equipped basement workshop where I planned to build a grating spectrograph and accessories. A spectrograph separates the various components of light into lines in a spectrum. One way of accomplishing this is to use a concave mirror with thousands of lines ruled on the surface. This is known as a diffraction grating. I wanted a 15,000 line per inch, three meter focal length grating. In 1948 such gratings were expensive and available only from a few universities that had ruling machines. However, technology had improved the process, and better gratings were being produced. I therefore expected that earlier gratings, used in research, were being replaced. A surplus grating would be adequate for my purposes. A suitable grating had to be found before the spectrograph could be designed.

Having graduated from the University of Toronto in Physics, specializing in spectroscopy, I knew the physics department had several surplus gratings in storage. I approached Professor Ireton, who had been our professor in spectroscopy, to buy one of their surplus gratings. Instead, he offered to rent me one at a reasonable rate and after four years I could keep it; a generous offer. His department had spending money and I had four years to pay for it. It was a 3 meter, 15,000 line per inch original Wood's grating, ruled on speculum metal, which was a soft alloy that took a high polish and was less affected by temperature than others. Now that I had the specifications of the essential component, I could continue with the design and construction of the spectrograph. For simplicity of construction, I decided that I would build the frame of mahogany. Wood has a very small coefficient of thermal expansion, and although it is affected by moisture, mahogany is less affected than many other woods. To have built it of welded metal presented greater thermal effects as well as distortions due to aging. A glued and screwed mahogany frame appeared to offer ease of construction and thermal stability. The changes due to humidity would be small and gradual, and could be compensated for in operation.

I bought three 2 x 12 inch mahogany beams, twelve feet long, and constructed a triangular frame to match the calculations I had made to suit the grating. A woodworking shop cut for me, from quarter inch plywood, four circular arcs a meter in length on a three meter radius. These formed the photographic plate holder. The grating came with an adjustable mounting. I bought a spectrographic adjustable slit and an optical bar to mount lenses and excitation stands from Hilger in England.

Years later the spectrograph was finally dismantled as new instrumentation had replaced it. Paul, who had grown up with the spectrograph, being always at my work, was working in the lab and came in one weekend and slowly dismantled the spectrograph. He still has the grating and slit in his curio cabinet and some of the mahogany in his wood-working shop.

With these components I assembled a spectrograph that served TSL for forty years. A few years later, when Dick Jarrell of Jarrell-Ash visited my lab, he was impressed with my mounting and used a modification of it in Jaco's Wadsworth spectrograph. (Note: Jarrell-Ash became Thermo-Fisher of today, which is a multi-billion dollar per year international company selling analytical instruments and supplies.) Originally some difficulty was experienced with vibration. This was overcome by mounting the mahogany frame on shock mounts, on an angle iron frame, which itself was mounted on shock mounts. The mahogany frame, although criticized by other spetroscopists, performed exceptionally well. Humidity did cause focus changes, but these were small and gradual and were easily corrected with a small adjustment of the grating. In fact, the resolution of my spectrograph was superior to commercial spectrographs of the same size. I could resolve .02 ångströms where others had difficulty resolving .08.

Besides the spectrograph, I had to design and build a power source to excite the samples, and a projector-microphotometer to evaluate the photographed spectra. A 250 volt 20 ampere DC arc source was built using a special transformer from Hammond in Guelph, Ontario. As a spark source I used a 15,000 volt .5KVA luminous sign transformer and three 30,000 Volt .01MF war surplus condensers. These sources were rebuilt using the same components a few years later to improve handling, but served us for forty years. The projector-microphotometer was somewhat more difficult to build. Using lenses and front surface mirrors available from war surplus I designed a projector with a movable photographic plate holder that formed a 20 times image on a sloping screen at table height. In the centre of the screen was a slit with a photocell. The photocell was connected to an amplifier and a large scale milliamp meter. Charts were prepared by using spectra of all the elements the spectrograph could identify against an iron spectrum for reference. In this way I could do both quantitative and semi-quantitative analyses.

To design and build this equipment took me about two months. At the same time, arrangements with various spectrographic suppliers of equipment and supplies were going forward. Jarrell-Ash (Jaco) of Boston was interested, agreeing to give me a 15% commission on any of their equipment I sold. Hilger of England (later Hilger-Watts) agreed to let me sell their equipment through an agent in Ottawa (Instruments Limited) with a 10% commission. The Hilger

Equipment was based on prisms, while Jaco used gratings. I also arranged to sell spectroscopic supplies. I got a 30% discount on these items.

I did not get an exclusive Canadian agency on any of these. As I proved myself, I did later get exclusive representation for Jarrell-Ash. I got an exclusive from United (later called Ultra) Carbon Limited. Kodak Canada never gave TSL an exclusive, but referred all requests for scientific films to us, although they allowed a drug store in Montreal to accept orders. Unfortunately the Aluminum Company of Canada (who was a large buyer) refused to buy from us and purchased from the drug store. TSL stocked the supplies and covered all shipping and customs.

Hilger-Watts never gave TSL an exclusive, but tolerated us. They could not afford not to, as we sold about 80% of Hilger-Watts sales in Canada. We even marked the price up 10% on items that needed installation and sold against the official agent in Canada. Instead of recognizing our value to them, they always maintained that anyone buying optical equipment would automatically think of Hilger, and they did not need sales people. No wonder they later went bankrupt.

TECHNICAL SERVICE LABORATORIES

In January of 1948 I registered Technical Service Laboratories (TSL) as a partnership of John E. Burgener of Lorne Park, Ontario, and Monroe Fraser of Galt, Ontario. At this point I had already sent out circular letters to all the spectrographic labs I knew of, advising them that I was supplying graphite and photographic supplies as well as Jaco and Hilger equipment. In order to start doing analyses, I needed somewhere to set up my laboratory. I found a space in a heated garage at the back of a large house on Bedford Road in the Bloor Street and University Avenue area of Toronto. It was a three car garage with living quarters above it. I set the equipment up and stayed there about six months. The electrical service was not capable of handling both the spectrograph and the cooking requirements of the upstairs resident. The frequent fuse blowing was annoying to both of us.

While here I developed a semi-quantitative procedure that covered most metals that were encountered in metallurgy, mining, and industry in general. I called this "A 30 Element Semi-Quantitative Analysis." I prepared a circular on this procedure with the help of Paul O'Neill, Elinor's brother, who was the PR director for the Canadian National Institute for the Blind. Using directories in the Main Library at St. George and College Streets, I made up a mailing list of companies and institutions that I felt could use my services. Elinor was my Girl Friday, and she addressed and mailed these circulars. She also did any typing needed as well as accounting. I sent a special letter to all commercial laboratories, offering my 30 Element Analysis at a discount of 50%. I was offering it at $7.00, and pointed out that they could extend their services into this new field profitably at no cost.

I got an almost immediate response from several assayers and concluded that mining was probably where the market lay. I then started a mailing to exploration companies and geologists expounding on the merits of spectrographic analysis. I also called on several geologists and exploration companies in Toronto and got a favourable reception. The concept of the 30 element spectrographic analysis was a new approach, making determinations of compositions available that were not previously possible. As an example, during the construction of the Toronto Dominion Centre in the sixties, some of the steel girders were the wrong alloy by mistake. To find those girders was impossible and may have required the dismantling the entire structure. However, a few grams of fillings from each girder spectrographically analyzed by TSL found the girders that had to be replaced.

During the six months I was on Bedford Road I did not get a lot of business. One of the exploration companies that I had called on phoned one Thursday afternoon and said they had 800 sample pulps that had been assayed, and they did not trust the results. If I could have them all analyzed by Monday at noon, they would pay $4.00 each. I accepted the challenge. Elinor and I worked almost continuously for those three days. Elinor got an infected tooth, which caused her face to swell and gave her a great deal of pain, but she kept on working. Each of the 800 samples, although already a fine powder, had to be thoroughly mixed by rolling and quartering so that a small representative sample could be taken. Elinor did this boring and dusty job, carefully, and she did it well. As the samples were prepared, I put a small amount of each sample into a graphite crater and burned it in an electric arc. The light from the arc passed through the spectrograph, was broken into spectrum lines, and recorded on a photographic plate. The intensity or blackness of the copper spectrum line indicated the amount of copper in the sample. If the copper line on the photographic plate was very weak or not present, it meant that there was little or no copper in that sample. If the line was strong, then the sample was analyzed quantitatively.

Quantitative analyses are similar with more controlled conditions and photoelectric measurement of the photographic plate. We finished the job Sunday night. Elinor typed the results Monday morning. I delivered them about 11:00 AM and picked up a check for $3200. In those days that amount was enough to last us some time.

Most of the time during those first six months was spent making contacts. One of the contacts I made was the Ontario Research Foundation, which at that time was on Queen's Park. They were considering purchasing a spectrograph, however, they decided that they could use my services instead. They never bought a spectrograph but continued to use TSL throughout the years. Toronto Testing Laboratories (TTL) on Adelaide Street was another contact. It was an old laboratory, founded before World War I. The son of the founder, Frank Ross, was not a chemist. He had an older chemist named Ernie Bolton managing the lab. Ernie was a good chemist, but not a manager. Frank, seeing me as a good manager, suggested that TTL had some surplus space where TSL would be better off than in a garage. He also offered to accept work in lieu of rent. It was a good offer and I gladly took it.

THE MOVE TO TORONTO TESTING

I moved the lab into Toronto Testing Laboratories' fourth floor location on Adelaide Street in the fall of 1948. Toronto Testing was a complete laboratory with all the equipment for fire assaying as well as good chemical facilities for mining and industrial analyses. TTL was one of Ontario's major assaying labs. As a result, 30 element analyses got to be known throughout the mining industry. By the very nature of the exploration process there will always be many mining samples - in any batch - that will contain little to none of the metal sought. TTL benefited from the use of the spectrograph to sort out the samples worth analyzing chemically. For fifty cents I would run the mining sample on the spectrograph giving a semi-quantitative estimate. The nils (nothing noticeable) and traces (something noticeable but not enough to be significant) were reported from spectrographic tests, and the higher values (something potentially significant) by wet chemistry. Ernie Bolton found this to be a great advantage both from the labour saving and the confirmation of the wet chemical. At that time there was a lot of interest in the metal niobium and the chemical procedures were not well established. On spectrographically checking the residues Ernie had separated by his chemical procedure, which were supposed to be niobium oxide, I found that instead of niobium oxide he was weighing titanium oxide. This saved him from reporting erroneous values. He reported to the customer the difficulty in wet analysis for niobium and the possibility that other labs were making the same error. I worked out a spectrographic procedure and we became known as the lab to analyze for unusual metals.

TTL had a number of industrial customers, such as Toronto Iron Foundries and Dominion Bridge. Malleable cast iron was coming into use, requiring analyses for magnesium in low concentrations, which was a difficult procedure by wet chemistry. Spectrographically, it was easy. TTL and TSL both benefited. TTL received the samples for other work as well as magnesium, but the spectrographic reports for magnesium went out in TSL's name. TSL continued to analyze magnesium in iron for many years.

Although I stayed at TTL for only a little more than a year and a half, TSL became known in mining exploration and industry. Frank Ross offered to buy me out, making him the owner and hiring me as manager. I might have gone for a 49% interest, but no way was I going to be an employee. I offered to buy **him** out but this antagonized him and he insisted that I find another location.

Chapter 11

OUR FIRST HOUSE

TSL was not making much in the way of a profit during these early years. If we had not had Monroe Fraser's backing we would have had to give up. Until the summer of 1948 we lived with my parents. This was cheaper than living on our own, although we always paid our share of the expenses. In the summer of '48 my sister Jennie, who lived on Third Street in Port Credit, told us that a low-rent house was available on her street. We rented it. My parents were sorry to lose their grandson Paul, and Elinor and I had to give up the comfortable accommodation, but we had moved here to start a new life and we had to go the whole way. It was basic with an outdoor toilet, only a cold water tap in the kitchen, two tiny bedrooms, and a small living room with an oil stove for heat. Storage space in the attic was reached by a pull-down ladder. Every cold night in the winter the water pipes froze and I would have to crawl under the house with a blow torch to thaw them. It was modest living, but we were independent. The location gave us the advantage of living near my sister Jennie and her husband Jim, who was Elinor's brother. Our son Paul had his cousins, Maureen and Caroline, to play with, Elinor had a sister-in-law, and I a brother-in-law. In the late summer of '48 Elinor developed a false pregnancy, which we were not aware of and was a potentially dangerous condition. Shortly after we moved in she slipped while going up the pull down ladder, resulting in a very painful miscarriage. Having Jennie nearby was a great help. Elinor became pregnant again in the fall of '49.

As a result of the war and soldiers returning home there was a serious housing shortage; to rent a suitable house was difficult. We had no money for a down payment to purchase a house. The alternative was to build a house, where my labour would constitute a down payment. About half of the cost of building a house is labour. So if I provided the major part of the labour I could cover the down payment. Elinor agreed that building a house was a solution, but pointed out that building a business and a house and raising a family all at the same time could be too much. We both agreed that it would be tough but it seemed to be our only alternative if we were to get a suitable house. I pointed out that God had put us in this situation and I expected He would see us through it. Elinor said she could handle it, but most of the burden would be on me. I felt the burden would not be that great and we did need a better house. Therefore we would have to build one. Before one can get a mortgage, one must own a property. Since we had no money we had to find an inexpensive lot. We also decided that this lot would probably determine where in the Toronto area we would settle, so schools, church, ease of getting to work, family location and shopping were important factors. Driving around in our old DeSoto, we looked at many locations around Toronto and came to the conclusion that the best location was the Port Credit area. Lots there were cheaper than areas closer to Toronto and it was close to my parents and Jim and Jennie. We found one on Pine Ave South in Port Credit, a 50 X 150 foot lot for $300. It was half a block from the lake with lots of trees. It was a bit low, had a very high water table, and backed on to an oil refinery. It suited our needs and proved to be a good place to start.

We did not have 300 dollars so we borrowed it from our good friend Amby MacNeil. At that time a new construction company, Saco Panel, was promoting a reinforced concrete panel construction with some attractive offers. They would provide the plans, the foundation, the sub-floor, and the outside concrete walls for a one-and-a-half storey, 750 square foot house for $1500. Furthermore, they would have it erected in ten days. Using their plans and quote I worked out the cost of materials to finish the house, including the cost of a plumber to install the drainage system, an electrician to install the electrical service, and a furnace company to install the heating system. Everything else I planned to do myself, including the internal wiring and plumbing. The estimated total cost of materials and Saco Panel came to about $4500. The estimated cost of labour in house building was 48% of the total. I added $3800 to the total and went looking for a mortgage on a house and a lot worth $8300. Since the house would be built to NHA specifications, it was possible to get a mortgage of 80% of the value - $6400. However, since I was not a registered contractor and was building for my own use, the mortgage companies would only talk about 60% - $4800. I could have lived with this. However, they would not loan me anything on a reinforced concrete house. They argued that the concrete would crumble in twenty years. I asked, "What about bridges and overpasses?" and they answered, "That's different."

I called on every mortgage company I could find but got the same reaction. It became evident that any different form of construction was taboo, regardless of whether or not the form or method was efficient or even superior. It began to appear that I would have to change my plans and build a house in the conventional way. I told my troubles to my Uncle Chris (Dad's brother). He had a friend in the Confederation Life Mortgage Department and he said he would see what could be done. As a result he got me a mortgage for $5800 and I could now cover my costs. To get my first draw on the mortgage I needed money up-front to pay for excavation, Saco Panel, and lumber sufficient to get the roof on. I did get a $2000 loan from the bank, which did not cover my requirements, and so I had to depend on credit at the lumber company to cover my shortfall.

BUILDING THE HOUSE

I hired a carpenter as a consultant, who for a reasonable price gave me advice on the various problems in house construction, thus avoiding potentially costly mistakes. With these arrangements completed, we started the construction of our Pine Ave. house in the early summer of 1949. It was a busy time for both of us as we tried to start a business, build a house, and raise a family. By fall, with a lot of help from my father and Elinor's brother Jim, we got the roof on and our first draw of 40%. By the time we paid off the bank, there was only $300 left. I tried to get another loan at the bank, but they said that my business did not seem to be progressing well and so they considered me a poor risk. We had paid some of the lumber bill but we still owed a lot and we needed $800 cash for the furnace. The heating had to be installed to get the next draw; I managed to scrape together the $800. However, the furnace had to be installed on a concrete floor and to get a concrete floor for the basement was another $400. I did not have the $400, so I hand mixed concrete and poured a section of the floor large enough to hold the furnace and a coal bin. The furnace people were not happy to install it. There was concrete floor for the furnace, but they had to work on a mud floor and had to use a ladder to go to the basement. We did not get the basement floor finished for several months after we moved in. With the furnace installed we got another draw of $1700. With this we paid off the plumber, the electrician, and most of the lumber.

By now it was the end of January, 1950, and the house was closed in and the furnace installed. I had finished the internal wiring, the plumbing, and the fibreglass insulation, and decided that the house was livable. Up to this point I had used the temporary electrical service installed on a post on the lawn. I called for the mandatory inspections. The plumbing inspector was a friendly and caring person who checked everything carefully, discovering a couple of minor errors, which he helped me to correct, and approved the house. The hydro inspector spent a full hour inspecting the wiring, including opening up almost every splice, following every circuit, and taking out every outlet. He could not find any errors. Finally he asked for a ladder and measured the height of the service inlet, which a licensed electrician had installed, and found it to be two inches less than the required height. However, he was measuring to the top of a two foot pile of building sand, temporarily put against the building. I offered to remove two inches immediately. He stated that the house did not pass and that he was too busy to come back for at least a month, even though I told him I had to move in since our lease was up. He was clearly a union official who had no regard for anyone but the union. It was obviously his god. I was very annoyed at such obvious disregard for others and at the stupidity of his agenda. On calling the hydro, they said it was up to the inspector. I heard from others who were similarly building their houses that this inspector did the same to them. If the hydro wanted to play dirty, I could too. I connected the house to the temporary service and had free electricity for the three months it took for him to send an approval in the mail. If I had not been resourceful, we could not have moved in for three months. He never came back.

At the beginning of February we moved in. The drywall panels upstairs were installed, but on the first floor the inside walls were studs, the kitchen counter was a plywood sheet with a sink in it, all the floors were sub-floors, and lumber was stacked all over the house. It did have a bathroom. We had stairs from the first to the second floor, but none into the basement, which had a mud floor. A ladder was used to go to the basement to attend to the furnace. It was primitive. Once we moved in Elinor and my mother did the painting and fixing up wherever they could to make the house comfortable and liveable, while my father, Jim, and I continued with construction. Not many wives would have

A Broader Vision

put up with it, but Elinor never complained and she supported me throughout. Without her support I would not have made it. These were stressful times and we always got a sense of relief on Sundays when Elinor and I, along with our children, attended Sunday Mass. I will mention here that as good as formal praying is, I have always felt that God wants to be our Father and one does not need to kneel before your earthly father to make a request: you simply ask him. In this same spirit, most of my prayer is just talking to God my Father.

Our house on Pine Avenue, Port Credit.

Unfortunately Port Credit Lumber had too many customers like us and the bank stepped in. The person the bank put in was a bully and he seemed to believe that the louder he shouted and the more he threatened, the quicker he would collect. He yelled and screamed at Elinor and he frightened our next door neighbour, who was also building their house, into making an unfavourable second mortgage. However, we still needed more lumber, and therefore more credit. I gave him a choice: he could give me more credit so I could finish the house and get another draw from the Mortgage Company, or he could sue me. I pointed out that I would acknowledge the debt to the court, but under my circumstances I would offer to pay $10 a month and there was an excellent chance the court would agree. He then insisted that I get someone to guaranty the debt, but refused any more credit. I pointed out that, with a guaranty, I could simply buy from another supplier. He could go ahead and sue me. Not being accustomed to creditors who fought back, he finally became reasonable. We agreed that he would allow me a total of $1500 credit if I got my father to guaranty a total of $800. We owed about $800 and the extra $700 was sufficient to finish the house. While this was going on I obtained an Ontario Government second mortgage for $1200 at 5%, which I could collect on completion of the house. We had $2300 to collect when the house was completed, which would cover all our outstanding debts and leave some to spare. It was winter 1950 before we got the last of the mortgage money. In the meantime we had a few more run-ins with our creditors, including the hospital and the doctor's expenses for Peter's birth.

OUR SECOND CHILD IS BORN

Our second child Peter was born on May 18, 1950, just two and a half months after we had moved in. We were still waiting for final draws so we were hard pressed for money. In those days the hospital required payment before a patient was discharged. I did not have the money and was concerned as to how I would get it. I could get it from my parents, but did not like the idea of not being able to stand on my own feet. Fortunately, I was paid by a client who had previously been slow in paying. I breathed a sigh of relief and thanked God: I could get Elinor and Peter out of the hospital.

Elinor was in a room with three other mothers. In the bed next to Elinor was a woman Elinor knew before she was married. This lady had married a chap named Bill Barringer. The babies were kept in a separate room and brought to the mothers at feeding time. Apparently the names Burgener and Barringer confused the nurse and they would mix the babies and give Elinor the Barringer baby. The mothers would then trade the babies. When we brought Peter home, he was so different than Paul. He was blond and Paul was redheaded; Paul was very peaceful and Peter was noisy and bouncy. Elinor often wondered if she got the right baby. Many years later our parish got a new deacon named Steve Barringer. One day Elinor asked Steve if his father was Bill Barringer and he replied that yes, he was. She told him how she and his mother traded babies. He agreed that he had a brother born at that time; however, he asked how tall Peter was. Peter is 6 foot 2 inches. The deacon said, "You can rest assured, the

Barringers are short people - the tallest Barringer is 5 foot 7 inches." And so, after many years of wondering, Elinor was assured.

When I brought Elinor home from the hospital she got an infection from the birth and was quite sick. Both mothers came to help but they spent a lot of time telling me how stupid I was to not get a steady paying job. As Elinor recovered they insisted that she should demand that I get a job. Elinor told them that my job was to provide for her and the children, and she trusted that I was doing what was necessary. We had both agreed to start a business and we would both agree if it was to end. We had both had the vision of our own business and we will put up with the difficulties to get it. Business was developing slowly, producing a meagre income. That summer was the worst we ever had. Total business for the month of July was less than $500; we decided that we had to give up. A chemistry professor at Ontario Agriculture College in Guelph had tried earlier to persuade me to accept a research position in spectrochemistry. I called him and he said the opening was still there, but he had to fill it by October. I told him I would let him know by the end of August. While I was considering the procedures to close down the business and working out how to sell our incompletely finished house, I got a call from Hal Champ at the Geological Survey of Canada. He told me they had approval for the purchase of $70,000 worth of Jaco equipment. My commission would be 15% i.e. $10,500. We decided to stay in business.

However, the order seemed slow in coming. I called the Public Works Department, who handled all major equipment purchases. I was told that their policy was to order from the manufacturer and if there was an exclusive agent in Canada, it was the manufacturer's obligation to advise them. TSL did not have an exclusive arrangement. At that time, there was considerable concern about Canadian graduates leaving Canada for jobs in the USA. I contacted the Department of Immigration and Citizenship, pointing out that, as a Canadian graduate, I was being prevented from making a living in Canada because of the attitude of the Department of Public Works. A few days later I got a call from Public Works saying they had canceled the order to Jarrell-Ash and were reissuing it to TSL. We thanked God and breathed a sigh of relief. By the end of the year I had sold another installation to the Canadian National Railway Research Laboratories in Montreal. Plus we got the final draw on our mortgage. We could pay all our debts, finish the house, and still have enough left to improve our lifestyle.

ST. GEORGE STREET

Early in 1950 I moved the lab from the Adelaide Street premises of Toronto Testing to 46 St. George Street. It was an old house, owned by Canadian Research Institute, which was a private electronic research company founded and owned by R. Spencer Soanes, who had graduated four years before me in the same course at U of T. I rented two rooms on the second floor and set up my spectrograph. Over the next several years TSL slowly expanded into more space until we had taken over most of the second floor and the entire third floor. It was a good, quiet location, close to the university and libraries. It did have some drawbacks. Parking space was limited so I had to rent a garage several blocks away to park my car during the working day. I often worked late and when walking to my car I frequently passed drunks or others who could present a problem. On two occasions I was accosted. The first incident was when two men stopped me: one asked for a light while the other went behind me. I was already aware of the common trick to get a victim to put their hands in their pocket while the second man crouched behind the victim; then, the first man would push the victim over the crouching man. Recognizing this, I jumped to the side and prepared for a fight, but they took off. After that I carried an iron bar about 14 inches long with me when leaving late. The second time I was accosted I raised the iron bar and they ran off.

One of the first new customers I had when I moved into St. George Street was a scrap metal dealer. He was a friendly person and often brought in the work himself. We often talked and he told me his story. As a child the family was hard up. So after elementary school he decided that he should help the family instead of going to high school. He started collecting scrap wherever he could find it, and sold it to scrap dealers. He did not make much, but every cent helped. At sixteen he got a job working for a scrap dealer and by the time he was twenty-five he owned his own scrap company. He said he often wondered if schooling was that effective. He pointed out that with high school and university, I must have spent at least nine years before I started to learn a business and no doubt at least another two years before I was good at it. Eleven years during which time a person like him was progressing and establishing himself. He also pointed out that during those eleven years, by reading and personal interest, he acquired probably all the general knowledge that a so-called educated person had. However, he was established and reasonably wealthy and I was just starting out. I have often wondered since if all the education people pursue is that indeed effective. In my case I had started my own business when I was thirty-one years of age, and started to earn a decent income at about thirty-five. He was ten years ahead of me. Even if I had remained with Alcan I would have been thirty-five by the time I would be earning a good living, and would probably be fifty by the time I had income and position equivalent. So he would have been way ahead of me. This scrap dealer developed into a major supplier of reconditioned machinery, even to the extent of reconditioning military hardware. He remained a customer of TSL.

By the time John was born in August 1951, the laboratory business had improved; with commissions from equipment sales, our income had risen substantially. Elinor (who was doing all the typing, bookkeeping, and general administration) also did a lot of direct mail advertising in the form of a monthly newsletter, explaining spectrochemistry and analytical services in general. We even had requests to be put on the mailing list. Of course this was a lot of work for Elinor. After we got the order from the Geological Survey, Elinor suggested that a former co-worker, Doris Crouse, would be interested in earning some extra money typing at night. We arranged this and I would drop reports and letters to be typed at Doris' on my way home, and pick them up in the morning on my way to the lab. This worked well, was inexpensive, and relieved Elinor of a lot of typing. It was at this time that I hired my first lab assistant, Millie Brown. She had been a neighbour when we lived on Third Street. Millie had no formal technical training, but learned fast and well, becoming TSL's senior spectrographic technician, serving TSL for many years.

In the spring of 1952 we decided that Elinor was too busy with two babies to also do our bookkeeping and other clerical jobs. The time had come to hire a full-time typist. A young Greek immigrant named Marta applied and became TSL's first full-time secretary. She had escaped from a Communist-controlled part of Europe with her husband. She told us quite a story of her encounters with the Nazis and the Communists. In both cases she lived in constant fear and starvation. Her father was killed by the Nazis, and then her brother was killed by the Communists. Getting to Canada was like heaven by comparison. Unfortunately for TSL, her husband got a job in New Brunswick and she left six months after joining us.

When Marta left, I advertised for a receptionist typist. An Ontario government department head phoned saying that he understood that we were looking for a secretary and he had a terrific secretary on a short term contract, who was about to be released. She was Chinese and had worked for Imperial Chemicals, a British Company, in China as the president's private secretary. He wondered if I would be interested. I pointed out that I could not afford - nor did I need - such a highly qualified secretary. He replied that since she was Chinese, and not a young woman, it might be difficult for her to get a job at that level. I agreed to see her. When I interviewed her I was impressed. I offered her a job and she accepted. When Mao's Communists were taking over Shanghai, Imperial Chemicals ask her to take five million dollars in gold to England. Since her father was Portuguese and her mother Chinese, she had a Portuguese passport and was able to leave China. She took the gold in her luggage and boarded a ship for England with her two sisters and her mother. On the way to England, her mother died. Stopping in Portugal, she buried her mother and continued on to England, delivering the gold, and from there to Canada. If the Communists - or anyone else for that matter - had discovered the gold, she would no doubt have been killed. Julia was a brave and honest woman. TSL got a superior secretary in Julia Remidios, who eventually became the administrator of our spectrographic sales business. Julia stayed with us for twenty years, retiring when she was seventy years old.

At about the same time, another immigrant came into the lab looking for a job. She had a master's degree in industrial chemistry from the University of Kiev in Russia. Her credentials were impressive, but I pointed out that I really could not afford her, nor did I need her at that point. She was working as a seamstress at minimum wage and offered to work without pay to gain Canadian laboratory experience. Since she worked nearby on Spadina Avenue 7:00 AM to 3:00 PM, she could come in after 3:00 PM and work till 5:00 PM or 6:00 PM to get experience. I agreed, but after one week I was so impressed that I hired her full time. Nadia Rudnik became our senior spectrochemist and was a valuable member of TSL's staff.

Nadia had a story of courage and resourcefulness that is rarely heard. She graduated from university about three years before World War II and married her sweetheart, who graduated at the same time in engineering. However, on applying for a job, it was discovered that his family had been White Russians (a term for Russians with tsarist sympathies in the period directly following the 1917 Revolution). Because of this, they had been executed by the Communists. As such he was not entitled to a university education and was sent to Siberia to a labour camp. Just as the war was starting he was released, and he returned as a physical wreck. Both of them were not enamoured with Communism, to say the least. When the Germans invaded Russia, Nadia and her husband decided that they would look for the opportunity to escape from the country. As the Germans moved through Russia, Nadia, her husband, her two sisters and her mother walked through the battle lines and surrendered to the Germans. Apparently many others fed up with Communism did the same. In fact, Nadia said that if the Germans had treated the Russians as humans, the Russian population would have surrendered.

When Nadia and her group reached the Germans, they were locked in cattle cars to freeze to death. Where Nadia's group was locked there were five cattle cars packed with Russians. There were a few guards. She managed to attract the attention of a guard and pointed out that there were at least five hundred people who would make great slave labour for the German factories and therefore it was foolish to kill them all. The guard apparently told his superior, who came to talk to Nadia, and agreed that she made sense. As a result they were moved to a barracks and treated as slaves for the rest of the war - but they survived. After the war they were moved to Belgium as displaced persons, and again they were treated as slaves. Her husband, who was in very poor health, was forced to work in a mine, finally breaking down completely, physically and mentally. She and her husband finally got to Canada, but her husband was a physical and mental wreck and died while she was working for TSL. Unfortunately Nadia was herself killed in a car crash shortly after retiring from TSL.

With Nadia on the staff I rented from Soanes an analytical balance, hot plate, and fume hood, which allowed me to set up an analytical chemical lab, expanding our services to include chemical analyses. The lab staff for several years was Millie, Julia, Nadia, and I, with occasional part-time help. Towards the end of TSL's stay at St. George Street, my brother-in-law Jim O'Neill was looking for a job. As I was spending a lot of time on sales, and since he had previous sales experience, I hired him as equipment salesman.

WORK FOR THE ONTARIO PROVINCIAL POLICE

One of our good customers at that time was Dr. Smith of the Forensic Laboratory of the Ontario Provincial Police. He used our services on a number of cases and finally bought equipment from us. Some of these OPP cases were quite interesting. In one case, some thieves had stolen several cans of platinum dust (belonging to International Nickel Company of Canada) from a railway station platform in Port Colbourne. Apparently the theft went unnoticed until the express arrived. No one saw anything and there were no suspects. However, on the same day, a station-wagon driving along a back road hit a culvert and flipped over into the ditch. The driver was killed and two others were seriously injured. The car was a write-off. The local police, wondering why this car was driving so fast on a back road, discovered the driver had a record, and asked the forensic lab to have a look. Dr. Smith noticed a round impression on the ceiling of the station wagon but could find nothing in the car that would make such a mark. He brought a sample of the covering to me to be checked on the spectrograph. It was platinum dust. There were no cans in the wreck, but the mark fit the size of the cans. Looking over the scene of the wreck, Dr. Smith found the cans in the culvert. One of the thieves must have rolled them into the culvert after the accident.

In another case a farmer's wife in Northern Ontario was accused of murdering her husband by shooting him with a .22 caliber rifle from her kitchen window through an open window in the barn, which was about 50 yards away. They were known to be quarrelling and she was known as a crack shot. There was a .22 caliber revolver beside the man and a .22 caliber rifle in the kitchen with a partly used box of ammunition. The bullet that killed him was too distorted to identify the weapon that fired it. The location of the wound and other circumstances seemed to indicate that he had not shot himself, nor that the wife could have used the revolver. Dr. Smith brought me the bullet that killed him, plus two bullets from the revolver, and two from the box of bullets in the kitchen. On comparing them spectrographically the bullet that killed him was of the same trace element composition as the two from the revolver. The two from the kitchen were obviously from a different batch. The local police decided that they did not expect that different boxes of bullets could be that distinct, and she was certainly not bright enough to have anticipated the difference, and to have therefore taken a bullet from the same box that the revolver bullets came from in order to cover her tracks. The conclusion was that the farmer had committed suicide, and she was released.

A head-on automobile crash in a small Ontario town occurred between a car traveling south and a car traveling north. The two elderly men in the car that were traveling south were killed. The driver of the car going north survived, but was very seriously injured. Both cars ended up in the ditch, with the northbound car a hundred and fifty feet from the apparent point of impact.

The northbound driver (who was known as a drinker and was probably drunk when the accident happened) claimed the southbound car was on his side of the road. I went with Dr. Smith to look at the scene. There was a scratch on the road starting on the southbound side from the point of impact to the place the northbound car ended. I took samples along the scratch and analyzed them spectrographically. They showed the composition of an electroplated bumper, chromium to nickel to copper to iron. The bumper had been forced down in the collision and scraped along the road as the car progressed to the ditch. On checking the car bumper the wear was evident. I don't know what happened to the obviously guilty driver.

We worked on many other similar cases; as our work became more widely known, the defence lawyers wanted to cross-examine the chemist. I appeared as an expert witness on a few cases but I never felt comfortable testifying against hardened criminals. I may have worried needlessly, but I felt that I could become a target. My suspicions were confirmed when a lawyer for a high-profile criminal case approached me to be an expert witness for the defense. When I explained that I worked for the police, he implied that it was not only more lucrative, but much safer to work for the defense. In that case I refused to testify for either side, but instead got Dr. Smith, who was a chemist, to go through all the steps of the test so that he could testify that he had done the work. At that point the OPP decided to set up their own spectrographic lab, which I organized for them.

JOHN IS BORN

In the fall 0f 1950, Elinor unexpectedly became pregnant again. Between Paul and Peter, Elinor had three miscarriages. We wanted more children and Elinor and I did a great deal of praying to Saint Gerard, the mother's Saint. When Peter was born we expected that he was the last, so we stopped praying, and John was a surprise. There were only fifteen months between Peter and John.

By the summer of 1951 the house was liveable, but the landscaping left much to be desired. The water table was only three feet below the surface so the basement floor was almost at ground level. Also, the lot was the lowest on the street, so a great deal of fill was needed. Clean fill was $50 a load and I estimated that we needed at least 45 loads. We had decided that when we got our last draws from the mortgage, if we bought two loads a month we would get our lot properly graded in less than two years. Fortunately the town decided to put in sewers on Pine Ave. When the sewers were finally installed, there was a huge pile of fill left over in front of our house. Elinor talked to the foreman, pointing out that it would be much cheaper to give the fill to us then pay to have it trucked away. The foreman was glad to get rid of it, and suggested that Elinor make a deal with the bulldozer operator to move it onto our property. For $80 he moved about 45 loads of fill onto our land and properly graded it. This moved our landscaping schedule ahead at a tremendous saving.

The sewer installation took place at the time Elinor's pregnancy with John was nearing its end. The street was impassable. To leave our property we had to cross a six foot ditch on a plank, and the nearest place a vehicle could come was the next street. We were concerned that getting Elinor to a hospital was going to be difficult. Fortunately, John waited till the street was open. However, it was still a rush. When the time came, Elinor was typing an urgent report for the lab and felt she had better finish it - plus the kitchen floor needed washing. When we started for St. Michael's Hospital in downtown Toronto (a slow twenty mile drive since the Gardiner Expressway had not been built yet), we ran into traffic leaving the Canadian National Exhibition, making progress **very** slow. By the time we got to the hospital, Elinor was in serious labour. She was rushed into the delivery room and John was born shortly thereafter.

Elinor is Rh negative. John's birth, following so close after Peter's (fifteen months), resulted in John being seriously affected. He was a "Blue Baby". His blood was reacting to the Rh factors and he was dying for lack of blood. At the time, most of the medical profession was not aware of Rh complications, and although the hospital had called in a pediatrician, he took the attitude that nothing could be done. Miraculously, our family doctor, Dr. Watson, who had been away on holidays when John was born, returned a week early. He heard that Elinor had had the baby and went to visit her at the hospital. When he saw John, he rushed off with him. John was returned a few hours later looking perfectly normal. We assume that he had been given a blood transfusion, which is the standard treatment today. If our doctor had not arrived home early and decided to visit Elinor, and not been up to date, John would have died that day. Certainly God wanted him to live.

Our three sons, Paul, Peter & John.

The business prospered during this time and in the spring of 1952 I was able to buy a 1950 Pontiac from John Holland at Bruce MacDougall Motors in Port Credit. This vehicle was a big improvement over our previous old cars. With a good car I bought a tent and the accessories needed for camping. Camping was inexpensive and did not require reservations, and both Elinor and I liked the outdoor life. Starting that summer we were able to take camping trips to Algonquin Park and Georgian Bay. Although Peter and John were babies, Paul was seven years old and it was time that he started to experience different ways of living. He enjoyed camping and looked forward to more the next summer. The following summer Peter was three and John two years old so they were able to enjoy camping. We drove to the Adirondacks in New York State. Here we visited Lake Placid. At White Face Mountain we took the elevator to the peak. While there, a violent storm occurred with lightning flashing around the observatory. It was a spectacular sight and the boys were at first frightened, but as I explained to them, they were safe inside. They were awed by the display and enjoyed it. We also visited the North Pole Park where they had pony rides. In the petting zoo John was not taking any chances with the goats and kept his distance. Peter wandered away and fortunately we found him. In the Amusable Chasm we took what was probably one of the first white-water rafting rides. In 1954 I bought our first new car, again from John Holland, a Chevrolet Bel Air, a beautiful two-tone blue and white car. It was the first of many new cars I would buy for myself (and for TSL) over the next forty-four years. With good cars we did a lot more holidaying. We all enjoyed the relaxed life of camping, and we did camp in many places, particularly as Peter and John got older.

Camping in Algonquin Park.

HURRICANE HAZEL

In October of 1954 Hurricane Hazel was heading for Toronto area. The media were, of course, predicting serious damage due to the violent winds expected. On my way home I drove up to my parents' house on Indian Road in

A Broader Vision

Lorne Park. My parents were in Florida at the time and I wanted to make sure everything was securely fastened down. It was a windy night, but nothing like what had been predicted. I went to work the next morning and forgot about Hazel. However, as the day wore on it started to rain, and the rain turned into a heavy downpour. About 6:00 PM I started to drive home. The streets were flooded and traffic was standing still. At about 7:00 PM I got to the Humber River—it should have only taken fifteen minutes at that time of the evening. There were police there allowing one car at a time to cross the bridge. At about 7:30 PM I got across and saw why there was a hold-up. The river had swollen to just under the bridge, with the occasional wave flowing over it.

I made it back to my house safely and I was glad to be home and out of the downpour. After supper I decide to turn on our home-made TV (I had bought a war surplus radar unit and added a tuner and made a TV). What I saw amazed me. At 7:30 PM they had closed the bridge at the Humber River. By shortly after eight the bridge had washed out. I must have been one of the last cars to cross. There were scenes of flooding, with houses being washed away, cars floating down rivers, and even a fire truck being washed away. In the trailer park in the Etobicoke Valley trailers were being washed into the lake with firemen trying to rescue the occupants. The rain was still pouring. The next morning I drove around to see if any help was needed. Many were homeless and our church organized accommodation for those washed out. We took in several children for several days. Then stories started coming in of other areas. My parents had a friend who had a hobby farm on the Humber River. They had two horses and at about 7:00 PM he went to the barn to see how things were. As he walked to the barn the water was up to his ankles. He checked things out and as he started back, the water was up to his knees. Astounded that the water had risen so much in a few minutes, he decided to lead the horse out of the barn and take them to the house, which was on higher ground. By the time he reached the house the water was up to his hips. He yelled for his wife and they got on the horses and rode bareback up to a hill. By the time they reached the top of the hill the water rose to the roof level of their house. If he had not gone to the barn they would probably have drowned. This was the story on all the rivers in the area. Eight inches of rain fell in twenty four hours. Hurricane Hazel more than lived up to predictions.

Chapter 12

GROWTH IN THE COMPANY

The house on St. George Street was taken over by the University of Toronto, which had an option on it, and TSL had to move. We rented a 2700 square foot space on the second floor of a building at 22 Harbord Street. It was off the street and tucked behind the buildings. It was a quiet pleasant place with lots of windows and even a small balcony, which served as a fire escape. The property also included a separate 700 square foot building and a lawn. In the good weather, lunches could be eaten there, and even a game of baseball played. As mining exploration assays had become a major part of our business, the separate building was also rented to set up rock crushing and pulverizing equipment.

With this move I made some major changes. This was a large increase in space: 3400 square feet as compared with 900 square feet at St. George. I bought a Hilger spectrophotometer, an analytical balance, hot plates, a fume hood, glassware, along with all necessary equipment to set up a sophisticated chemical lab. I also hired several new people. Shortly after we moved into Harbord Street, Toronto Testing went into receivership and we got a senior analytical chemist, Ernie Bolton. We also hired John Gurney as an assistant manager. He had worked in the spectrographic lab in Arvida. We lived with John and Julie while we waited for Alcan to assign us a house. They left Alcan in 1946 and went to Kansas to establish the co-op system there. John had been involved in the cooperative movement at St. Francis Xavier University and they recommended him to the people in Kansas. He was in Kansas for several years, had finished the job, and came back to Canada.

A Broader Vision

Lunch break at Harbord Street.

An ore-dressing lab was established in a 1200 square foot space a few blocks away, on Classic Ave. Dr. Berkovich was hired to head up this section. We carried out a few ore testing programs but our major program was for a promoter, Mr. Guy McKay. He had an andalusite deposit in Cape Breton that he hoped could compete with bauxite. It was on the North American continent and not subject to the vagaries of the equatorial countries. Our objective was to convert the andalusite to aluminum oxide by metallurgical and chemical processes. This might have succeeded if the ore had been uniformly as rich as the early samples received. There were apparently pockets of almost pure andalusite, but the general grade was too low. Fortunately for TSL, this program paid for the investment in the metallurgical equipment.

When we set up the ore-dressing lab we moved the rock preparation equipment to Classic Ave. We then bought a Jaco 2.4 meter direct reading spectrometer and installed it in the separate 700 square foot building. In this instrument, the photographic film was replaced with photo multipliers, very sensitive photocells. The photo multipliers were placed behind slits that were positioned on the spectrum line of the metal to be analyzed, thus reducing the errors introduced by the photographic emulsion. It also eliminated the time-consuming photographic processing and the evaluation of the photographic record. This was a unique spectrometer using a Wadsworth mounting: it had two parallel focal curves, making it very versatile. The spectrometer cost $25,000. A similar instrument in 2010 would cost $200,000. TSL was the first commercial laboratory in Canada to have a direct reading spectrometer. We developed procedures for mineral samples and used it on several major analytical programs. It was a major selling feature of our analytical services, as well as instrument sales. Not only did we sell the equipment; we used it and could assure our customers of a true understanding of their needs.

On Harbord Street we finally got the Aluminum Company of Canada as an instrument sales customer. Jim made a substantial sale at Alcan. They bought a Hilger direct reading spectrometer for the Arvida plant and one for Isle Malign, and later bought one more. I went to Arvida to install the equipment. Since I needed some equipment to do so, I decided to drive. It was March and the weather was not a problem. It was a two day drive: the first day to Quebec City and then through the Laurentide Wilderness park to Arvida. It was an uneventful drive. It was pleasant to be back in Arvida and to see some of our old friends. I stayed at the Saguenay Inn. Even one of the single girls who had been there during the war was still there. I was asked to give a talk to the Chemical Society meeting, as they did not often get outside speakers. I gave a talk on the differences in approach in a commercial laboratory. It was well received. I also spent an afternoon skiing on the hills Elinor and I had skied on.

When finished in Arvida I had to go to Isle Malign, which was about 30 miles north; I spent two days there. On the way south I skidded off the road into a snow bank that buried the station wagon. It was impossible to open the doors. Fortunately the rear window was electric. I opened it and crawled out. At least I could get help if someone came along and I did have an arctic sleeping bag in the car. The first vehicle was a big dump truck and he pulled the station wagon out of the snow bank. After de-snowing the car I started for Quebec City. By the time I reached the Laurentide Park it was getting dark and a warm spell had set in, with snow melting and water flowing across the highway. The temperature was just above freezing, so there was the possibility of frozen areas. I drove slowly and a car passed me. I decided to follow at as safe distance and if he hit ice I would have time to stop. He did not hit ice, but at a dip in the road he ran into deep water and came to stop on the other side of the flooded area. Hitting the water at high speed flooded his engine. I had time to stop. I drove up to the edge of the water and turned my engine off and coasted through. The fan in the engine spreads water over the electrical wiring and stalls the engine. I offered to take the driver to get help but he said he would dry the wiring with a cloth and expected that within a half hour it would start again. I left him and continued on to Quebec City. While in Quebec City I called on the department of health lab and closed a complete spec lab sale. It was a good trip.

About three months later TSL got a call from Alcan that the equipment had not performed properly; they wanted a meeting to discuss it. Jim O'Neill and I went to Montreal and met with the person who had called. A meeting was set up that included the person in charge of the Arvida Spectrographic Lab, a person from the purchasing department, and the chairman of the meeting, who was a person I had worked with in my Arvida days. The meeting started with the lab person listing a series of problems with the equipment and ending with the comment that he did not know why the equipment had been bought from a "pig in a poke". Jim (who sold the equipment) had brought a copy of our quote. He handed the quote to the chairman and said, "You will note that we included an unconditional service contract for one year and have not had any requests to service the equipment." The chairman turned to the lab man and asked, "Why did you insist on this meeting if the equipment was not working? The first step is to have it serviced under the guarantee." He ended the meeting. At the end of the meeting I asked the lab man why he did not call us. He had no answer because none of his complaints were equipment problems. The problems could be fixed by the company instrument service department. I suspect his boss was the chief chemist who never liked me, probably because I had questioned some of his results. I knew that he was annoyed that the equipment was bought from TSL instead of Applied Research Laboratories. When installing the equipment he stated several times that the equipment should have been bought from a well-known international company, not some small Toronto outfit.

I heard no more complaints from Alcan - in fact they bought another complete installation.

AN ARCTIC LABORATORY

At this time we ventured forth on our first on-site laboratory. We had a client who was going to start exploration of a nickel deposit in Ungava on the Arctic Ocean. The site was remote with no regular flights, so they wondered how they could get samples to us for assaying and get the results back quickly. I suggested that they put a minimum lab at the site – they would get results every day and save significantly on transportation of the samples. They liked the idea and we got a contract to provide their analytical services in Ungava. All equipment was to be provided to crush and pulverize the drill core, as well as for chemical analysis equipment, all supplies for a season, and a building. It all had to be flown to the site. We had a limit of 4000 lbs. The building had to withstand 150 lbs. per square foot snow load and winds of 140 miles per hour. After studying several books and consulting a mechanical engineer, I designed the building of aluminum angle and aluminum sheet that was bolted together. The building was the lab proper. The sample preparation equipment was under a roll-up canvas and plastic awning supported on an aluminum angle frame. In bad weather the awning could be rolled down, but could be left open for normal conditions, so that the dust produced could be blown away. The windows in the building were glazed with thick nylon plastic sheet that would endure the rough handling. For the chemical analyses we used a torsion balance instead of a delicate analytical balance and a colorimetric procedure. Since the only electricity to be provided by the camp was for lighting, gasoline motors powered the crushing and pulverizing equipment.

On-site lab flown to Ungava Bay on the Arctic Ocean.

As delivery was by air, we had a maximum weight allowed of only 4000 lbs. for the entire shipment, including the building, the rock crushers and motors, and all supplies. We managed to get everything under the allowed 4000 lbs. This set-up lasted at least six years. TSL operated it for four summers and another company operated it for two more that we know of. This was the first of several on-site laboratories supplied or operated by TSL over the years.

By now the uranium rush in Ontario had started. The assaying of mineral samples for uranium introduced new techniques in the assaying business. A rather long and relatively insensitive procedure was available. However, the Manhattan Project (the atom bomb, of which I was familiar from having worked on it in a minor way in Arvida) had developed a very sensitive method using a fluorometer. Jaco sold such a device. TSL bought one, becoming the first commercial lab in Canada to offer such a service. Of course our instrument sales department sold fluorometers to other labs. The procedure involved fusing the sample with Lithium Fluoride in a platinum dish. A spectrographic procedure was developed that covered the range above .05%. An investment was also made in a Beta and Gamma ray counter. Using a radiometric method developed by the Mines Branch of the Dept. of Mines in Ottawa, it was possible to obtain a true uranium value by compensating for other radioactive components. Ernie Bolton added to our versatility by his excellent chemical procedures. With the various methods we were able to counter-check our results. With these tools TSL became recognized as the best lab for uranium assays.

However, we had an unfair competitor. The Mines Branch laboratory of the Canada Department of Mines and Resources offered similar services at half the price we charged. They were set up to provide services not available commercially. Their cost calculations did not include capital cost and overhead. I got nowhere with the Deputy Minister in charge of this lab. He argued that they had the equipment and staff, so capital cost and overhead did not figure into their charges. I again approached the Minister of Immigration and Citizenship. The result was the Mines Branch laboratory continued to offer the services, but at our price. This was fine with me, since their turnaround time was three times longer than ours. There were many government laboratories offering services that competed with commercial laboratories, but their turnaround was poor in general. If a client complained about our prices, we often suggested they go to a government lab. They usually came back.

John E. Burgener

ON-SITE LAB IN BANCROFT, ONTARIO

TSL set up its second on-site laboratory at Bancroft, Ontario, to analyze uranium ore using a beta gamma counter for Grey Hawk Mines. We got a contract from Grey Hawk to provide all their assays with fast turnaround local analyses on site, and the results to be checked in our Toronto lab. They also offered to provide space on their property for our lab.

Several other exploration operations were being carried out in the same district; we wanted to be able to serve them as well. For this reason we decided to set up outside Grey Hawk, and offered to buy a lot a local farmer had for sale. The purchase seem to be going satisfactorily, although slowly. Two weeks before we were to start operations, the farmer backed out. He would only consider selling if he either got a percentage of the billings we did, or if we paid a ridiculous price. He thought he had us over a barrel. I told him to go to hell and I set up the lab on Grey Hawk's property. For the several years we were there, the property was still for sale.

A three-roomed prefabricated cottage acted as the lab and living quarters for the operator. The mine provided meals. Since the analyses were radiometric there was no fume problem. A prefabricated two-car garage was insulated and provided the sample crushing and pulverizing area. Oil space heaters heated both insulated buildings. Grey Hawk provided electricity and water and we used their washroom facilities. When the supplier erected the buildings, I went up to supervise, set up the equipment, and got things started. Andy Pitett, who was to operate the lab, was to come to Bancroft when things were ready. The fuel oil supplier did not show up for the first three days after the buildings were set up, and I had a deadline for starting the operation. This was December and a real cold snap had set in: it was -25°F. I bought an electric heater, which probably raised the temperature to 0°F.

The hotel space in Bancroft was very limited and I only had reservations for two nights. The first night I went to my room I found someone sleeping in my bed. I complained to the desk and their response was, "Oh, that's the local drunk—we'll chase him out." I asked for clean sheets and they replied that if I insisted, they would change them. I insisted. After spending all day setting up the equipment at -25°F, I had to spend the third night sleeping in the lab with only the electric heater. It was cold, especially so in the morning when I crawled out of my sleeping bag. Finally the fuel truck arrived; Andy came in and we got the lab in operation.

A Broader Vision

* * *

Blind River was the major area of uranium exploration in Ontario. The ore from this area also contained significant copper values. Since we were doing the uranium, many samples were also checked for copper. Samples to be analyzed chemically were first checked spectrographically. Where nil or traces of copper were found, these were reported without chemical analyses since the spectrographic method was many times more sensitive than chemical. Those that showed significant values were run chemically. A saving to the customer resulted, since we charged one half the chemical price for traces and nils. It also reduced the possibility of an error in chemical analysis. If spectrographic and chemical results did not agree, then we found out why. Our chemical analyses were probably the best available. However, on one sample, which was reported to a Blind River customer, the typist typed 0.6% instead of .06%. This was discovered immediately after the report was mailed. I phoned the client and explained the error before he got the report, and sent a corrected copy. We never got another sample for copper from that client and the word among the mining people for years after was that TSL could not do copper assays.

TSL was at the same time progressing in equipment sales. After the sale to the Geological Survey of Canada, I doubled my efforts on equipment sales and it paid off. Over the next three years I sold a spectrographic installation to the Canadian National Railway Research Laboratory in Montreal to develop procedures for wear analyses on their Diesel Locomotives. Another complete installation was delivered to the Ontario Forensic Laboratory, and a similar one to the RCMP in Ottawa. The National Research Council of Canada Laboratories bought an installation, but in this case they decided that the source unit at $15,000 was too much and they would build their own. However, to have one specially built 30,000 volt transformer that could allow a dead short cost about $12,000. Along with other components that required one-of-a-kind purchases, I expect it cost them at least $20,000 to build it. By now both Hilger and Jarrell-Ash (Jaco) began to appreciate us. I was invited to both companies to learn more about their equipment. In 1956 I went to London and by 1958 we had sold three Hilger direct reading spectrometers, along with several UViSpect spectrophotometers. TSL had also expanded the sale of supplies, producing a substantial return.

John E. Burgener

FLIGHT TO EUROPE

During the years TSL was at Harbord Street, our personal standard of living improved steadily. In 1956 I took up Hilger's offer to increase our commission to 15% if I spent a week in London at their factories learning about their existing and some new equipment they were offering. This was to be at my expense. However one of the advantages of having my own business was that I could make a business trip a family trip, instead of leaving the family at home while I was away. So I went to London with Elinor and Paul, who was ten years old, leaving Peter and John with my sister. Flying in 1956 was not as common as today, especially overseas. Very few people flew overseas. It was an occasion and you had to dress appropriately; you were not welcome on the plane in jeans. The Malton Airport was a collection of frame buildings. The check-in area was six counters, one for Trans-Canada Airlines, one for British Overseas Airways, another for Trans World Airlines, and a couple others. The observation area (where you could watch the planes load, take off, and land) was on the roof of the main building. There was no security; passengers walked out to the plane parked in the field and climbed up the stairs. There was no seat selection, you sat wherever you wanted. The plane was usually not full. The planes were much smaller. Most flights in Canada were on DC3s although some four engine planes were in use: North Stars and Viscounts. We flew to London on BOAC in a Britannia (which was a British plane), stopping in Gander, Newfoundland, and then in Ireland to refuel. The flight from Toronto to London took more than nine hours.

The director in charge of Hilger sales met us at the airport in his chauffeur driven Bentley. We had reserved at the Regent Place Hotel at Piccadilly Square. It was an old hotel with lots of character, and it was centrally located. While Elinor and Paul enjoyed London, I spent the days at Hilger. I did manage to see some of the sights in London. One evening Elinor and I decided to go to a nightclub, leaving Paul in the hotel. I had noticed a sign near the hotel advertising "Murray's Cabaret Club". We decided to go to it and asked a taxi to take us. The driver asked, "Is this your wife?" which seemed like a strange question. "Yes," I replied, and he shrugged and took us there. When the show started, the dancers were scantily clad, but there were others standing totally nude. Elinor was shocked. However, this was not as shocking as after the show: the girls came out nude and sat with the patrons. Well, we wanted to see the world, so we were seeing it.

A Broader Vision

On the weekend one of the technical men I was dealing with took us on a picnic to Canterbury. We visited the old Cathedral where Thomas, the Bishop of Canterbury, was murdered. On our last two days in London I did some sightseeing. We took a boat from London to Hampton Court, the castle of King Henry VIII. It was a pleasant afternoon and we enjoyed the castle, the gardens, and the boat trip on the Thames River. After my week at Hilger we rented a Hillman car and drove from London to Dover and saw the White Cliffs. From there we took the ferry to Calais and set out to explore continental Europe.

On leaving the ferry we drove to Paris. In 1956 there was still evidence of the devastation due to the war and we witnessed this on the way. In Paris we spent a couple of days visiting the Louvre, the Arc de Triomphe, Notre Dame, Montmarte, Sacré Cœur, and the Eiffel Tower. The Eiffel Tower gave one the choice of walking up for a fee, or riding the elevator for a larger fee. What I did not expect was another fee to get down. We walked in the Tuileries Gardens and sat on a park bench and were advised that there was a charge to sit on it. We also discovered that when you bought a meal in a restaurant there were other charges like bread, butter, and water, which were unexpected and not listed on the menu. The French customs were different than Canadian. However, that's why we were there: to see and enjoy other ways of life.

We leisurely drove south from Paris to the Riviera on the Mediterranean. On the way we passed many medieval towns and beautiful countryside. It was early summer and the drive through Southern France was beautiful, especially in the hill towns. At one point getting off the main highway we found a pretty little village named Vienne. A bridge built by the Romans crossed a river flowing through the town. We also found a small church where a body was laid out in a casket and there were mourners in attendance. A plaque on the church wall said that the church had been erected in AD 62. It surprised me to realize that Christianity had reached that far in less than 30 years after Christ's death. Later I learned that it is claimed that the first Bishop of Lyon was the same Lazarus who was raised from the dead by Jesus. We stayed in Nice for a couple of days, staying in a small hotel called Hotel Canada. The proprietor was French Canadian.

At Nice I saw my first bikini: the girls standing on the beach took their clothes off and put on their bikinis, surprising me, but shocking Elinor. Somewhere on the trip Paul picked up a song about a "teeny weeny yellow polka dot bikini" and sang it often as we drove along. From Nice we drove along the Mediterranean coast to Pisa, where Paul and I climbed the Leaning Tower. To do so there is a stairway on the inside wall. With the lean of the tower you appear to walk up on one side and down on the other side, causing a feeling of falling. Elinor started but gave up; Paul and I continued to the top. It was bell-ringing time and the bell ringer let Paul do the ringing.

Paul at the top of the Leaning Tower of Pisa on our 1956 tour of Europe

Then we drove to Rome. Staying at a beautiful pensione, we visited the Vatican, including the Sistine Chapel, which was not crowded in 1956. We sat and enjoyed the magnificent art. On another visit in the '80s it was so crowded that the pressure of people pushed us through. There was no stopping to admire it. On our 1956 visit we had a letter from our bishop that would have given us a private audience with the pope. Unfortunately, the pope had died. Many other sites were visited, including the Catacombs, the Coliseum, and the many fountains. We threw our coins in the Trevi Fountain and many years later we did go back. Paul also went back in 1976, twenty years later. He was on his way to work in Kenya and stopped for a few days. With his nine month old baby and his wife Suzanne, he was still able to remember the sites he had seen and led his family through the streets of Rome to the Trevi fountain where they threw their coins in the fountain.

Elinor and Paul at the Vatican.

From Rome we drove north to Florence, where we stayed in a hotel that overlooked the Duomo, and we viewed Michelangelo's statue of David. At that time the actual statue was in the open. Now the statue that people see is a copy. We visited the famous bridge Ponte Vecchio, and Elinor bought a gold necklace. I was impressed with the statuary of the Duomo and the artwork of the big main entrance doors. Leaving Florence, we drove north through Verona, which was Romeo and Juliet's town, stopping to look at Juliet's balcony. Many towns had obviously suffered much damage from the war, but in general they were rebuilt.

Proceeding north we passed through Siena with its beautiful Cathedral, and the square where they have the furious Palio Horse Race. We drove through some medieval hill towns on our way to the Brenner Pass to Austria. We stopped overnight in a village in the Pass. Here, in a small inn, we got a room on the second floor with a large balcony, overlooking the mountains. After supper, as we sat on our balcony, we noticed people coming into the inn. Soon there was singing and music. We went down to see what was happening. One of the local young men had been called to do his Army service, so the village was suitably sending him off. We were asked to join in, and although we did not speak Italian or Austrian, we enjoyed their joie de vivre.

The next day we spent in Innsbruck, a beautiful city in a valley between two mountain ranges. From there we drove through Salzburg on our way to Neuschwanstein, mad King Ludwig's fairy tale castle on a mountain top. Unfortunately for King Ludwig, he went for a walk with his doctor along the nearby lake shortly after the castle was finished, and they were never seen again. It is believed that someone murdered them and threw them in the lake. I have no photographs of the visit because I used my movie camera; I only took photos of people. We were able to go through the whole castle enjoying its beauty and fairy-like structure and decoration. We visited the throne room, the king's chambers, the dining room, ballroom, the balconies, and even the kitchens. When we returned in 1980, very little was open to the public.

After our visit to Ludwig's castle we drove on to Munich, staying for two days. Elinor bought some new eyeglasses and I bought a Zeiss movie camera. We spent an evening in a beer garden, leaving Paul at the hotel. We expected that children would not be allowed, but Germany had a different attitude and there were many children there. Elinor is not a beer drinker, but in Munich she made a small exception and appeared to enjoy it. To see the barmaids carrying half a dozen big beer steins at a time was amazing. The entertainment included bell ringers, yodelling, and lively dancing. People were singing, talking, laughing, and everyone treated everyone else as a friend. In a Munich beer garden it is hard not to enjoy yourself. When we started to return to the hotel we apparently had enjoyed the beer garden to the full. Neither of us could remember the name of the hotel. There was a minute of terror since we had left Paul. Fortunately I had parked my rented British car on the street in front of the hotel. I asked the driver to drive past the downtown hotels, looking for a Hillman with an English license plate parked in front of it. Thank God, after the fourth hotel we found it. Needless to say, I now always make sure that I have the name of the hotel on me, especially when visiting a beer garden.

SWITZERLAND

Switzerland was next, passing Lake Constance (the Boden Sea), which my father had described as a beautiful calm sea. Our first night was spent in Stein am Rhine - a pretty town where many of the houses have the history of the house painted on the wall, in some cases in caricatures. We found a hotel with all the auto club endorsements and checked in. Having enjoyed an excellent dinner, we went to our room. At about 10:00 PM there seemed to be a lot of activity, with cars coming and going, and much walking along the corridor. Elinor was convinced that we were in a house of ill repute. I pointed out that even if we were (which I doubted), the patrons had their own interests and would not bother us. Nevertheless, she sat up all night in a chair against the door. The next day was spent in Lucerne, visiting the church that was built in 800 AD. We walked across the Chapel Bridge, which is the longest and oldest covered bridge in Europe. Visiting Bucherer's, we bought a Cuckoo clock and I spent $80 on a self-winding Rolex watch. I am still wearing this watch more than fifty years later. Elinor bought a Tissot watch made by Rolex for women (also for $80), which she wore for the rest of her life.

The next day we enjoyed the riverfront with the stores and restaurants. In the square a mountaineer played his big alphorn, which was used in former times for signalling in the mountains. Leaving Lucerne, we drove through the Grimsel Pass. I must say the name suited it. It was a winding, narrow road without guard rails, with vertical drops of hundreds of feet. To add to it, the Swiss post buses that traverse the mountain regions have the right of way and drive the buses through the passes like sport cars. Personally I enjoyed it, but Elinor was worried through the whole pass. I have driven it four times since, but each time it had been improved. The third time was on a visit to Switzerland with our friends the MacFadens. The pass was improved, but it was still a challenge. Ross wanted the experience of driving it, so I let him. When we reached the bottom, he pulled off the road and sat there while he smoked two cigarettes to calm down. The last time I drove it a few years ago, it was widened and paved and had guard rails in the dangerous stretches, and more room on the switch backs. I felt the excitement was taken out of it.

After the pass we drove through valleys surrounded by mountains and made our way to Grindelwald, the village in a valley where my ancestors came from. When we registered at the hotel we were told that many Burgeners lived there; they tried to arrange a get-together, but a storm came up and the proprietor had to leave to look after a restaurant up the mountain. A few days were spent there while we enjoyed the town and the mountains. There was a flower store named "Blumen Burgener". We went in and explained that we were from Canada, but their English was poor and our German even poorer.

Burgener Flower shop in Grindelwald, Switzerland.

In Grindelwald, Elinor took her first ride on a chair lift. She did not plan to do so, but Paul, the attendant, and I got her to sit on the chair. The next thing she knew, she was airborne on her way up the mountain to First. After a few minutes of terror, a passenger coming down told her to open her eyes and enjoy the beauty. This prompted her to do so and she discovered that it was beautiful. She enjoyed the remainder of the ride and has taken many chair lift rides since. My father had told me of the cog rail to the observatory and ice palace on the Jungfrau, so we took the 7:00 AM train to Jungfraujoch. The train travels to Kleine Sheidegg and then travels almost the whole nine kilometres in a tunnel in the Eiger and Momk mountains to the peak at Jungfraujoch, which is the highest station in Europe. Although this was June, it was minus 25°F at the top.

We were lucky to have a clear day with spectacular views of the mountains and the valleys. I have been up twice since and each time I could not see the valleys, despite the clarity and bright sunlight at the mountain tops. We were above the clouds.

After Elinor and Paul had a dog sleigh ride on the mountainside, we each rented skis. On renting them I asked how long we could keep them. He replied as long as we wanted. This should have alerted me. Within a very short time the effects of high altitude (10,500 feet), started to take effect. Paul began to collapse, Elinor got tangled in the towrope and pulled it off its pulley. I began to get weak. It was a struggle to get back to the hut to change our boots and then to walk to the station. We were all so weak that the 500 foot walk back to the station felt like five miles. We did not eat lunch or visit the ice palace; we just sat until the next train. Not until we got down almost to the valley did our strength return.

When we left Grindelwald we visited Interlaken, a beautiful town between two lakes. Then we went to Thun, near where my father was born. At Bern, Paul and I climbed the steeple of the cathedral that my father had climbed as a boy. We watched the famous clock strike the hour and visited the bear pit.

GERMANY

From Bern we drove through Switzerland into Germany following the Rhine. One of our notable stops in Germany was at Rüdesheim, a famous wine cellar resort. After checking into a hotel, enjoying a delightful dinner, and putting Paul to bed, we went out to sample the wines. There were several places listed in our guidebook. We found one and went in. People sitting at long tables were talking and singing, all drinking wine. The host sat us at a table with three young chaps. They spoke a little English and we spoke a little German. We soon became friends and they ordered a bottle of wine to share. Of course we had to reciprocate, and then they did, and so on. After several glasses the young fellows (who were students) decided it was time to go, so we felt we had better head for the hotel too. On the way, finding another even more famous wine cellar, we stopped for another drink. After one bottle, we again started for the hotel. We were both feeling pretty good and Elinor was having trouble walking. At the hotel we had to ring to get in, as they locked the doors at 10:00 PM. Elinor was concerned that the hotelkeeper would be shocked if he saw her hanging on to me. When he came she was struggling to keep her balance. He was a short man in a nightshirt with a little cap on his head and Elinor could not keep herself from saying, "Oh, you are such a cute little man!" right before she staggered up the stairs. I am sure she was not the first guest who had enjoyed Rüdesheim to the full.

Continuing up the Rhine, passing through Karlsruhe, Koblenz, and Cologne (which were still dead cities from the devastation of the war), we spent a day at Heidelberg, visiting the ruined castle and its wine cellars. The story goes that the keeper of the wine cellar drank only wine. One day when he was half asleep someone gave him a glass of water and one gulp killed him. Proceeding up the Moselle River to Zell on the Moselle, we stayed in the Black Cat Castle. Paul had a room in one of the turrets. A wine festival was in progress and we enjoyed the free wine, the re-enacting of Charlemagne's arrival, and the dancing both in the street and at the hotel. Leaving Zell, we followed the Moselle into Luxemburg, and then made our way back to France. It was a very rough crossing across the channel to England. On returning the rented car, the proprietor was amazed at the 2000 miles we had driven in two weeks. No one ever drove that much in such a short time. I pointed out that in Canada one thought nothing of driving from Toronto to Miami, an 1800 mile drive each way on a two week holiday. We then boarded a Constellation aircraft (which was at the time the fastest passenger plane in the world) and flew home at 425 miles per hour air speed, stopping in Gander, Newfoundland, to refuel.

Talking to Paul after he had taken a similar trip with his wife, I was surprised at how much he had remembered from this trip. Apparently the impressions that had been made on him of the effects of World War II have never left him. He told me of staying at a campsite across the river from Koblenz and spending a few hours looking at the modern city across the river. His recollection of driving past Koblenz in 1956 was a pile of rubble with almost no buildings standing. He was amazed that a city could be restored after such devastation. He had a similar experience when he revisited the Cathedral in Cologne. In 1956 we had to walk through pathways dug through the bricks and stones that were the remnants of buildings that had surround the church. From the tower there was almost nothing standing as far as we could see. When Paul revisited it, there were buildings surrounding and a large paved plaza.

Chapter 13

A BIGGER HOUSE

In the spring of 1957 we started looking for a larger house. The 750 square foot house on Pine Avenue was a little tight, especially as we were considering adopting a girl. In Fairfield Manor in Clarkson we found a builder who seemed to have a careful approach to his work. He quoted for a house on Elite Road in Clarkson a price of $25,000. The house would be an 1800 square foot stone-fronted bungalow on a 100 foot frontage lot, with four bedrooms, two bathrooms, two fireplaces, and a double garage. It was a big improvement over our Pine Avenue house. Completed by fall of 1957, we moved in. My parents thought we were foolishly showing off and that we were in over our heads. They were quite cool to the new house, but they eventually accepted it. It was a nice house in a good location and we enjoyed it for many years.

Our house in Clarkson, winter of 1960.

The local separate school was St. Christopher's and had just been built and the parish formed. The parish bought a former church that had been used as carpet store and we took part in the renovations. It served the purpose very well but as the parish grew we eventually raised enough money to build the present St. Christopher's Church. The school was about two miles away. All of our children attended this school. They walked the two miles twice a day; there were no school busses. They did not have a problem with obesity, nor were we worried about their safety.

In the summer of 1958 we bought a sixteen foot travel trailer. It was just big enough to accommodate us, and small enough not to be hard to pull. We also bought a new eight cylinder Plymouth station wagon. As I had a number of prospects for sales out west, I felt that a trip out west should be made. With the trailer we could take to whole family, as was in keeping with my attitude that long business trips should be family events. We set out the second week of July to drive to the Pacific. After the first couple of days on the road the boys became restless. We started playing games such as who could first see a police car, or number games, I Spy, story-telling, and singing. We would find a pleasant campsite at about 4:00 PM so the boys could get out and run around before dinner. We went to bed early and we got going early in the morning. As a result we all enjoyed the driving. We did not have TV or computer games - we used our imaginations. Driving through Chicago to Iowa, we visited the Corn Palace, Mount Rushmore, and Wall Drug Store in Wall. At Mount Rushmore we started up a road and missed a sign that advised trailers not to use the road. We came to a tunnel in the rocks on the road and looking at it was obvious that my trailer would not fit. I did not try to drive through. I pulled onto the shoulder. As there was a continuous stream of traffic, we had to sit there for a couple of hours till traffic slowed down at dusk. Then I had to maneuver the trailer in a very limited space to turn around. I had to uncouple it twice to get the car in a position to move the trailer around. I paid careful attention to signs on the rest of the trip.

The boys thought that Yellowstone National Park was straight out of a horror movie with its boiling pots, hot springs, and large areas where boiling water flowed across the ground. There was a boiling river, geysers, and many other amazing natural phenomena. They also enjoyed the many black bears, with some even climbing on the car. As we drove through Wyoming we saw a sign advertising caves on the top of a mountain. The boys said they had never

A Broader Vision

been in a cave and wanted to see them. Leaving the trailer at the bottom, we drove up a one lane road to the caves on the top of a mountain. The caves were quite spectacular and we all enjoyed the stop. As we started down we met a car coming up. Since we were closer to the top than the other car to the bottom we had to back up about an eighth of a mile. Elinor and the boys got out and waited for me to come back down. It was a narrow road with a straight drop without guard rails. If I was going to go over the edge, I figured that there was no point in all of us going.

Camp in Yellowstone National Park, on our trip across America.

We viewed other attractions such as the Grand Teton Mountains, which are the kind of mountains an artist would love to paint. We visited Cody, which was Buffalo Bill's birthplace. The boys had to buy Buffalo Bill hats. A mock gunfight on the main street of Jackson Hole was so realistic that Peter started to cry because he was certain the victim was dead.

After Wyoming we drove through the Idaho Badlands and marvelled at the different levels and colours in the eroded landscape. Then we continued to Salt Lake City, where we swam in the salty water of Great Salt Lake. The water was so buoyant that we could float without any physical activity. Then we drove across the desert to Reno. Since it was very hot we decided to start out in the late afternoon, but it was still unbearably hot in our non-air-conditioned car. I drove till midnight and found a campsite at an oasis. Early the next morning we started out, reaching Reno late that afternoon. We stayed in a motel that night to cool off. Reno did not have much to offer a family.

We moved on to Lake Tahoe. Here we found a nice campsite in a beautiful location with a lake to swim in. It was a weekend and we found a church to attend Mass. Although traveling, we always tried to attend Mass on Sundays. After enjoying a few days at Lake Tahoe, we traversed another stretch of unbearable heat on our way to San Francisco. In the early afternoon we saw a sign advertising a private lake for swimming. We drove in and found the lake: a watering hole for cattle. It didn't matter. It was cool. Elinor, who loves children, was very attentive to the proprietor's three-year-old daughter. The proprietor stated that she could not stand her and did not want her. Did Elinor want her? Elinor felt this poor lovable child did not have much of a chance for a good life and wished she could do something about it. If we had been in Canada we probably would have looked into it, since we had applied to adopt a child.

Late in the afternoon we got out of the hot valley and came to a pleasant restaurant that advertised all the root beer you could drink for a fixed price. We all had root beer. Paul had three big mugs, drinking so much that I was afraid he would be sick.

The boys at Buffalo Bill's house

We camped for several days near San Francisco. We drove across the Golden Gate Bridge into the city and enjoyed Chinatown, where we each bought a Chinese puzzle box. We ate at Fisherman's Wharf, rode the trolley, and even took a boat trip around the bay. From San Francisco going north along the coast we spent a couple of days in the redwood forests of Northern California. There was something inspiring here, and I experienced a feeling of peace in this forest of huge old trees. We saw a 2000 year old tree growing over a fallen tree, which itself was 2000 years old. Continuing up the coast we stopped at several pleasant campsites, some on the ocean, as we passed through the States of Oregon, Washington, and into Vancouver.

BACK TO CANADA

In Vancouver we all took a ride on a chairlift (now replaced with a gondola) to the mountaintop restaurant called The Grouse Nest. We had lunch there and enjoyed the magnificent view of Vancouver. We visited Stanley Park and watched the seals play. The boys thought a totem pole would look great on our lawn and wished we could buy one. We drove around the university, a water front park, and along the hazardous coast road to Squamish, where Elinor and the boys hoped to see some Indian settlements. I think they expected to see Wigwams, but they were living in houses. From Vancouver we traveled east along the Fraser River into the Fraser Valley. At Capilano we stopped to cross the long pedestrian suspension bridge across the Fraser River. Some teens started swaying the bridge. Seven year old John grabbed Elinor's hand saying, "Don't be frightened Mom, I will help you."

From the bridge we drove into the Rockies. Along the way we took the Great Bend route, which was about to be flooded by the dams on the Columbia River. It was an uninspiring route, dusty and uninhabited. On the whole 150 miles there was one habitation, a gas station. In 1958 the new Trans-Canada Highway was being built and in some places the road was a mud track. In one place I did not think I could pull the trailer through it, as it was a sandpit. A bulldozer went ahead to level and pack the sand, offering to pull me through if I got stuck. I made it.

At Lake Okanagan we stayed for a couple of days to see the dragon of the lake, Ogopogo. He did not appear, much to the boy's disappointment. Camping in a pleasant campsite in the Yoho National Park, we explored all the natural wonders in Yoho and Banff. The black bears roamed through the camps and we were cautioned not to disturb them or to leave any food around. On one occasion Elinor sent John to put some garbage in the garbage cans. He didn't come back for a while and when he did, he still had the garbage. When asked why, he said that there was a bear in the garbage can and it would not let him put the garbage in it. Bears were heard outside our trailer at night and we were glad we were not in a tent. Finding an abandoned mine tunnel in a mountain, the boys and I went in but there was little to see.

Bear in Yoho National Park, BC.

One afternoon the propane tank on the trailer next to us started venting. The woman came over to ask us what to do about it, as her husband was away with the children. Elinor told her that I would certainly know what to do because I was a physicist. It happened her husband was also a physicist. Looking at the tank, I concluded that it had been over-filled, and the heat of the sun was causing it to vent, so there was no danger. When her husband returned he came over to thank us and we got to talking. He was Professor of Physics at the University of Alberta in Edmonton and had just taken delivery of $70,000 worth of Jaco equipment. As sole agent for Canada, I should have been informed. Obviously Jaco was trying to cheat me out of my commission. I told him that I would go to Edmonton to set up the equipment on my way home. When I got there I called John Shuch, the sales manager at Jaco, who said he was about to advise me. That I doubted. However, my chance meeting netted TSL $10,500, plus about another $5,000 in commissions on needed accessories.

After Yoho we stopped and watched a freight train locomotive coming out of the spiral tunnel at one level while the caboose was going in at a different level. We drove into Banff and had lunch at a restaurant. Visiting the hot springs, we all bathed in the hot sulphurous water. We then visited Banff Springs Hotel, a beautiful castle-like hotel in a lovely location in the mountains. It was built in 1888 and was reported to have two ghosts: a bellman who loved the hotel and a bride who fell down the stairs on her wedding night and died. Many guests and employees reported strange happenings. In later years Elinor and I have stayed there several times and certainly never experienced any strange happenings. We also visited the Johnson's Canyon; at that time the water flowing through the canyon was a raging torrent. When we returned twenty years later it was only a stream.

The next stop was Lake Louise with the beautiful Lake Louise Lodge. We had lunch with a view of the lake and the glacier. After lunch we drove up to the Columbia Ice Fields where we took a six passenger snowmobile ride on the glacier; we got out and walked on it as well. In recent years we have been back and are amazed at how far the edge of the glacier has receded. In 1958 the edge of the glacier was right up to the highway. We continued up to Jasper Park, stopping at Angel Glacier on the way. Some years later I painted a mural on the wall in the studio in the Springhill house drawing inspiration from pictures taken on this route. On all our trips I took many movies and some still photographs, some of which I used as scenes to paint in oils. I was not a great artist, but I did enjoy painting and found it relaxing. I gave most of my paintings away to people who thought they were interesting. What I did keep got lost in our recent moves. I know that one of my Grandson's, Michael, had wanted one of the pictures. Michael is now an Australian citizen living in Sydney. When his father (Paul) went to visit him, as they were expecting their first child in June, 2012, he brought one of my paintings with him to give to Michael.

From Jasper we drove to Edmonton, stopping on the way to visit a ghost town where our friend from Arvida, Shelly Donvito, had lived as a boy. The town serviced a coal mine that is now closed. The boys wandered around looking in some of the deserted buildings. There were also two white horses there, probably left to pasture when the owners left. Shelly earned his way through university working in that coal mine.

WORKING AGAIN

We checked into a hotel in Edmonton and stayed for three days while I set up the Jaco equipment and sold accessories. Elinor drove the children around town and enjoyed the sights of Edmonton. From there we went on to Regina. On the way we stopped at a park east of Edmonton where there was a herd of Buffalo. We got out of the car and walked towards the herd that appeared to be behind a fence. As we approached, a large buffalo put his head down and started to charge toward us and then the whole herd started to charge. I yelled for everyone to run for the car. I guess the fence stopped them. I did not wait to see - I drove off.

At Regina I had an appointment with the Commissioner of the Royal Canadian Mounted Police. Spending two days there I sold them a complete spectrographic set-up worth about $100,000. The boys wandered around the establishment and watched some RCMP officers on parade. While in Regina, I called on the university and the department of health, but made no immediate sales. We all visited the parliament buildings and were even escorted up to the roof for a better view of Regina. The next stop was Winnipeg, where I made some sales calls without any immediate effect. By now it was the end of August, with the weather turning cold. Spending a couple of cold nights in a campsite on the edge of Winnipeg, John and Elinor each had a birthday; John celebrated it by getting a very bad cold.

After that we headed for home. In 1958 there was very little in the way of campsites or motels along the Trans Canada Highway. One night at about 10:00 PM, not having found anywhere to stop, we pulled into a truck weighing station and asked if we could spend the night there. The operators were very courteous and loaned us an electric heater for the trailer, as well as the use of their washrooms. We spent one more night on the road at Sault Ste. Marie and then we went home. It was a great six week family holiday, while netting TSL $30,000 plus many thousands more over the years in additional sales of equipment and supplies.

Putting this trip in perspective: the top-of-the-line eight cylinder Plymouth Station wagon that we had traveled in cost $2,700 and the trailer cost $700. The $30,000 earned in the six week trip had the buying power of at least $200,000 in 2012 dollars, and our family had a great experience. It is also to be noted that the many business trips like this with our family would never have happened as an Alcan Manager.

Chapter 14

AGAIN THE LAB MOVES – AND OUR DAUGHTER ARRIVES

Again the university wanted the space we were occupying and gave us notice to leave. We still had two and a half years on our lease so we got a settlement that helped to cover our moving cost. I found a space in a building at 350 King Street West in Toronto. The fourth floor was 8500 square feet with an exhaust system venting on the roof. It had lots of windows and a freight elevator. Parker Pen had used it for manufacturing their pens. The space was divided into rooms and it was well suited to our use. In the late fall of 1958 we moved in. The front of the space was divided into offices, with a large room used as a conference room and library. Behind was the spectrometer room with the spectrograph and the direct reading spectrometer and the microphotometer. We installed a dark room for photographic developing. The back room had the exhaust and we set it up as a chemical lab with fume hoods and hotplates. Lab tables with sinks and drawers were installed, as were the usual glassware such as distillation glassware, burettes, and beakers. Also in the same room were the ovens and high temperature furnaces, along with the instruments used in modern laboratories, spectrophotometers, and colorimeters. Another room had the X-ray equipment along with its associated computer. Near the freight elevator we had a sample receiving and preparation area, including a rock crusher and pulverizer, a lathe for physical testing preparation, and a drill press for obtaining drillings from metal samples. In the same area were the fire assay furnace and the working tables to place the red hot cupolas. Between the sample preparation and the office was a space for maintenance and electronic servicing, which included a precision lathe, along with all the test equipment for electronics testing. This area was used for much of the original design and development for the ThermoCarbs. It was possible to include all our operations in one space.

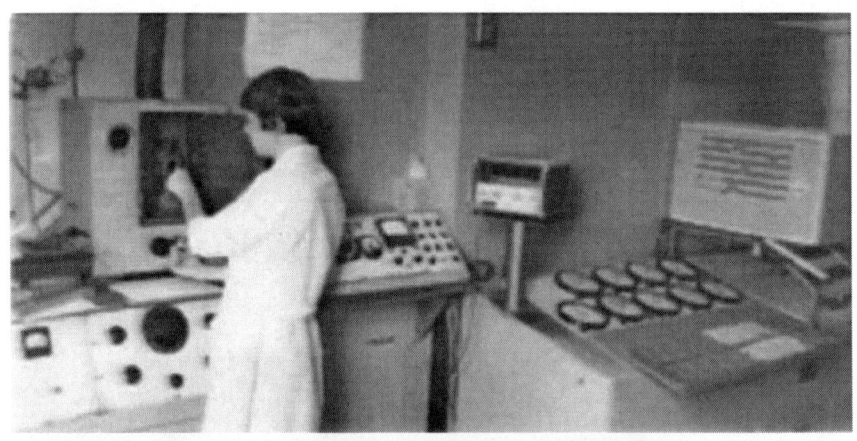

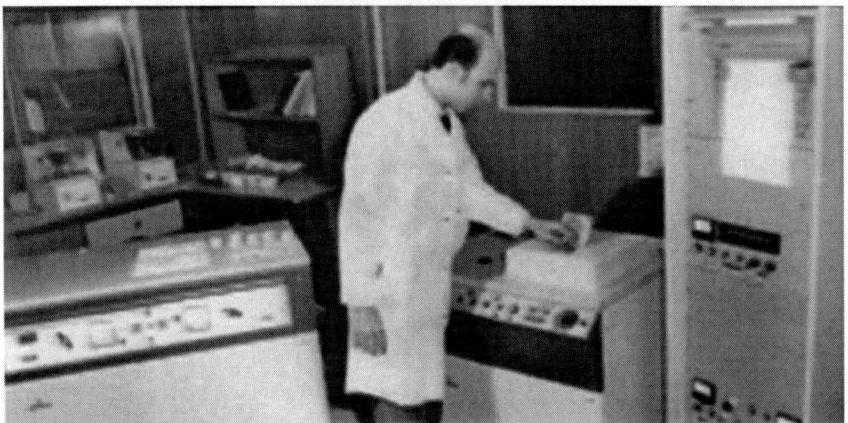

Upper picture: Direct Reading Spectrometer. Lower Picture: X-ray Fluorescence Spectrometer.

Shortly after we moved to King Street we developed a procedure to evaluate the wear condition of truck engines by analyzing lubricating oil. Under the name Wear Check, we started to market it. To prove its value we arranged with Canada Cartage to run a test program. Ten trucks were put on a program in which lubricating oil samples were taken every 2000 miles, and a record of their use and maintenance kept. We were able to identify the trucks carrying the heaviest loads, the trucks operating in dusty conditions, and the trucks nearing an overhaul. Management was impressed. The mechanics insisted that it told them nothing they didn't already know. On a truck that was showing serious wear, it was agreed that the best procedure was to tear down the engine and check everything. The condition of the engine confirmed our predictions. However, the chief mechanic complained that we had only produced more work for him. The engine could have gone another 5000 miles before a breakdown. The fact that minor repairs put the engine back into use before a breakdown (rather than creating the need for a $4000 total rebuilding cost after breakdown) had no weight with the mechanic. He insisted that wear check told him nothing. Canada Cartage continued to use Wear Check on a reduced basis for scheduling. Management would have a wear check before sending a truck on a long haul, minimizing breakdown on the road, thereby avoiding all the associated cost of towing, upsetting a client, etc. We tried to get them to use it as a means of scheduling rebuilding but the mechanics would not take samples regularly. Although Canada Cartage did not accept Wear Check, TSL gained confidence in the technique. As a result we had brochures, promotional literature, and press releases prepared and distributed. Tom Murray, our lab services salesman, called on many trucking firms, the Toronto Transit Commission, Montreal Transit, the CP Rail, and Air Canada. In general, management in those companies showed interest, but few commitments were made.

✻✻✻

It appeared that we were not going to have any more children and we wanted a daughter, so we had a family discussion to get the boys opinion on adopting a girl. The boys thought it was a great idea and suggested we should do so right away. Application was made to the Catholic Children's Aid to adopt a girl. We were interviewed and placed on a waiting list. In the early summer of 1959, just as we were about to leave for a holiday trip to New Brunswick, the Children's Aid called to say that they had a girl for us. As the trip was both business and vacation, a number of appointments had been arranged. I had to go. It did not seem wise to take her immediately on a trip. We asked the Children's Aid if they could hold her for about three weeks, they agreed. Our plan was to stop in Montreal and make some calls and then cross the St. Lawrence and take the south shore, where there was a super highway.

A late call came in which caused us to choose to stop in Quebec City. Since we had go to Quebec City, we decided to visit the shrine at Ste.

Anne-de-Beaupré. Here we prayed and went up the steps of the chapel on our knees, asking that we would be a good family for our new daughter, and that she would fit in. We then continued on to St. Andrews, New Brunswick, where a mine was interested in a contract lab, and I made a sale. After spending a few days around the Bay of Fundy, we continued to Maine. We spent about a week in a campsite on the ocean, swimming in the cold Atlantic, and enjoying some good lobster dinners. One of our fellow campers ate some seafood that made him deathly sick. There was a doctor camping nearby and I asked him to see the sick camper. The doctor agreed from the symptoms I described that the sick man was in serious condition. Unfortunately, the doctor said he could not help because of the legal possibilities that he could be sued. He did phone for an ambulance. I was amazed; I expected a doctor to help in emergencies. When I returned home I asked my doctor if that was the case in Canada. He said it was, but he pointed out that suing was much less of a problem in Canada. In recent years Canada has become as bad as the United States when it comes to people seeking legal action. In fact most medical activities are now controlled by the possibility of being sued, greatly helped by the insane law that permits a lawyer to sue at no cost and split the proceeds if they win.

DEBORAH ARRIVES

On our return we immediately contacted the Children's Aid. At the end of September 1959, the Children's Aid called for us to come to see our daughter. She was a pale little girl of a year and a half old. She was unfriendly and sullen and did not want to come with us. She was tiny in stature in comparison to other members of our family; Paul at 14 years old was six feet tall.

Her name was Deborah Anne and we felt that since we as a family had prayed to St Anne, this was an indication that she was meant to be our daughter. As we drove home she stood on the front seat beside us, crying and pointing back. She obviously did not want to go with us. I realized how upsetting it must be for this little child to be moved from place to place. I knew whatever problems we may have, she was now part of our family and it would stay that way.

On the way home we stopped at a children's store to buy Debbie clothes, as well as whatever else we felt she would need. She only came with the clothes she had on, which did not fit her. Her feet were jammed into shoes that were much too small. The boys made a fuss over her, which seem to please her. She was especially attracted to Paul, probably because she had never seen so tall a person. Debbie settled in quickly, although there were problems. For a long time she would wake up in the night screaming, as if in terror. She was very possessive and would show her anger by kicking people in the ankle or biting the shoulder of the person holding her. She wanted to be the centre of attention. However, with Elinor's good direction and love, she slowly became the loving daughter we wanted. Our way of handling children was based on a set of rules and practices that Elinor and I had agreed on.

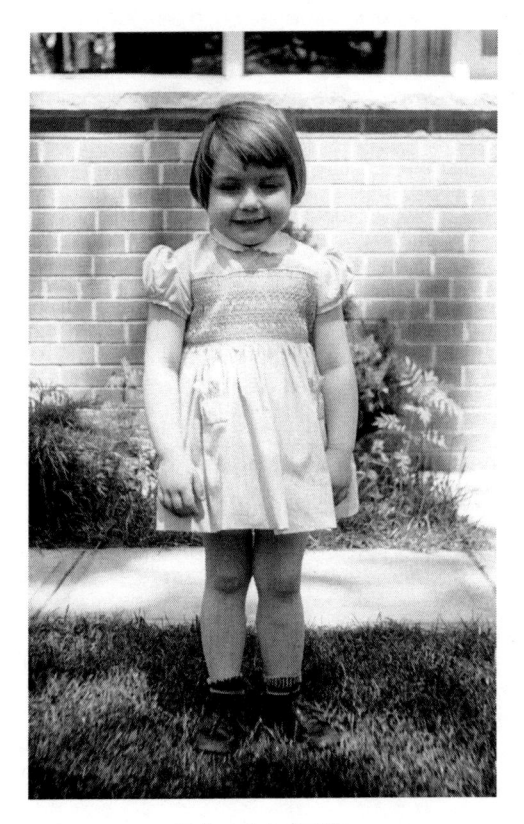

Deborah in 1959.

The most effective means of parenting is to love the child and to demonstrate it practically. Unfortunately there is a lot of misunderstanding and a great deal of sentimentality associated with the current popular notions of love. Love is an act of the will, and in its purest form it is offered for the benefit of the recipient. The objective of our rules and practices was to raise a good, kind, and loving adult, and to impart to them a sense of self confidence that would make his or her life useful. Our approach to parenting our children highlighted the importance of laying a solid religious foundation, enjoying travel, cultivating as many experiences and skills as possible, and encouraging generosity, love, and respect for others. This often meant doing things that were not easy. Many people confuse permissiveness with love. To let a child have his or her way is often tolerated because the parent does not want to upset the child. If the child is allowed to do something that will not make it a good adult, the parent is not showing true love. In fact, the parent that allows such actions is actually serving themselves rather than the child. Often in such cases the parent will say, "I can't stand to refuse the child". Who is being loved in those instances? A set of rules that will lead to a good, successful, generous and loving adult, and the firmness to apply those rules is a demonstration of true love. This was how we raised our family, and all of our children are good, loving, successful adults.

ANOTHER BUSINESS AND FAMILY TRIP

It was time for Debbie to become accustomed to our traveling. The next summer we decided to take another trip - this time to the Maritimes. On our previous trip we only visited the western part of New Brunswick and had not seen Nova Scotia or Prince Edward Island. The trailer had a double bed at the back; the dining area benches folded into a double bed for John and Peter. Paul slept on an air mattress in the corridor. To accommodate Debbie I built a crib over the dining table with a folding gate to prevent her from falling out. This gate proved to be a blessing. We could close her in after dinner while the rest of us had a little peace. We stopped at St. Anne-de-Beaupré on our way to thank St. Anne for our Deborah Anne, and continued on to the Maritimes. We visited all the points of interest such as Moncton, the Tidal Bore, and the Magnetic Hill, where the car appeared to coast uphill without power. It took some explaining to the boys to point out that we only appeared to be coasting uphill because of the general slope of the land and the horizon. We had stopped at a restaurant for lunch and they had an all you can eat pancake offer. Paul, now in his teens and still growing, took to eating pancakes. After the fourth refill the owner refused to serve anymore. Paul raised a fuss that this was unfair but Elinor and I, who had long before finished our eating, told him we had to go and left. Elinor was embarrassed that we had been refused service because of Paul's huge appetite. I called on the RCMP in Sackville and sold a complete spectrographic laboratory and I also looked at a mining client's property and concluded that it did not justify the expense of a contract lab. We spent a couple of nights in Fundy National Park.

Family in 1960

On the second night a tent was pitched in the lot beside us by four rough-looking young men. At about 10:00 PM there was some yelling and a woman started screaming. This went on for some time. Finally the screaming stopped and they started walking around our trailer. I suspected they gang-raped the woman and were wondering about us. I had a citizen band radio in my car and wished I had brought it in at night. On these trips I always had a .22 caliber rifle under our bed. I took it out and loaded it and would have used it if attacked. Fortunately I did not need to use it. They left early in the morning.

We then took the ferry to Prince Edward Island where we camped at a seaside camp with a beautiful beach. Incidentally I took my CB into the trailer at night from then on. A man who was photographing at the beach asked if we minded if he took a photo of Debbie, since she was such a cute little girl, and of course we agreed. We looked at Anne of Green Gables' house and that evening we read some of the story. We also visited where Canada's confederation was signed in Charlottetown. On the ferry ride back John amused himself by counting jellyfish. I think he counted at least a thousand. We visited Halifax and several fishing villages, including Peggy's Cove, where I took many pictures, some of which I later used as inspiration to paint. After this we wound our way home.

After that trip we decided that our trailer was too small for our growing family, so we sold it and I built a collapsible trailer. It was designed so that the top would fold down over the bottom to make it less wind resistant. Since the upper part was raised when set up, it was possible to make it higher and to have a lower double bed and an upper double bed, which fit into one another when collapsed. This allowed for more sleeping area in the same size trailer. The dining area still converted into a double bed and therefore had beds for six instead of the four in our original trailer. A fold-out canopy protected the entrance at the back in rainy weather. The first model was rather ugly as it had steel levers on the side that raised the roof with electric motors in a scissors-like operation. As the mechanism was unreliable, I removed it and mounted a large jack at the back and front. This improved the appearance and reliability, but two people were needed to jack it up.

Homemade collapsible trailer.

This trailer was used on a number of camping trips. Several times we spent a weekend at Brighton on Lake Ontario, along with family and friends. We have pictures of Peter in a 1920s bathing suit he bought for a lark. On one of these trips John found two large foam floats and tried to use them to walk on water. They supported him, but he could make no progress. When he pushed one foot forward the other floated backwards. Debbie learned to swim on these trips. On several occasions we also visited Algonquin Park, Rondo on Lake Erie, and the Elora Gorge. The many camping trips taught the children to be self-reliant and to do things and enjoy them, even when they had to put up with inconveniences. We continued to camp after the children grew up, but used a tent rather than pull a trailer.

Chapter 15

THE THERMOCARB

In the summer of 1961 the Steel Company of Canada approached TSL regarding a device they had developed for the fast determination of carbon in steel. Steel refining was undergoing major changes. Oxygen was being bubbled through molten iron to burn off carbon, which significantly sped up the refining process. With the old open-hearth procedure, up to eighteen hours were needed to refine a charge. Using oxygen the metal could be refined in the same furnace in two hours or less. With specially built furnaces, the refining time was as short as twenty minutes. This necessitated many changes in the handling and control. Previously samples were taken at intervals and sent to the laboratory in another part of the plant. The turnaround was typically forty-five to ninety minutes. With eighteen hours this was rapid enough. A much shorter turnaround time was needed with the oxygen process. Stelco developed a carbon determination system that shortened the turnaround time to two minutes. It involved a sample taking procedure, sample preparation, and a fast determination of the carbon content of the sample. A combustion technique was used, with the combustion gasses measured by chromatographic techniques. To take advantage of these improvements, the furnace personnel should do the carbon determination. Stelco had two experimental set-ups in operation when they approached us. We undertook to develop the system on a commercial basis. We had on our staff Peter Mladenovich and we hired a young electronics engineer, Joe Shock, and put them to work on developing the system. Stelco, since it was their own development, were prepared to live with shortcomings in the system, which we had to overcome to make it saleable.

The standard procedure in a laboratory was to burn a weighed sample in oxygen and absorb the carbon dioxide produced. The absorbent was weighted before and after combustion to measure the amount of carbon burned. This was time consuming, requiring a delicate balance and a laboratory environment. Using an induction furnace, the combustion could be completed in less than a minute. By replacing the absorption step with a thermal conductivity cell that sensed the carbon dioxide in a stream of oxygen, the quantity of carbon dioxide produced by the combustion could be measured as fast as the combustion.

Stelco used an evacuated glass tube, which was widely used for spectrographic analyses, to obtain a sample of the molten steel. Such tubes were available commercially, however, they were very unreliable. One had at best a 50% chance of getting a useable solid rod sample. When a solid rod was produced it had to be cut to useable length and then weighed. Our first problem was to get a sample that did not have to be weighed. It was easy to cut a fixed length of rod. Since the inside diameter of the glass tube varied by 20%, a cut segment of fixed length varied in weight by the same amount. If the diameter were constant, a fixed length would be of constant weight, eliminating the weighing of the sample. To get a constant length was easy to arrange by using a heavy-duty motor grinder with two carbide cut-off discs separated by a spacer and a heavy-duty clamp to hold the sample rod. The cut-off device could cut a segment with precision of 1%. To obtain precision inside diameter for the class tubing we used gauges to select tubing of the right diameter. Being able to produce samples that did not have to be weighed was a necessary step in the development of the fast turnaround carbon analysis. It was also marketable.

BURTEC INSTRUMENT CORP

The US Steel Companies had a policy of buying American. As the major market was in the USA, we knew that we had better "be American". An operation in a storefront on Seminole Blvd. at Largo, Florida was set up. Florida was chosen because my father, who was a good manager, had recently retired to St. Petersburg. The new company was called Burtec Instrument Corp., and my father was director and manager. The plan was to send Toronto personnel as consultants and use local help for production. To get the sample taking system into production, Peter Mladenovich went to Florida to set up a vacuum tube operation with our precision glass. He experimented with the shape of the tubes, and reasoning that if the molten metal entered from the side instead of the bottom, there was a better chance it would not run out. He made up a few with a bubble on the side near the bottom and sent them to Stelco. The side entrance was amazingly better.

We applied for and got a patent in Canada and USA. Then we proceeded to market the Burtec Pin Tube. It was so reliable that we guaranteed there would be less than two spoiled samples in 100. Our tubes were more than double the price of the tubes on the market, but the reliability and the ability cut a segment that did not need to be weighed in the lab were real advantages. The sales increased slowly. On investigating why several large steel companies were placing only small orders, I discovered that the purchasing departments claimed that although the lab liked the tubes, the furnace rooms were using as many of our expensive tubes as they did when using the much cheaper tubes, hence they saw no advantage. This was not only disappointing, it was also unbelievable. I got one of Stelco's technical men to go with me to Bethlehem Steel in Buffalo to talk to the furnace room people. I felt that he could speak their language. We discovered that the sample takers were accustomed to taking a handful of tubes, then thrusting the end into a ladle of molten steel. With the old tubes this was necessary to be sure they got a good sample. After some argument the Stelco man got the sample takers to try Burtec tubes and pointed out that the handful of Burtec tubes were all good, and got them to try using one tube. A good sample was obtained every time. We showed the foreman and he was impressed. However, as he pointed out, pin tube costs were negligible in the steel making costs, and therefore he was not about to upset his operators by changing the rules. Stelco's man pointed out that the cost of the tube was negligible, but handling of a handful of tubes instead of one was not negligible, especially as turnaround time for control was involved. That won the day. Burtec changed its marketing to stress time savings, and Burtec Pintube sales increased, eventually becoming the standard.

As pin tube sales increased, hand making of the tubes became a problem. Several people worked on automating the production with little success. One day as my niece Sharon O'Neil's husband Rick Barrette was visiting the lab where work was being done on the automation, he suggested that the tube should be lifted, carried, and dropped in its next position instead of rolling or pushing. This was the answer and I proceeded to design and build such a design. It had problems and did not work, but it looked like it should work. My son John had recently returned from his world travels and I asked him to see if he could get the machine working. He solved the problems with the design and a month later we had a working machine that sealed and bubbled the tubes at the rate of eight per minute. This machine and its duplicates are still making pin tubes.

Several attempts were made to automate the evacuation of the tubes. Unfortunately none were successful. The last couple of years before I retired I devised a way of evacuating and sealing the tubes. I built an experimental machine and successfully evacuated and sealed a batch of tubes. There were a number of bugs from a production point of view. I did not have time to pursue it and since retirement did not have the facilities.

THE THERMOCARB

The other component of this project was the fast determination of carbon in the pin tube sample. As noted above, it used an induction furnace for fast combustion of the sample, and a thermal conductivity cell that sensed the carbon dioxide in a stream of oxygen. There were a number of problems with this system: the temperature needed exact control, oxygen flow rates needed to be the same hour after hour, and moisture in the oxygen would ruin the results. The finished system covered these problems. However, the operators had to use moisture-free oxygen or change moisture traps frequently. Similarly dust traps had to be maintained.

After a few months of development we designed and built our first production model. It was designed to operate on the furnace floor by furnace room operators. Much testing showed that our ThermoCarb performed exceptionally well with repeatability and accuracy beyond our expectations. However, it would occasionally produce a completely erroneous value. At times it would work perfectly for several hours and then suddenly act up. In the meantime, marketing was progressing with much interest on the part of the steel business. A number of demonstrations were set up and in general they were successful. The average accuracy was so good that the prospective customers tended to assume the problem could be solved. Actually, if the accuracy had not been so good most of the time, the erroneous values would not have seemed too bad. On a 1.50% carbon the ThermoCarb would vary between 1.49 and 1.51. A bad value would be low and could be 1.40. Occasionally it might be worse. A routine chemical lab value would vary between 1.40 and 1.60, which was acceptable, and occasionally it might be worse. However, since the ThermoCarb was capable of high accuracy most of the time, it was demanded all of the time.

The ThermoCarb furnace room carbon analyzer.

Jim O'Neill was our sales manager and he arranged and conducted several demonstrations. We got a few orders. Bethlehem Steel bought one for their Buffalo Works and one for their research lab. Inland Steel in Chicago and West Virginia Steel each bought one. The steel publications carried stories about the ThermoCarb and as a result we got several inquiries from Europe. Jarrell-Ash, for whom we were agents in Canada, had a factory in Switzerland and agents all over Europe; we appointed them as our agents in Europe. They had a booth at The Frankfort Industrial World Fair and suggested that the ThermoCarb should be on display. We provided a ThermoCarb and I attended the fair to demonstrate. Considerable interest was raised, resulting in a demonstration for several German steel makers at Jarrell-Ash's factory in Lelocle Switzerland. The steel prospects said that every time the ThermoCarb came up with a perfect value they would have a schnapps. We had so many perfect values that they were quickly inebriated. We sold two ThermoCarbs. Jaco's Italian, Swedish, and British agents each sold one. Five units sold in Europe to four in USA. Unfortunately the ThermoCarb continued to produce spurious values on a random basis. The requirement of moisture-free oxygen also gave trouble. Jarrell-Ash backed away from it.

In the early sixties there were frequent flights to London and Paris, but less frequently to other European cities. Thus it was easier to fly to Paris and then fly to other cities. With ThermoCarb problems and promoting Wear Check, I had to make several trips to Europe and was in Paris a number of times. On one of these trips I was there overnight. The next morning I called a client and asked if I could see him as I had some new services to offer. He said it was not possible to see me without an appointment at his office, but could see me after hours and suggested that we meet at a restaurant for dinner. Dinner in Paris was whole night event, so I cancelled my continuing flight and renewed my hotel reservation. We did meet at the restaurant. He explained that to see me without an appointment was just not done in Paris. We had a good business meeting and a good dinner, however that night I came down with a severe case of diarrhea. The next morning he called to ask for more details and I told him my situation. He was very concerned and said it must have been the mushrooms. I did not remember eating any mushrooms. It dawned on me that he was referring to the mouldy cheese that we ate. After all was said and done, he became a long-term customer.

On another occasion with a different client the same thing happened and I met him at a restaurant. This time we were in a restaurant that had staff that spoke only French. At the table next to us were two women who obviously could not speak French, and the waiter had walked away when they spoke English. My client suggested that we should help them and invited them to eat with us so that he could translate for them. They accepted. They were from California and were sisters. One was married and had come to this restaurant on her husband's recommendation. He was often in Paris and spoke French, so he probably did not realize that French had to be spoken. It was an enjoyable dinner. My client ordered a special liquor to finish dinner and it came in a bottle wrapped in a towel. It was certainly different and I was intrigued; I asked to see the label. When he unwrapped the bottle there was a snake inside. We were surprised but we had to admit that it was interesting and different. After dinner we escorted the ladies to a taxi and said goodbye.

On another trip I was to meet Carlton Joyce, a member of my staff, in Paris. I arrived on a late flight and asked a taxi to take me to the hotel where I was to meet Carlton. The taxi driver said that the hotel had a serious fire the day before and was closed. Of course cell phones had not been invented and I could not contact Carlton. Since I arrived late in Paris without a reservation, my only option was to go to the tourist bureau. I asked the driver to do so. When I asked for a room they said that due to the fire, a large number of people had to find alternate accommodation and the city was booked up. They could get me a room in a nearby town, but in Paris the only available rooms were in some rough parts of the city. As I had appointments in Paris the following day, I accepted a room in a rough part of town. After all, I was traveling to it in a taxi and would leave it in a taxi. So I had the taxi take me there. By the time I checked in it was after midnight. There were a number of women sitting in the lobby. The room was clean and reasonably furnished and as I was settling in the phone rang. It was Carlton. He said he knew I would have to go to the tourist bureau and kept phoning them to see if I had arrived, and thus was able to contact me. He had a room with two beds so I checked out and went to Carlton's room.

ANOTHER BUSINESS AND FAMILY TRIP

In 1963 we were still having troubles with the ThermoCarb, so I had to go to Europe again. Since the other three children did not have a chance to see some of Europe like Paul had, I decided to make this business trip another family holiday. Paul remained at home as he was in his last year in High School. We arranged with our friends Madeleine and Bob Welter to watch over him and they offered to feed him on weekends. Their oldest daughter, Suzanne, was fond of Paul and after he graduated from university they were married. I had several days work in England and contacts in Paris, as well as in Milan, Italy. Renting a car and driving to these appointments would make a nice family trip. This time I decided I would rent a car on the continent rather than in England where the driver is on the wrong side. Since I had to spend several days in England working, I decided to go ahead and have Elinor and the children follow me so that when they got there I would be free to spend time with them. However, when I was in England I was asked to go to Amsterdam in

A Broader Vision

Holland. Before I left England I arranged with the people I was working with to meet Elinor at the airport, settle her and the children in a hotel, and then arrange a flight for them to Amsterdam. When I got to Amsterdam I found that the parent company was there, but I was needed in Stockholm and had to fly to Sweden. I hoped I would be back in Amsterdam before Elinor got there. I arranged for them to meet her at the airport and take her to the hotel in case I did not get back in time. I also phoned England and told them to give Elinor the name of the hotel. The work in Sweden took longer than expected and I phoned Elinor in Amsterdam and told her I would come there when finished. I did not get back to Amsterdam, but ended up in Paris a week after she arrived in Amsterdam.

I phoned her when I got to Paris and said I would fly to Amsterdam the next evening as I had a day's work to do. She said that she would prefer to go to the airport and fly to Paris and could be there that evening. I immediately arranged flights and called her back with the information. She was fed up with delays. I could not blame her. In fact, most wives would have been angry enough to seek a divorce after twice missing meeting her with three children. However, the delay did give them opportunity to see Amsterdam, enjoying boat rides on the canals, visiting the miniature village of Madurodam, going to Anne Frank's house, and to see the famous painting "The Night Watch". Elinor and the children arrived in Paris that evening and this time I did meet them. The hotel was in the Sacré-Cœur area, so she and the children spent the day sightseeing as I finished my day's work.

The next day we rented a small station wagon that had seats for four, but we arranged a comfortable place in the back for Debbie, thus accommodating the five of us, and we started our family holiday. Although I had been to Paris several times, they were all business trips (except for the visit in 1956) and I'd had very little chance to enjoy it. I intended to enjoy this trip with the family. We visited the Louvre, where we saw the Mona Lisa. We rode up the Eiffel Tower. We visited Sacré-Cœur, Montmarte, the Tuileries Garden, the Arc de Triomphe, and the Champs-Élysées. Paris was much busier in 1963 than it had been in 1956. In 1956 there were still the after effects of the war but in 1963 it was a very active city. After spending a few days in Paris, we drove south through beautiful country, passing many medieval towns and visiting a couple of castles. We chose to stay overnight in the small towns where we found quaint hotels that had atmosphere. In some of the small hotels or guest houses we could get two rooms adjoining; otherwise Elinor slept with Debbie and I slept with the two boys.

Accidentally taking a wrong road, we ended up in rough part of Marseille, so we took a side road to turn around and leave the city. Suddenly the car in front of me stopped and another car pulled up behind me. The occupants of both cars got out of their cars and started towards us. I expected that we were about to be murdered. I was just putting the car in reverse to push the car behind far enough back to get around the car in front when the suspected gangsters suddenly started to run for their cars. Fortunately a group of American Navy Sailors in a jeep saw us turn and, anticipating this sort of thing, they followed us. As the Americans showed up these gangsters ran for their cars and drove off. The Americans said that we should get out of Marseille and led us to the road I had missed. Our Guardian Angels were certainly looking after us. If the Americans had not followed us, I expect I would not be writing this.

Verigotti on the Mediterranean.

A Broader Vision

After Marseille we stopped at Beaulieu sur Mer, which translates to "Beautiful Place on the Sea". It was exactly that, and we spent a couple of days there staying in what had been a beautifully furnished mansion. We slept in canopied beds and ate our meals in the garden filled with flowers. Then we spent a few days in Monaco, Cannes, and Nice. At Cannes I was surprised to see that their famous beach was pebbled and not sandy, and of course there were lots of bikinis. A few miles across the Italian border we stopped for three days at Verigotti, a pleasant village on the Mediterranean. We had accommodation for five including meals and wine at dinner for ninety dollars a day. It was the best bargain I had on the trip. The hotel was on the Mediterranean and it had a beautiful beach.

One afternoon as we sat on the beach watching Debbie and the boys playing in the sand, an almost naked woman started talking to us in Italian in an angry voice. We did not know what she was saying but another person told us that she was complaining because our children playing on the beach were casting a shadow on her and thus spoiling her tan. We moved to another location.

After our time there we headed for Milan where I had an appointment, and drove into the city. The traffic was so heavy and the driving so different from my way of driving that I left the city and found a hotel in a village not far away. The next day I took a commuter train that was standing room only. At the end of the day I returned to the village by train. The village was a pleasant place and the family enjoyed it. The next day we headed for Switzerland. As we crossed the border going north, the lineup of trucks going south into Italy extended for miles. These trucks must eventually return to Switzerland, and there were only a few trucks at the northbound border. I guessed that the Swiss had less red tape at the border than the Italians. We drove through the Valleys region of Switzerland, where the valley Burgeners come from, as we made our way to Grindelwald.

We spent a couple of days at a small hotel in the Valleys. This hotel was built like a castle. The dining room had an alcove with a throne in it so we sat Debbie on the throne; along with the waiters, we bowed to her. She really thought she was a princess. It was a pleasant place with great mountain scenery all around. We then continued through the valleys to the Grimsel Pass. This was July and on the way up we were on the sunny side and there was no ice. When we reached the top there was lots of snow and ice, so we all got out and had a snowball fight. We also visited St. Christopher's Church on the mountaintop.

On the way down - on the shaded side - there was much ice. Three cars at a time followed behind a bulldozer as protection against skidding. If you skidded you hit the bulldozer instead of possibly dropping a few hundred feet. When we got to the bottom we drove through beautiful valleys surrounded by mountains until we reached Grindelwald, the home of the mountain Burgeners. We spent a few days there enjoying the mountains.

At one point we took the chairlift to "First", a mountaintop restaurant. After lunch the proprietor suggested that we should walk down instead of the taking the chair lift as it was a beautiful walk and not difficult. Elinor and I agreed that it sounded great and we were assured that the children would have no difficulty. The children started down with enthusiasm and we could not keep up with them. After about an hour we began to realize that we must have got on a different trail. Five hours later we reached the valley about two miles from Grindelwald. On the way Debbie, who was five years old, had to be carried. We had to cross a mountain stream, which was flowing too fast for the children to cross, so I helped Peter, John, and Elinor across, and carried Debbie. The water was just above freezing and by the time I had crossed it seven times my feet and legs were almost frozen and hurt for several hours. It was a spectacular walk, but after the first three hours we lost interest in the spectacle and were striving to reach the valley. In the last hour the knee Elinor had injured many years before in the toboggan accident, that caused me to visit her in the hospital, began to hurt, and she collapsed. I had to support her. Peter helped with carrying Debbie.

When we got back to the hotel and described our walk down, they said we obviously got on one of the trans-mountain trails. Hikers use them to travel from mountain to mountain, because the trail down from First takes 30 to 40 minutes. The next day we all rested. We spent another couple of days in the valley visiting the face of the glacier and other mountain streams and views. On one of these excursions we met two older ladies, probably in their late seventies or early eighties, and spent some time chatting with them. They had come from a village ten miles away for a walk. I offered to drive them home but they refused, saying it was less than a three hour walk home. I understood why a five or six hour walk in the mountains is only a walk. On a different trip to Switzerland I met an aunt of my father who was 94 years old. She walked three miles and up four flights of stairs to visit her daughter, a retired professor, several times a week. I guess Canadians have lost the ability to handle regular and vigorous walking due to the use of the automobile.

On the top of the Grimsel Pass in July.

Leaving Grindelwald we drove through Interlaken, a beautiful town between two lakes, and then to Bern, where we watched the famous clock strike and viewed the bear pit originally built by the Romans. We bought Debbie a Swiss mountain dress and looked at some lederhosen for the boys. The boys said they would never wear them. I bought myself a mountain curved pipe, which I occasionally smoked. On our way to Geneva we stopped at the castle of Chillon, built in the eighth century, on an island near the shore in Lake Geneva. It is in perfect condition and beautifully furnished in medieval furniture. The boys enjoyed climbing in the turrets, while Elinor and I, who had visited before, again enjoyed its beautiful furnishings. Debbie on the other hand said she would sooner be home playing with Julie.

When we got to Geneva there was an international conference and the hotels were booked up solid. While eating supper at a restaurant I asked the proprietor if they knew of a guest house that might have room for us. He replied that even the guest houses were booked up, but he had a couple of rooms in his house where we could spend the night. We accepted and the next morning when I offered to pay him he replied that tourists like us kept Switzerland rich, and that he was glad he could help at no charge. The next day we headed for Paris and flew home.

PROMOTING WEAR CHECK AND THERMOCARB

Back in Canada we were promoting Wear Check. Carlton Joyce had made some promising contacts with British Airways, Lufthansa, and Scandinavian Airways. He traveled to Europe and called on the airlines. Lufthansa and British Airways went on limited programs. With Wear Check samples being generated in Europe, and with more interest in the ThermoCarb there than in North America, we decided that a presence in Europe was indicated. We set up an English company in London and transferred Dr. Adrian Debnam, our senior vice president, to London on a two year trial. Adrian contacted a Belgian company that had expressed interest in the ThermoCarb. They agreed to look into it. However, nothing came from it. He also promoted Wear Check and arranged to have the samples analyzed in England to speed up service. The interest and use remained limited.

While Adrian was in England the Ontario government sent a trade mission to an industrial fair in Budapest Hungary. I was invited to be part of it. Hungary was a major steel producing country behind the Iron Curtain and I decided to go. Adrian decided to spend a few days there, but not the full fourteen days, which was a wise decision because the trade show actually was less than a week and the remainder of the time was a public show. Our family physician was Hungarian. He and his wife and baby daughter had escaped from Hungary during the war and were afraid to go back. His wife, Ann, begged me to take her as an interpreter. She felt that as part of an Ontario mission she would be safe. I talked to the mission leader and he pointed out that as members were paying their own expenses he would be glad to include her.

I brought a lab model of the ThermoCarb with me. The first six days of the fair had an industrial focus, but the remainder of the time it was open to the public, who certainly were not going to buy ThermoCarbs. Since my work was done, I decided to leave. One had to fly on the Hungarian airline, so I went to the airline office to get a flight out. I was told that the mission was for 14 days and I had to stay for the appointed time. To ensure that I would stay, the ticket agent took my ticket and put it in a drawer and said I would get it back when it was time to leave. I asked to see someone in authority and was told that he was a commissar and there was no one of higher authority. I talked to the mission leader and was told that a mission in a Communist country was carefully regulated and that no deviations were allowed. He said he would get my ticket back, which he did, and commented that if I wanted to leave, there was an embassy car that drove to Austria every day.

Budapest was an interesting city. There was a somber atmosphere, and although the store windows displayed interesting merchandise, when you went in to buy they were out of stock. One evening the mission leader (who was Hungarian) took us out to an interesting nightclub. Suddenly everybody stood up and lined up against the wall. We were surprised and our leader told us to line up as well. When we lined up I saw two soldiers with machine guns and another soldier looking at the patron's documents. I ask my leader what was going on. The leader explained that this was normal and that the soldiers (who were Russian) were checking for persons who did not have work permits up to date, as well as seeking out anyone not registered. When they got to our group our leader explained who we were but they still inspected our passports. One of the group was not carrying his passport and for a few minutes it looked like he was going to be arrested. Our leader finally convinced the soldier he was a Canadian.

One evening Ann and I took a taxi to visit her brother, who lived in a small town some distance from Budapest. When we arrived I asked the driver if he would return about 10:30 PM and drive us back to Budapest. He replied that it was no problem and that he would just wait. Anticipating he was going to charge for waiting I asked how much it would cost. His answer was, "I am assigned to sit in this car for twelve hours, whether or not I have a passenger, so I will wait." Ann's brother, who was an orthopaedic specialist before the Russians took over, had been ordered to practice as a family physician in a small community. After practicing for five years he got permission to buy a designated car. It was a worn out Russian car. He had refused to become a card-carrying Communist. Ann's sister lived in Budapest and before the Russians took over she had been a teacher. She was assigned a job as a street sweeper when she refused to be a card-carrying Communist. I assumed that the taxi driver was not a card-carrying Communist. No wonder the Russian Empire collapsed. Canadians should recognize that too much government control leads to lack of incentive and innovation, and it demoralizes talented and skilled individuals.

The first Saturday that we were there the Canadian Ambassador, who had his office in Austria, had a banquet for the mission. A number of Hungarian officials were also invited. At the banquet I sat beside the Hungarian minister of finance. I needled him on free enterprise. As the wine flowed and the noise level increased, he finally said, "I agree with you; if only we could get rid of these d*mn Russians!" After the banquet I talked to the embassy driver, who drove from Vienna to Budapest and returned every day, and I asked him if he had room for Ann and me. He replied that most days he was alone and would gladly take us to Vienna. He did point out that there was some risk if we were caught fleeing the country. I checked with the mission leader and he said that he had no problem if I left in the embassy car.

The next day Ann and I left in the embassy car. When we were about two miles from the border, soldiers with machine guns stopped us and ordered us out of the car. The driver commented, "This is standard, don't worry." The soldiers opened the trunk, poked around the wheels, looked under the car, asked to see our passports, and then let us go. When we got back into the car the driver said, "They were looking for people who were trying to escape the jail that Hungary is to most people."

At the border there was a 100 meter strip of ploughed land that was devoid of any vegetation, with a four meter barbed wire fence with towers stretching as far as one could see. We drove into a concrete bunker where again we were ordered out of the car. After checking our passports, we were herded into a room and the door was locked. After about half an hour we were allowed to leave the room. The car had been stripped - the seat cushions, the spare tire and luggage were lying on the road. We had to put it back. Then we were allowed to continue to Austria. The driver went through this every time. It was a great relief to leave that prison. From Vienna we flew home.

From the contacts we made at Budapest, Adrian did sell two ThermoCarbs to a steel company in Hungary. These units operated for several years, buying supplies from Burtec Canada. The revenue from the sale and supplies to Hungary covered the cost of our London office two year trial.

Back in North America we were still trying to sell ThermoCarbs. To simplify demonstrations, a ThermoCarb was set up in a trailer so that it could be pulled into the furnace room and operated there. Such a demonstration was in progress at Great Lakes Steel at Detroit, when it became evident that the ThermoCarb was dead in the USA. Their union gave notice, insisting that if the ThermoCarb was not immediately removed they were going on strike. The union pointed out that all testing had to be done by laboratory personnel in a laboratory environment. If Great Lakes Steel purchased a ThermoCarb, there would be an immediate strike. Great Lakes Steel asked us to remove the demonstrator and the word went out that no other steel company was going to risk a strike. The next planned demonstration was at US Steel. They canceled it. The steel union decision to stop the ThermoCarb effectively killed the steel business in the USA. Fast turnaround control and different ways of handling were needed to gain the economic advantages of oxygen produced steel, and steel made in USA became uncompetitive. US Steel, once the largest steel producer in the world, now buys its steel offshore. Although the ThermoCarb did not produce the return we hoped for, it was not a failure. We did sell sixteen units, including the sulphur model. These sales produced a revenue of $250,000. The Burtec pin tube, developed as part of the ThermoCarb development, was a real success and is still producing profits.

THE GROWING FAMILY

During this time our family was growing up. As mentioned earlier, the children all attended St. Christopher's School. With encouragement from Elinor and me, they did well at school. The boys went to Michael Power High School (a Catholic private school for boys), and then they went on to university. Paul graduated in Materials Engineering, Peter in Architecture, and John in Physics and Geology. Deborah started high school at a private school for girls but she missed the boys. Having lived with three brothers, an all-girls school did not appeal to her, so she transferred to Lorne Park high school and then went to Sheridan College. All have been successful in their careers.

Paul, being five years older than Peter, finished high school while in the house on Elite Road and he decided to be a priest. He spent his novitiate near home at what is now the Glen Erin Inn. At that time it was the novitiate for the Basilian fathers. During the year at the novitiate we often saw him out walking, but the novitiate year is to see if you can be separated from family and friends, so we had to pass him by. It bothered Elinor that she could not stop and talk to her son. After the year in the novitiate, he was sent to Windsor to go to university to become a teacher. After a year in Windsor he told us that he decided that he was not cut out to be a priest and hoped that we would not be disappointed. We were disappointed, but we agreed that it was his decision. He had been studying English and Mathematics with the intention of becoming a teacher. He decided that engineering was more interesting and applied to the engineering department. With much discussion, and by making an agreement to take special courses, he convinced the engineering department to credit him with first year engineering. He had to do a lot of studying to catch up. He succeeded and graduated in Engineering Materials.

As mentioned above, TSL was having a hard time as Paul started engineering. I would have been happier if Paul had gone to Toronto where he could have lived at home. Paul would have lost a year if he did so and he struggled at various jobs during the school year to cover his expenses. During his second year of University, after leaving the Basilians, he had five jobs. The hardest was shoveling coal in a multi-resident building that the university owned. The furnace had an automated feeder that pushed coal into the burner. However, the hopper had to be filled with over a ton of coal in the morning and in the evening to keep it burning for half a day. He never asked for financial help and when asked he always said he was doing okay. I believed him, but later found out how difficult it was for him. After graduation he married our friends the Welters' daughter, Suzanne. He worked for Burtec manufacturing the ThermoCarb and other equipment that Burtec produced. The ThermoCarb principles were applied to measuring sulphur and Paul traveled about installing and demonstrating the ThermoSulf to mining companies. This took him to Texas and Arizona in the US and to Belgium and Cyprus.

He later left TSL and started his own business, Quanta Systems, with a fellow graduate from the University of Windsor. They worked on a number of projects. One project they developed used a television set to assist people suffering from certain forms of near blindness. Unfortunately the Canadian National Institute for the Blind (CNIB) rejected their design and chose to standardize on a more expensive, less useful American design. They felt that products made in Canada were not desirable. His partner's wife became impatient with the struggle to develop a business and demanded that her husband get a job. Paul then accepted a job in developing instrumentation used in remote sensing of air pollution, geophysics, and for heavy water detection. Later, an engineer I had known in Arvida, who was now working for the Canadian International Development Agency, phoned and asked me if I would be interested in going to Kenya to develop a geological lab for the department of mines in Kenya. I suggested that Paul might be interested. Paul was subsequently interviewed by a person at the Bureau of Mines, who was an x-ray spectroscopist, and considered optical spectroscopy as an inexact science. He disapproved of my promoting it, thus I did not expect him to approve of Paul. However, Paul convinced him that he was capable and was offered the position. It was a big change leaving family and friends, plus a house they had just bought. It did fulfill a desire to make a useful contribution to the world.

Paul and Suzanne's Wedding.

Paul accepted the position and left with Suzanne and their nine month old son Brian for Kenya. The initial contract was for two years. Kenya appointed him as the Chief Chemist of the Department of Mines and Geology with a mandate to setup a modern analytical chemistry laboratory and train Kenyans to operate the lab. The person who was supposed to take over as chief chemist was completing a master's degree in Holland during the first year and they asked Paul to stay for a third year to provide a two year training time. At the start of the third year his Kenyan counterpart was murdered. A new Kenyan was recruited and Paul was then asked to stay on for another two years. Overall he stayed in Kenya for over five years. On his return to Canada he worked for TSL. After TSL he worked on various engineering projects and later worked with The National Research Council of Canada as a consultant for government supported industrial research. In this position he helped dozens of companies on the road to success.

***

In 1966 TSL set up a mobile laboratory at Sainte-Anne-des-Monts on the St. Lawrence River. Paul, who was a third-year university student, operated the lab alongside Peter, Gerry Thompson, and science teacher Don Roberts. The lab was performing geochemical soil analyses collected in the surrounding area. To check how things were going, I decided to drive down using our trailer, taking Elinor, John, Debbie, and Suzanne Welter. She had begged to come with us so she could see Paul. When we arrived, I found that they were doing a great job, but were taking the "service" in Technical Service Laboratory a little too seriously. Geologists would show up at 3:00 AM and expect the lab to start right away to run their samples, so that when the geologist awoke the next morning, the results would be ready. I recommended that they set a deadline for samples to be received for results the next day. That made their lives more endurable. Hydrogen was used in the lab and on a couple of occasions they filled some garbage bags with hydrogen, and let them float over the village. The locals considered them to be "mad scientists". Spending several days there, we even had Debbie washing test tubes. This kind of summer job for the boys was excellent training. Don Roberts was a mature adult but the boys were in their teens. Paul was the technical authority and assumed full responsibility for the technical operation.

After leaving Sainte-Anne-des-Monts we continued traveling and spent a few days in a pleasant hotel overlooking Percy Rock. We took a boat trip out to Bonaventure Island. Sea birds by the tens of thousands occupied the island. On the way home we detoured to Arvida. Elinor had never been back and wanted to see it again. We called on our former neighbours, Grace and Joe Bowden. They were pleased to see us and, sharing our food supplies, we had dinner together. That evening we pulled our trailer across the Saguenay River to a campground where we spent the night. It turned out to be a children's day camp and the next morning we were surrounded with kids. We left as quickly as we could. From there we headed home.

On-site lab in Gaspé, Quebec.

Chapter 16

THE MIDDLE YEARS

With TSL's move to King Street in 1958, the family was growing up and the company had reached a point where it was no longer struggling to survive; the company continued to strive to expand and to remain on the leading edge of its field. As in the course of any business, particularly one that is striving to be a leader, there were ups and downs. I will not attempt to list them all but I will mention a few outstanding events. Often there were several activities occurring at the same time.

Soon after our move to King Street in 1958 we perfected a technique for the spectrochemical analyses of ores using a DC Arc procedure, suggested by Dr. Stalwood at the Canadian Bureau of Mines. The DC Arc had previously been limited to semi-quantitative work. In this procedure, as the sample burned in an electric arc it was cooled by a stream of air. It was effectively a plasma to analyze solid materials. It required little sample preparation. Mixing the sample with a buffer and internal standard, it was loaded into the crater of a 1/8 inch diameter graphite electrode and arced. The method gave an accuracy of about 2% coefficient of variation at the 97% level. We were able to sell this not only as a service, but also as complete spectrochemical installations to several mining companies. One of these companies flew drill core pulp samples on a daily basis from Ireland. We would receive the samples at about 2:00 PM and would phone their Toronto office with the results by 4:00 PM the same day. At the end of their exploration, they bought a complete spectrochemical lab from us.

This procedure was very successful and provided us with both laboratory and equipment sales revenue for several years. The air jet procedure also provided revenue for all three of our sons. The small diameter graphite crater used had to be precision machined. I made an offer to my son Paul that I would buy a lathe and would contract with him to produce the electrodes we needed. This proved successful. Paul paid for the lathe and earned his tuition at Michael Power High School, as well as his spending money throughout his high school years. This business was passed on to Peter and then John.

First ICP Spectrometer in Canada.

The air jet procedure was replaced in the late 1970s by the inductively-coupled argon plasma (ICP), which produces greater accuracy. However, the sample must be put into solution. The standard technique was to fuse the sample with a flux in a platinum crucible with a flame or electric furnace. This was time-consuming and frequently did not produce a stable solution. At TSL John developed a method for sample dissolution by fusing the sample with a flux in a graphite crucible using an induction furnace. The fusion was completed in a few seconds at a very high temperature and produced a stable solution. This was part of what enabled us to produce what became our famous Whole Rock Analysis that helped the company grow dramatically, and remains as the standard technique for Whole Rock at Activation Laboratories, which was part of TSL, and is the successor to TSL. At the time we developed the Whole Rock procedure, most labs were not able to use the ICP spectrometers at all. They were essentially still experimental, or used for very simple samples. None of the other labs had John's software or digestion method. As the Stalwood Air Jet method enabled us to provide unique services, so also our ICP techniques put us years ahead of other labs and helped encourage the instrument manufacturers to develop ICP spectrometers to the present situation in which they are the most commonly used instruments for elemental analysis. Most ICP spectrometers today use routines first developed by John on our spectrometers, and most labs today use the ICP as the main instrument for elemental analysis.

GEOCHEMISTRY AND ON-SITE LABS

In the early sixties mineral exploration started to use geochemistry for exploration. Samples of soil or vegetation were analyzed to find underlying mineral deposits. Trends were important. Hence, large numbers of samples had to be taken. TSL's instrumentation was exceptionally well suited to such analyses. A geochemical lab was set up and quickly became a large part of our mining business. Jim O'Neill, our equipment salesman, met a young post-doctorate at the Geological Survey in Ottawa who was working on geochemical methods for oil exploration. Jim was impressed and suggested that I talk to him. The net result was that Dr. Adrian Debnam became our Chief Geochemist and vice-president.

Atomic Absorption, which is based on spectrographic analysis, was just starting to be applied at that time. The dissolved sample was sprayed into a flame. Passing light produced by specific metals through the flame (and measuring the absorption of that light) resulted in an accurate and specific analysis. We were among the leaders of this technique. It was well suited to geochemistry. A suitable digestion extracted the sample. There was no need for separations, calorimetric evaluations, residue weightings, or titrations. The atomic absorption procedures were fast, simple, and specific, and able to handle hundreds of samples per day. The most time consuming part of the operation was the drying and sieving of the samples, handling, sorting, and recording the samples as received. The analysis was simple and fast. Extensive laboratory facilities for geochemistry were not required, and as such the procedures were readily adapted to field laboratories. As geochemical surveys depended on soil or vegetation samples, they could only be collected in non-freezing weather. With so short a season, field laboratories reduced turnaround time and provided quick feedback to the survey team. TSL operated many geochemical field laboratories.

Atomic Absorption Spectrometer with automatic feed.

INTERESTING CUSTOMER PROBLEMS

TSL was involved in diverse activities such as solving problems in construction and developing better methods of analyzing materials. When the Toronto Dominion Centre was being built, a mistake was made in a shipment of steel girders. They were not the alloy specified but since they looked the same as the alloy they were expecting, they were approved by the inspection team and were installed. Sometime later the mistake was discovered and as there had been several shipments stockpiled, there was no way of knowing where the wrong steel had been installed. It appeared that only option was to dismantle the structure and rebuild it. I called the contractor and pointed out that with a few grams of grindings from each girder, the spectrograph could positively identify the type of steel in each girder for as little as $3.00 per girder. Knowing which girders were wrong and replacing them was a lot cheaper than rebuilding the whole structure. They accepted my suggestion and found that relatively few girders were the wrong alloy. The spectrograph saved the building.

In another case, the glass roof of the Roy Thompson Theater in Toronto constantly appeared dirty. TSL was asked to identify the cause. We obtained samples of the dirt by absorbing some in a cloth and using infrared spectroscopy we were able to identify the dirt as a solvent used in sealants. We found out who had provided the sealant for the glass, obtained some of it, ran an accelerated weathering test on it, and found that the sealant would take about five years to completely cure and to stop leaking. Working with the sealant supplier, we devised a system similar to the swimming pool Kreepy Krauly^{tm} cleaner to continuously clean the windows until the sealant completely cured.

A large condominium development in Oakville used a new surface coating that was guaranteed to withstand weather and sunlight better than previous surface coatings. However, in a couple of months, large areas of the coating had fallen off. The developer sued the supplier for false advertising. The supplier of the coating asked TSL to investigate. We checked the material that had fallen off and found that although the outer surface was hard and dry, the inner material contained considerable solvent. On reporting this to the supplier, it was pointed out that the instructions clearly stated that it must be applied as a very thin coating, preferably less than one eight of an inch, and never thicker than one quarter inch. We then did an accelerated weathering test and found that when applied in less than a quarter inch it had the durability claimed, but at one half an inch thickness the top quarter inch hardened; the lower part could not release the solvent and thus did not dry and harden. The failure was due to improper application by the contractors, who had originally applied the surfacing.

Tip Top Tailors had a fire and the insurance company brought TSL clothes that may have been contaminated by smoke in order to check for smoke contamination. Tip Top Tailors wanted to be sure that our tests were sensitive enough, as they did not want to sell clothes that were affected. I suggested they bring some cloth they were certain had not been affected and I could show how sensitive our techniques were. We checked the material for smoke contamination and found none. We then put the cloth in a closet for twenty minutes and again tested it and no contamination showed. I asked the Tip Top representative to go in the closet, light up a cigarette, take two puffs and come out. The cloth was left in the closet for five minutes and when tested it showed a strong positive indication of smoke. They were convinced. TSL was involved in many similar endeavours where our unique facilities and personnel provided solutions to problems.

A NEW HOUSE

Front and back view of our Springhill House.

On an afternoon in the spring of 1969 a real estate agent knocked on our door and said he was looking for prospects. He was a friendly person and he mentioned that he was new at real estate and had to show some success. He said he had a very unusual house for sale at a good price and would appreciate if Elinor would take a look at it. She agreed and they went to look at it. When I came home that evening she told me about it and suggested I should look at it. After supper Elinor, Peter, and I did so. It was a flat-roofed 4500 square foot house on a ravine lot. It was appealing and Elinor and Peter both thought it was a great house. I agreed and contacted the agent. The asking price was $90,000, but it was the last house in the development and the builder wanted to move on. I told him I was interested, but not at $90,000; $70,000 was my limit. The next day the agent called and said that the builder would like to meet me and that we could probably arrive at a deal. We met, and with some changes in the final finish, he agreed to $70,000 cash and I arranged my mortgage.

It was a modified Spanish style on a ravine lot with four large bedrooms and a huge master bedroom suite. The floating stairs to the second floor and the lower level were off a huge foyer. The living room had a fireplace and a sliding door which led to the back deck. There was also a fireplace in the walnut-panelled family room. Another room that could be used as a den or office was off the foyer. The large kitchen featured a breakfast area and a small office space overlooking the deck. The dining room had a wall of windows facing the ravine. A large bar with glass shelves across the mirror at the back was at the foot of the floating stairs to the lower level. The lower level also contained a large living room with a fireplace and a sliding door to the lower level patio. Two smaller rooms were used as studio and library. There were also two large unfinished rooms where we had a pool table and a workshop. Across the back of the house was a deck with stairs to the lower level. It was a very nice house. It was also in a good neighbourhood and we acquired some good friends. Across the street lived the McClures and next door to them lived the Harts. Down the street lived the McFadens. Between the McFadens and our house lived Tommy Hunter the country singer and Dr. Kingleyside, a noted ornithologist. Elinor often played bridge with these and other neighbours The Hunters moved away and the McFadden's have both died, but the McClures and Harts are still living there and are very good friends.

The house was well suited for hosting parties and we had several. At the house warming party many friends and some of the neighbours attended. Elinor wanted to see how many she could pack into the main bathroom. She got twenty five people in it and could shut the door. It was a beautiful house and we all enjoyed it. Since Paul was already married we only needed four bedrooms. As a result, Debbie's friend Julie, who lived nearby with four brothers, probably spent more time in our extra bedroom than at her own home. It was also put to use when Peter's girlfriend Jocelyn was thrown out of her home by her parents because she let Peter visit her when her parents were not home. She lived with us for several weeks until Paul and Suzanne arranged to let her live with them. Peter and John were attending university while living here. Peter also had a part-time job as TSL's janitor and was making a reasonable income. He bought an MG Midget, which is a very small English car. It was cute but it was so small that he was hit several times because the other drivers did not see it on the road. Elinor and I were concerned that he would be hurt with a serious hit. After several hits he finally sold it to Jeff, Debbie's boyfriend, who reconditioned it and resold it.

PETER'S TRAVELS AND GETTING MARRIED

Peter and Jocelyn's wedding.

Peter graduated from Michael Power High School and registered at the University of Toronto to study Philosophy and English in the fall of 1968. In the spring of 1969 he and his friend Gerry Thompson decided to go backpacking in Europe for the summer. Peter was only eighteen and Elinor felt he should postpone it for at least a year. I preferred that he wait a year, but he said he was in the wrong course at university and that this was a good time to travel. I was glad he did not go alone. They traveled through France into Italy, then by boat to Greece. They purchased deck class, which meant that they slept on the deck with the animals. From Greece they went to Turkey. In Istanbul Peter bought and sent us a Christmas present, which did not arrive until March. When it did arrive it was a hammered brass tray that was a meter in diameter. It was a beautiful piece of art that we hung in a prominent place in our house. When we entered a retirement residence there was no place for it and we gave it back to Peter. When Peter came home just before Christmas of '69, his friend Gerry went to Israel. While there, Gerry got word that his father had a heart attack and so he returned home.

While he was traveling Peter had thought a lot about a university education and decided that architecture was the broadest field of study in a university context that related to his interests. It included philosophy and English, communication, anthropology, archaeology, science, engineering, photography, the arts, etc. In the winter he met with the Chairman of the Faculty of Architecture and was accepted for registration the next fall.

When Peter continued his backpacking the next spring, Gerry did not accompany him, so he went alone. He took the Orient Express to Athens. From Athens he went to Egypt. He climbed the Great Pyramid of Giza (which was illegal) in the middle of the night. He left his boots at the bottom. On looking down he saw three soldiers with rifles standing by his boots and they arrested him when he came down. The soldiers took his camera and started fighting over who would get it. While they argued he escaped and ran away in the darkness. Shots were fired as they chased him but he eluded them and ducked into in a tent that sold tea. He sat among some others drinking tea and when offered some to drink himself, he accepted. After he realized that he had given them the slip, he also realized that the tea was made with polluted water from the street gutter. He became very sick while in a Cairo Youth Hostel and was unconscious for three days. Fortunately an English backpacker who was also staying in the hostel gave him some of the medication that he had with him and looked after Peter. Once he recovered, Peter flew to Entebbe in Uganda to visit East Africa. He started walking from the airport to Kampala, which was 20 miles away. Fortunately the man that he had sat beside on the plane picked him up en-route and invited Peter to stay with him and his wife at the university, where he was a professor. The professor introduced him to others within the university and as a result he was invited to go to a backcountry research camp. He was welcomed there and then put up at Mweya Lodge in Queen Elizabeth National Park and provided with a jeep to use. He was taken on airplane flights counting wildlife - all at no cost!

He stayed several weeks at Mweya Lodge and then joined another researcher and traveled through the Budongo Forest and canoed up the Nile River to Murchison Falls. Unfortunately, Idi Amin was in power at that time in Uganda and the country was not a safe place. Peter witnessed some terrible violence and tragedies and decided to continue on to Kenya, where he stayed in Nairobi with a friend and his wife that he had met backpacking in Europe the year before. In Kenya he bought us a large wood carving of a man swallowing a snake that he carried in his backpack for the rest of his trip, which included going to Tanzania and climbing to the summit of Mount Kilimanjaro.

Our first grandchild, Samantha

When he returned home he continued his studies, and on finishing second year in architecture he married Jocelyn Rivers in 1972, who at that time was working for Ward Air as a stewardess. Peter was also working at TSL part-time as a janitor. Our first grandchild, Samantha, was born in 1973. Peter graduated in 1975 and took a job in North Battleford, where he designed a ten storey senior citizen apartment building, amongst other projects in that area. He then moved to Calgary in 1976, started his own firm in 1978, and he has since become a very successful architect. He is the senior partner of that firm, which is one of the largest in western Canada. He and his company have designed many significant buildings in Calgary and western Canada.

JOHN IN THE ARCTIC

In the autumn of 1970 John saw an advertisement on the University of Toronto's Biology Department's bulletin board for summer students as scuba divers working at Resolute Bay in the Arctic. It advertised long hours, little pay, dangerous work and a chance to see the far north. John applied and although the other students hired were masters or doctorate students in biology, and he was only a first year student in physics, he was hired. John had experience helping me build and repair spectrometers since he was about ten years old. At age fifteen he had spent a summer in Florida building our *SpectroChem*, a small mobile rapid sorting spectrometric instrument. He did the machining, wiring, and optics himself and built seven machines in two months – four times what was normally built in that time. With such experience, he was able to offer the ability to repair and maintain the equipment in the Arctic. It seemed that few biology students had the many years of experience repairing machines and electronics that John had, as well as being able to do the biology work. He needed a scuba diver's certificate, which he immediately studied for and obtained. Elinor and I would have preferred that he had chosen a more conventional job, but John was enthusiastic. We hoped the management of the project would not take risks. John apparently liked the job as he returned for a second year. When he came home at the end of the summer we found out that he was diving under six feet of ice in a frozen lake and in the ocean. It was much more dangerous than we had anticipated. He insisted that enough precautions were taken and it was reasonably safe. Not until we saw the photographs he had taken did we find out that they had often been in serious difficulties and very dangerous conditions. When the diver enters the hole in the ice he has a rope tied to his arm. This rope must have sufficient slack so the diver can work, but must be taut enough that it can signal if the diver is in trouble. It also guides the diver back to the hole in the ice. One time the person at the hole in the ice let go of the rope and it fell in the water and sank. When John started back, the rope was loose instead of being taut. He fortunately found his way back to the hole. He told us that accidents could happen – but no one was ever hurt on the project. He had many other escapes.

Chapter 17

CORPORATE BATTLES OVER WEAR CHECK

Wear metal analysis was becoming known. Most of the railroads and the US Air Force were using it. I decided that it had great potential and a huge market. Our new venture, Wear Check, had made more progress than others. We had developed a package consisting of a sample-taking pump, a small sample bottle, a form to list particulars, a mailing package, and diagnostic data. The client took the sample and entered data such as where the sample came from and any other relevant information. Then the client dropped the information in the mail, and the lab mailed the form back with the values of the wear metals found, along with a recommendation for action (if any). If any serious wear was found, a phone call or telegram was sent. At this point we had a few regular customers and had set up a section of the lab for Wear Check. I incorporated a company named Wear Check International and copyrighted the name. Carlton Joyce, whom I had hired some months earlier, was put in charge of the new company. Carlton pointed out that since the market in the USA was much larger than in Canada, the major effort should be in the USA. This made sense. One trucking company, Pacific Intermountain, had over 4,000 trucks, and there were dozens of such trucking firms in the USA.

Carlton and I attended several conferences in American cities where the US Air Force was giving papers on their use of wear metal analyses. We made contacts with British Overseas Airways (now British Air), the Danish Air Force, the Australian Air Force, and several aircraft manufacturers. Since the US Air force was still in experimental stages, Wear Check got a limited contract to do wear metal analyses for an air force base near Washington. An aircraft sample from this base showed abnormal wear and we telephoned the base. It turned out that the sample was from Air Force One - the American president's plane, which was at that moment airborne. The plane was ordered to land at the nearest airport. Wear Check got a phone call from the base thanking us for our service.

Paul had worked on setting up equipment for the Wear Check analysis and was aware of the advantages it provided. When he was in Kenya he met an American at an US embassy party who worked for GE. He had been sent to Kenya to help their air force establish a maintenance process for new F5 military jets that used GE engines. He told Paul that it was unfortunate that Kenya was unable to do wear metal analysis as that would double the time between engine overhauls. To his surprise, Paul said he was familiar with oil analysis and that his laboratory at the Mines department could do it if Kenya wanted it. The testing was setup and the air force was then allowed to double the time between engine overhaul. After about a year an analysis was completed on a Friday afternoon, which showed very high lead. This was a very surprising and potentially dangerous problem for the whole fleet of F5 aircraft. Paul tried calling his normal contact and then the next level of command. With a weekend about to start, everyone was away. He drove to the air force base and after some discussion at the gate managed to speak to the commanding officer, explain what they were doing and the potential problems that it could mean. The air force grounded all of its jets. Through the weekend, Paul and the lab people repeated the analysis, finding the same results, and only on the Monday did they find out that the air force had been so happy with the oil program they had decided to put their propeller planes with radial engines on the testing and had submitted the samples from these without any indication of something different. The radial engines ran on leaded fuel and that was the source of lead in the oil.

On one of his trips Carlton ran into a salesman in Detroit named Glenn Miller (**not** the famous musician). Miller was immediately sold on the potential of Wear Check and wanted to become our USA agent. We did make him an agent, but not exclusively. He went after the automobile companies to try to convince them that with Wear Check they could extend their warranties, provided the owner had a Wear Check twice a year or every 30,000 miles. Chrysler considered it and had us run some test programs but decided against it.

Massey Ferguson, the tractor manufacturer, decided to try it out on a test program they were starting. The test program involved a heavy-duty tractor to run on a test track pulling the equivalent of ten ploughs until failure. An oil sample was taken every twelve hours and analyzed for wear metals. On the basis of our analyses, we were able to predict that the engine would fail within the next two weeks. The week it failed we could predict within four hours of it happening. Wear Check was also able to identify the cause of engine wear resulting in failure. The research department was impressed and recommended that six Wear Check packages should be included with the sale of every tractor. If oil samples were taken at specified intervals, the company would extend the warranty. However, Massey Ferguson was running into financial problems and the department we were working with was disbanded and the whole project dropped.

Several other approaches were tried. Attempts were made to convince the bus and the transit companies with little success. Greyhound in USA did go on limited trial. Attempts were also made to offer it to the general public. Gulf did seriously consider putting the Wear Check package on their service station shelves. Logistics of handling, sampling, reports and their evaluation unfortunately doomed it. Another area was the small aircraft. The US Federal Aviation Administration required that an aircraft engine must be overhauled every 100 hours, and torn down and completely rebuilt every 500 hours. This is a major expense in the maintenance of a small aircraft. Carlton and Glenn worked with Cummings Engine to convince the FAA that with regular Wear Check analyses, overhaul and rebuild times could be extended by up to 50%. This took some time. It was finally granted and later extended to other engines. Wear Check's first success was with small aircraft. At the same time, Wear Check had managed to get a few trucking companies interested in limited programs. A steady flow of samples was being received. Wear Check was becoming viable.

With the US Air force's use of lube oil analyses and Wear Check's promotion, other labs were starting to offer the service. To benefit from the effort we had put into development of Wear Check, we needed to embark on a more aggressive marketing program before someone else did. This meant much heavier expenditures.

At the same time, Jarrell-Ash, our major equipment supplier, was unfortunately sold out to Fisher Scientific. Fisher believed that telephone salesmen, who were only order-takers for laboratory glassware, could sell complex and expensive spectrometers as well as we could. They canceled our contracts and we could no longer sell their equipment. We had good prospects for at least a million in sales, which would have been realized within a year. Losing this source of revenue meant a loss in excess of $200,000. To increase our marketing cost meant we would need outside financing.

OUTSIDE FINANCING

In 1972 we hired a management consultant to help us prepare a prospectus to aid in the raising of capital. He put us in touch with Helix Investments, a venture capital company owned by Ben Webster, who was the son of a Royal Bank director and a brother of the president of the Globe and Mail newspaper. Helix agreed to invest $250,000 in Wear Check for a 10% interest in Burgener Technical Enterprises (BTE), the holding company I had set up to own the various TSL related companies. They also had an option to buy an additional 15%. The agreement also stated that if more money was needed, they would put in another $350,000, but at that point, they would increase their interest to 65%. To protect their investment, they appointed one of their personnel as a financial manager of Wear Check. They also threw in a clause that if we did not perform satisfactorily, they could convert the investment to a demand loan but would retain their 10% interest in BTE.

I discussed this agreement with my lawyer and consultant. They both agreed that this was a fairly standard agreement, so I signed it. As far as not performing, I was not worried at all - and if Wear Check was a huge success, then 45% (which my holdings would have shrunk to) of a very large operation was better than 60% of a small operation.

The appointed manager, Michael McCabe, immediately started spending money. He hired four new salesmen and set up an office in New York City, in spite of my objections. I could not see why we needed an office in New York City, since the transportation center of eastern USA was Atlanta. Trucking and airline head offices and maintenance centres were in Atlanta. Furthermore, hiring salesmen without a sales plan made no sense. I put up a strong objection to New York so he agreed that we should open offices in both places. As the sales effort was in the USA, it made sense to set up a lab in USA. We both agreed that Atlanta was the logical location. A fully equipped lab was set up there. He argued that since Wear Check was a new company, and since the lab would cost about $150,000, it would expedite deliveries if BTE ordered everything. His next effort was an expensive advertising program, again without a plan. I began to realize that his objective was to spend the $250,000 as fast as possible, without regard for the value of the expenditure, triggering Helix's next investment, and giving them 65% of the company. I would become an employee. It may have made me rich, but I would lose my freedom. This was not my vision of how I intended to live. I started objecting.

I went to a conference in Texas to promote Wear Check. While I was away one of my employees (who was a graduate physicist and MBA) went to the bank, stating they should call their loans and appoint him as CEO, as I was doing a poor job. I suspect that McCabe planned this. I fortunately called my secretary on Friday afternoon and she suggested that I had better get back because there were a number of secret meetings going on, and the bank manager had been present for some of them. I was in Salt Lake City at that time and started driving home right away. I arrived home Sunday afternoon, having chosen the states with no speed limits. Monday morning I was in my office at 8:00 AM, and after talking to the bank manager, my secretary, and others, I left a note on the instigator's desk to come and see me. He argued that he and others felt that I was impeding the company by objecting to spending money on Wear Check. The company and I would both be better off if a more aggressive management had control. Maybe he was right, but I never found out since I fired him on the spot. A few years later this same person had become president of a large security company and he came back to ask my opinion on whether or not he should give up the big company and buy a small company that he had the opportunity of buying. He said that being president of the large company had many disadvantages as compared with the way I operated and lived.

The management consultant was the next to go and a big argument with McCabe ensued. Webster called and asked me to see him. He pointed out that I was restricting the progress of Wear Check. He stated that they put up the money to rapidly expand it. If I would not spend the necessary money, it would not expand, and Helix would have to assume that performance was inadequate. This meant of course that the $250,000 would become repayable and due immediately.

Webster's comments were a warning. The full $250,000 had not yet been spent but we were getting close. Whether it was Helix's plan to get rid of me, or McCabe's opinion that he would make hero of himself by getting rid of me, I did not know. Webster seemed to be a reasonable person, so I decided that I would fight to retain control of BTE. The other alternative was to let them put in more money and I would become an employee. The bank refused to loan me the $250,000 to pay them back. If I could pay back the $250,000 I could get

A Broader Vision

Wear Check back, however, I did not see any way to cover that amount. My lawyer pointed out that if I refused to go along with them - especially if we had not yet spent the full $250,000 - that it would become a matter of interpretation as to whether or not I was performing, hence they had to get a court order to demand their money. I decided to bring it to a conclusion.

On my lawyer's advice I sent Helix a letter pointing out that I had no intention of needing more investment and that their manager had not shown prudence in the handling of their investment. Needless to say, this resulted in a lawyer's letter from Helix demanding immediate repayment of their investment. Several meetings followed between lawyers, Helix's representative, and myself in which some backing down on the part of Helix occurred. Helix was represented by a Michael Needam, who was a much more reasonable person than McCabe. I suspect that McCabe got fired because I never saw him again, even though I had dealings with Helix for several years.

Helix made a final proposal that my lawyer advised me to accept. He pointed out that to continue would probably result in a court case at considerable cost, and I may not do any better. Furthermore, it contained a clause preventing me from being involved in analysis of engine oils anywhere in the world for five years. That clause would not stand up in court. He said that I should sign it and we would declare the agreement void later.

In the agreement Helix got 100% of Wear Check and would not exercise their option of 15% more interest in BTE. BTE still had to repay the $250,000 "loan" even though all of it had been spent on Wear Check. They allowed $90,000 for the Atlanta lab even though it had cost me $150,000, and I still had to pay $160,000. The debt was to be paid in $20,000 increments every quarter and Helix was to have a director on BTE's board. Any major expenditure had to have Helix's approval until the debt was paid off. The Canadian Wear Check work was being done in TSL's Lab, since Wear Check Canada had no facilities. TSL was to continue to provide that service at cost until the debt was fully paid.

It was not a fair deal for BTE, but it did leave me as owner of BTE. At the end of the first three months I paid the $20,000. Having established my willingness to live up to the agreement, I had my lawyer send a letter in which I pointed out that Helix was using the name Wear Check on which I had a copyright. More negotiating ensued with Needam and I agreed to sell the copyright for the next two and the last two of the $20,000 payments. This covered me for the next six months plus another six months at the end.

The lease at 355 King Street was nearing its end. The new owners of the building were neglecting it to the point that even the entrance looked like a garbage dump. Frequently the elevator did not work. The heating system broke down on a very cold day, and the building superintendent's attitude was that it would take two or three weeks to repair and that he didn't want me to bother him. I checked out the furnace and found that a fuse on the circulation system was blown. I replaced it and the pump worked. I got a letter from the owners pointing out that if any damage occurred as a result of my tampering, they would sue me. Obviously they were just trying to cut costs on heating. This was the general attitude and I decided that a move was necessary.

As we had to move, we decided to move away from the parking, transportation, and other difficulties the city presented. Since all of our mining business came from Bay Street, a move to the suburbs could be disastrous. I looked for a short-term lease so that we could move back to the city if needed. A two year sublet was eventually found on Evans Avenue in Etobicoke with the possibility of renewal.

THE HELIX PROBLEM

I still had The Helix problem since we had to continue providing service to Wear Check. I wanted to get out of moving the Wear Check facilities. I decided to pay the next $20,000 instalment and hold off on my next deal until we were ready to move. To make sure that the next deal would stick, it was necessary that Wear Check was prospering. As their business was improving, time was in my favour.

About two months before the end of the lease I pointed out to Needam that we were going to move. Since I had to continue to provide service to Wear Check, I planned to set up the operation in our new premises, but was going to start competing with them. This started the lawyers talking again. It was decided that the non-competition clause was not binding and possibly the whole agreement was not valid. Carlton Joyce, who had continued as Wear Check's manager, commented that all hell broke loose at Helix. This went on for some weeks with threats of suits on both sides. Finally I decided to play my trump card. One evening while using the spectrometer used on Wear Check, I accidentally damaged a circuit board. It was not serious damage and I could have repaired it in an hour. However, I refused to have anything to do with it and suggested that they get the manufacturer to send a service man. Wear

A Broader Vision

Check was doing a good business on aircraft engine oil analysis, where turnaround was guaranteed in twenty-four hours. It took more than twenty-four hours for the Jaco service man to arrive, and after a quick look at the spectrometer, said it had been modified and that he could not fix it. Jaco had a more experienced man but he was not available for at least two weeks and it probably would take him a week to solve it. Carlton suggested that Helix talk to me and meet whatever terms I demanded, or wind up Wear Check.

A most unfriendly meeting resulted in which I laid out my terms: I would fix the instrument and get it into operation immediately for the remainder of the debt. I would also put the instrument back to its original circuitry and would deed the equipment to them. We would no longer operate it, nor would we move it to our new location. When we moved we would leave it where it was and it was their problem. If they agreed to this then I would not go into competition. If they did not, I would move the equipment, repair it, and set up a complete oil analysis lab using TSL's experience with Wear Check.

This resulted in some rather heated name calling, to which I responded by pointing out that if they wanted an example of unethical actions, then they could look at the scheme Helix perpetrated in which the obvious attempt was to oust me and take over BTE. Their actions were about as dirty as one could get. As it was, they got Wear Check. I got nothing, even losing another $20,000 worth of equipment - and I still had to pay off $70,000 on the Atlanta Lab. Helix agreed to the deal; they had no choice because I meant to follow through with a new service called Lube Check.

In spite of all this, Needam, who was on our board of directors, remained friendly. Since the space we had leased was 15,000 square feet, and we needed only 7,000 square feet, Helix rented the other 8,000 to store a stock of tires they had bought on some deal. Needam, after a couple of years, suggested that he would arrange to sell us back their 10% at less than what they paid. TSL did so, and that ended our direct relationship with Helix. I believe that had Needam been our contact man from the beginning, we would have had a more successful arrangement.

Wear Check went onto be a success in both Canada and the USA. Helix later sold Wear Check Canada to the manager and Wear Check USA to Carlton Joyce. Carlton later bought the Canadian operation and expanded Wear Check into an international operation with 3500 employees in several branches in North America, Australia, and Europe. When I think back on Wear Check, I realize that it was downgrading the mechanics. The mechanics were the technical authority in the trucking company. To have someone come in and tell them how to look after the engines reduced their importance, and obviously they would fight against that notion. If instead we had approached the mechanics and pointed out that they could *enhance* their position by convincing management that they could do a better job using Wear Check, we would not have needed extra financing.

As a result of our Helix troubles we needed money. At the same time, our Vancouver lab was showing signs of a slowdown because of the NDP government's attitude towards the resource industries. Fortunately, an American lab wanting to expand into Canada approached us on a buyout. I seized the opportunity and sold it for $90,000. At the time we had our 1967 Chevy van and trailer lab in Vancouver, and some other equipment and supplies that I did not want to sell. It was agreed that we could keep them but we had to get them to Toronto. Since I was in Vancouver, I decided to load up the van and trailer and drive the lot to Toronto.

This was the middle of March, and although it was spring in Vancouver, the mountains and prairies were still in the grip of winter. By the time I reached Kamloops I realized that the load was too much for the van. At Kamloops I shipped by rail everything that did not need special packing. It was a good thing I did: The van stalled twice climbing a steep grade while I was going through the mountains. I discovered that the hand brake on a steep grade could not hold the heavily loaded van-trailer combination. The reverse gear held it. In order to start the engine, it had to be out of gear. The foot brakes held it, but I could not have my foot on the gas pedal and the brake at the same time. Several attempts showed that a different approach was needed. Finally putting the van in reverse gear, I got out and put a large stone under each front wheel. Racing the engine while letting the clutch out, I swung hard to the left, hoping the back wheels would miss the stones. The first attempt failed and stalled the engine. On the next attempt, I put the stones behind the trailer wheels. That worked and I knew what to do the next time it stalled. Fortunately I ran into very little snow and in general I enjoyed the trip. Between Winnipeg and Thunder Bay the clutch and transmission started to give trouble, probably as a result of the strain in the mountains. By the time I reached Thunder Bay it would only go into second gear. I left it at a garage and flew home. When it was repaired I sent someone to bring it to Toronto.

TSL SPOKANE

We retained the Spokane lab when we sold the Vancouver lab. It had been operated as a branch of the Vancouver lab. The mining exploration activity in the US northwest was expanding. We had made some good contacts with the US Bureau of Mines. Unfortunately, the chemist who had been heading it up became more interested in running a hot dog stand at the World's Fair in Seattle than in running the lab and he had let the lab deteriorate. He was replaced with a chemist whose husband was a consulting geologist. Apparently he did not want his wife working in a mining lab because he felt that there was a conflict of interest. She was a very competent person and quickly brought the lab back to a good level. However, her husband decided to move to Arizona and we lost her. There were several good technicians on the staff but no other chemists.

When she left she suggested that a man she had hired to look after sample preparation a few months earlier would make a good administrator. With the experienced technicians, she felt that he should do a good job of running the lab. Her suggestion was followed and Marvin Colman became the lab manager. He did a good job for several years, expanding the lab to the point that an ICP direct reading spectrometer was purchased, and two chemists were added. The US Bureau of Mines designated TSL Laboratories as their lab in the North West. Business was booming. Then suddenly President Reagan canceled the ten year multi-billion-dollar exploration program the Bureau had embarked on. Exploration in the Northwest stopped. The result was that Marv and most of the staff were let go. We continued running the lab for a couple years as a small AA based geochem lab with the former chief chemist, John Trector, as the new manager. He eventually bought out the Spokane lab and continued running it. Marv was a good salesman and I heard that he was making a success as a motorcycle dealer.

***

With the loss of Wear Check, less space was needed. As mentioned earlier, a short term sub-lease was arranged in a property on Evans Avenue which had been a Lab before we took it over. It was 15,000 square feet and we only needed 7,000. However, the rent was reasonable and the sub-lease was for two years with the option to renew for ten years. As a former lab, it had a number of facilities installed, so I rented it and moved in. The move was easier because of its former use. The move proved that business was not lost by the move.

In fact, the customers approved, particularly because we had parking space, making it convenient for them to drive to the lab and park, and sales increased.

Evans Avenue was close to a residential area, thus we had difficulties with break-ins. The police, who we saw frequently, said that since it was a laboratory, the thieves expected to find drugs. They suggested we change the name on the building. Since the move to this location had demonstrated that business increased because of parking and easy access, we looked for a more industrial location rather than renew the lease. I found a nice freestanding building with good parking on Fewster Avenue in the Dixie Road area, and so we moved again. This building was only 5,000 square feet, but there were other buildings nearby that had space if needed. We stayed at the Fewster location from then on.

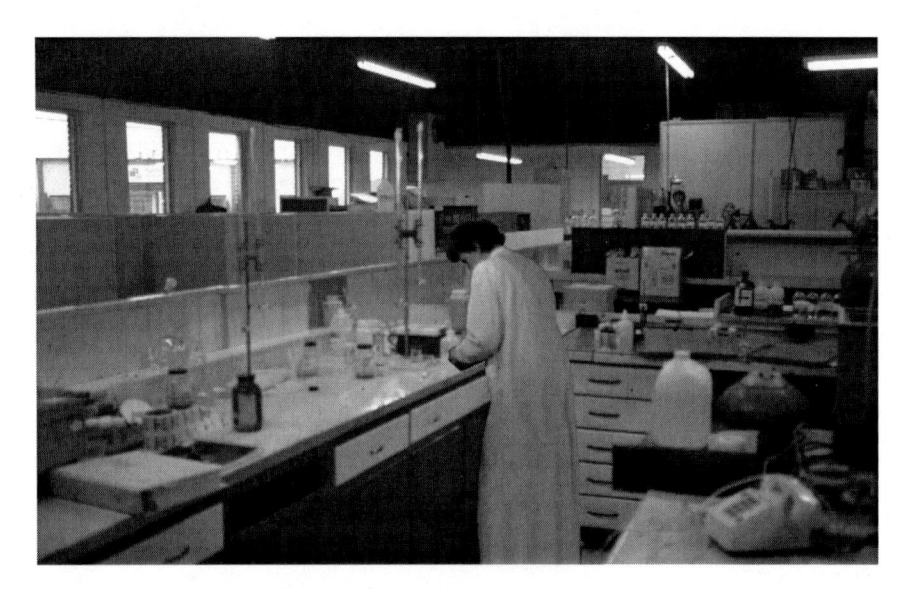

Inside TSL's Main Lab Mississauga

Chapter 18

MOVING ON AFTER WEAR CHECK – FAMILY EVENTS – THE KIDS GROW UP

In 1974 a real estate agent called and said he had a client who would pay a premium for a house in our district. This was a ploy used to get new clients. However, this also was in the middle of my difficulties with Helix, Wear Check, and the ThermoCarb (which I will describe later). I agreed to see him and said that I would sell for $200,000. I ended up selling it for $175,000, with a capital gain of $105,000. When one considers at that time a new top-of-the-line Chevrolet cost $2,500, the $100,000 had the purchasing power of $1,000,000 by today's standards. Elinor was very upset because she really enjoyed the house and had good relationships with the neighbours. Since both Peter and Paul were now married, we did not need a five bedroom house. I felt that a three bedroom house was all we needed. Since Elinor was so upset by the sale, I told her to find a house she wanted and that I would buy it. She found a house on Tecumseh a few blocks away. It was a five bedroom, 3300 square foot house. I bought it. Elinor's wisdom saw that the extra bedrooms were a real advantage, as they provided room for our grandchildren to spend more time with us. The extra bedrooms were soon put to use. Paul, along with his wife and three children (who had spent five years in Kenya working for the Canadian International Development Agency), returned to Canada, and they needed somewhere to live while they re-settled in Canada. They lived with us for several months. The extra space also made it possible for Peter and his family of four children to visit. Jocelyn and the children often spent several weeks in the summer with us. The house also provided the opportunity for me to improve it.

I always preferred to get my physical exercise accomplishing something rather than working out in a gym. In the basement there was a fireplace, but nothing else was finished. The basement was divided into three areas, running the full length of the house. I finished the north area, with a fireplace by installing walnut panels on the walls, a tile floor, and a ceiling. I built a bar, a lounge, and a studio in the central area, and I turned the south area into a large workshop. The front end of the workshop was setup as a wine fermentation and bottling area. Over the years some good wines were produced there. Outside at the back there was a small patio. I installed a partially in-ground pool and extended the wooden deck of the pool to include a deck across the width of the house. These activities kept me busy and physically fit for several years.

Tecumseh Park Road house, Lorne Park.

While living in this house, John graduated in physics and geology, and he worked as a geophysicist in the Arctic for that summer. He then spent a year trying to get into a PhD program but was not acceptable to the professors as

A Broader Vision

he wanted to re-write the basic laws of physics, which they did not want to happen. In the spring of 1976 I asked John to set up a mobile lab in Yellowknife for the summer. I offered enough to cover his expenses and a commission on any additional work he was able to get while running the lab for us. By the end of the summer he had done more than five times the work expected and had earned enough to go traveling for a year. He came home and announced to us that he was going to travel for a year before looking for a different job. John was twenty-five years old and had lived independently for many summers in many far-away places, not to mention that he was proficient in Karate. He was older and able to defend himself in any potentially problematic situations, so we were not as apprehensive about John traveling as we had been with Peter.

He started his travels by going to Kenya to visit Paul and Suzanne. While there he traveled to Tanzania to climb Mount Kilimanjaro. Tanzania closed the border to Kenya as he was climbing the mountain and he was not permitted to return to Kenya. While climbing Kilimanjaro, John had helped some Canadians down the mountain and was able to contact them and ask for help. They let him stay with them until the Canadian government was able to find a way to allow him back into Kenya. Eventually Tanzania agreed to allow people who were on a flight from Tanzania that was stopping in Kenya but continuing on to somewhere else to also let some people off in Kenya. With $200 as his total assets in Tanzania, John was able to survive for the two weeks it took to get back, and he flew from Dar es Salaam to Nairobi. He then began his cross-Africa trip, with its first stop in Tanzania. His truck driver was able to convince the border guards to let them through, but the travel group in a following truck were not allowed to pass. The truck he was on was the last truck to cross the Kenya/Tanzania border for five years.

John's trip took them through civil wars, peaceful towns, deserts, storms, and mud roads where they had to push. One night the group wanted to camp on the side of an active volcano and John insisted they move. The next day their first campsite was covered with molten lava. When the group reached the Mediterranean, John left the tour and flew to Nepal. Here he was supposed to meet a cross-Asia tour, but was a day late and they had left already. They left a message for him to meet them in India. He then flew to India and waited for two weeks for the tour to reach him – the bus had engine problems and it took them that long to get spare parts. The trip continued through Pakistan,

Afghanistan, Iran, and Russia, and then back through Europe to England, and then finally he headed home.

***

Debbie as a small child showed a real interest in art, which to some extent may have been encouraged by my interest in painting. Because of her apparent interest, Elinor had her take sewing lessons from a friend, who was a home economics teacher. She also took piano lessons but had less interest in these. It is possible that the teacher was too demanding and it could have discouraged her. However, Debbie utilized her sewing skills at high school by modifying her clothes to look spectacular. When she started her post-secondary education she registered in an art course. She did not continue in it because the professor did not control the idiots in the class. For example, one student lay on the floor through the lectures, commenting every few minutes, "Yeah, Teach." Others did other ridiculous things. The professor tolerated it and possibly even encouraged them. Debbie was there to learn and felt that this was wasting time, so she quit. I would also have quit. She did not go to school to act a fool. When she quit it was too late to register in another course, so she went looking for a job. She got a job as a letter carrier and worked at it until the following September. She enjoyed the letter carrying, except for some of the union rules, such as having to carry her entire load all the way up the west side of the street, where the houses were, and then down the east side of the street where the apartments were, which meant the heaviest load. She was not allowed to reverse it. She also found that after she had finished her letter carrying she had time for another job as a clerk in a teenager's clothing store at Square One Shopping Centre. She was one of their best salespersons.

The following September Debbie took a course in computer science, where she found students who were serious about learning. When she graduated she became a computer instructor, traveling across Canada for a major national company. Debbie has continued her interest in art. She made her children's special clothes, dressing them in very well-made and striking items. She does a lot of ceramics and has done some nice work in oils. She of course is encouraging her daughter Katlyn to nurture her artistic interests; since she was a young girl she has shown some exceptional talent.

A Broader Vision

Deborah at eighteen.

Debbie's son Spencer has suffered from a severe peanut allergy as well as a severe skin allergy from birth. This threw a huge burden on his parents, especially his mother. Debbie has handled this with persistence and she has consistently shown great care and concern without complaint. Even with these difficulties, she still spent time each week helping out at a shelter for the homeless. She belongs to a prayer group that prays for anyone who has need. Now that Spencer is no longer a teenager and can look after himself, Debbie has taken a job demonstrating food in supermarkets, where she shows her willingness to listen and be present to others, listening patiently to people as they tell her their stories. Debbie is in so many ways like Elinor, her mother, who taught her well. We certainly have to thank St. Anne for directing us to adopt Debbie.

Debbie never went backpacking but she did go to Spain for a couple of weeks with a girlfriend. Unfortunately they left their first destination quickly because the local males seemed to think that visiting females were there solely for their entertainment. Later she went to Monaco to visit with a girlfriend, who was helping her father maintain residency there. This trip of course was not like backpacking, but she had a very good time.

OUR VISIT TO AFRICA

In 1977 Elinor and I decided that this was a good time to visit Africa, since two of our children were in Kenya. John was in Nairobi when we arrived. After a few days of visiting, Paul and Suzanne drove us to Samburu Game Park, where Elinor, John, and I stayed in a Banda. Paul, Suzanne, and infant Brian stayed in the Banda next to us. The Bandas were huts made of stone. The kitchen had a propane stove and a sink with running water from a reservoir on the side of the building. The bedroom had four single beds with mosquito net covering and there was a shower. The hot water for the shower was obtained by building a fire under a tank outside. The windows were heavy screens without glass. Electric lights were from a generator for the group of Bandas. The first night we had dinner with Paul and Suzanne in their Banda. It is safe during the day but after dark one is advised to stay inside. It was dark before we finished dinner so we had to walk to our Banda in the dark. It was only a few feet and we felt safe. During the night something bumped into our Banda. A few minutes later there was a great scream, and then all went quiet. We got up and peered into the darkness, but saw nothing.

The next morning, as we started to walk to Paul's Banda, we saw two lions eating a water buffalo beside our Banda. We hurried into Paul's. The lions were not interested in us; they had their meal. Another day as we drove around the game park, the car got a flat tire. We changed it, but as we were finishing we saw a lion walking towards us. We quickly got into the car but the lion just walked by casually, showing no interest in us. For a few days we traveled around seeing elephants, lions, giraffes, impalas, water buffalo, rhinoceros, hippopotami, warthogs, ostriches, and many forms of antelope. We visited Lake Nakuru and saw thousands of flamingos standing and moving about in the shallow water.

We spent a day and a night at the famous Tree Tops Hotel. Queen Elizabeth had been visiting here when her father died, making her queen. To go there you start by having breakfast at the former residence of Lord Baden-Powell, the founder of the Boy Scouts. A Jeep takes you with an armed guard, the big game hunter, across a plain where wild animals are drinking at a water hole. I thought the big game hunter was only window dressing. The hotel was built on stilts in the trees overlooking the water hole, and upon climbing the steps to the main level and continuing up to the roof level, I saw many wild - and no doubt dangerous - animals. In the hotel there are pictures of a rogue elephant being shot as it charged a group of visitors. I guess the big game hunter was not window dressing.

Banda in Samburu Game Park, Kenya.

A buffet lunch was served and the afternoon was spent on the roof deck observing the wild animals at the water hole while enjoying some refreshments. The sliced pineapple was exceptionally good. We were also entertained by the big game hunter as the baboons felt in his pockets and crawled all over him. Supper was served in the dining room at long tables. The food was served in trays sent along a rail in the center of the table and you chose your food as it passed you, which was quite an effective way of serving food in a restricted space. The choices were good and it was an enjoyable meal. John and I sat across from an editor of a well-known periodical, who apparently saw John as a potential husband for his thirty-five year old university professor daughter. John had other ideas. After dinner we went to our rooms, which looked over the illuminated water hole. We were advised to remain dressed as we slept because as different animals came to the water hole, we would be awakened so that we could observe them from our window or go to the roof deck. We were advised to shut our windows, as the baboons would crawl in if left open. Several times through the night calls were heard and we got up to look at herds of elephants, water buffalo, antelopes, and rhinos. The next morning we were escorted back to Lord Baden-Powell's house where breakfast was served and then we made our way back to Nairobi.

Nairobi is a modern city with apartments, hotels, government buildings, and a very modern conference center. Poverty was not as apparent as it is in places like Mexico City, where people live in packing cases. In Nairobi we visited Hemingway's favourite bar, the conference center, and the dry goods sales, which were held in an empty field. We watched the wood carvers and bought some of their carvings. There were also some stone carvers and I bought a stone chess set. Elinor was intrigued by the warthogs who folded their front legs to eat so that they are leaning on their elbows. She of course bought a carving of a warthog. Paul and Suzanne had a nice apartment backing onto an arboretum; there were wild monkeys living there who roamed around the apartments. They had a servant who objected to Elinor having anything to do with her own grandson, Brian. He was her baby and no one interfered.

Lions in the game park.

Again Paul packed all five of us into his mini and we drove to Mombassa on the Indian Ocean. Here we stayed in a house that was built around a tree. Tree branches came through the bedrooms. Bush babies, a small animal that has a cry like a human baby, wondered along these branches all night. We were also introduced to tropical house cleaning. Brian, Paul and Suzanne's child, spilled some Coca-Cola on the floor. As Elinor started to clean it up, Paul told her to wait a few minutes. A swarm of ants appeared and cleaned it up to the last drop. A note in the bathroom asked anyone taking a bath to please put a stick into the tub before and after bathing to allow the lizard, who lived in the tub, to leave the tub and return. A few days were spent there and we enjoyed the surroundings, the beach, and swimming in the warm Indian Ocean. We then returned to Nairobi. When we got back, John's traveling group was ready to start their trip across Africa. We said good-bye to them as they drove off.

House in the trees, Mombasa, Kenya.

We stayed a few more days visiting the Nairobi Game Park. The park is in sight of Nairobi and has all the wild animals such as lions, rhinos, leopards, and is only a very few miles from the city. Paul has his pilot license and took me for a flight over the Great Rift Valley. As we flew, oil sprayed on the windshield of the rented airplane and Paul decided it would be wise to get this plane on the ground and headed immediately back to the airport for a landing. It was a short but interesting flight. A few days later, after a very enjoyable visit, we said goodbye to Paul, Suzanne and Brian, and left Nairobi for home.

MISSISSAUGA IS EVACUATED

On Saturday night, November 10, 1979, Elinor and I were playing bridge at the Welters' when we heard a boom. It was not thunder so we went out on the porch to see what it was. We saw a red glow in the sky to the northeast, and as we were looking, another explosion occurred. I had a Citizen Band radio in my car so I got in and turned on the CB. I found out that a train derailment had occurred and the contents of a train car carrying propane had exploded. The derailment was several miles from us, so we went back to our bridge game. The next morning on the radio and TV we were told that the explosion had damaged some tank cars. No one was hurt so we did not worry about it. We were invited for dinner at a friend's home in Scarborough, which is east of Toronto. In the afternoon we drove out, taking my 87-year-old mother with us. While having dinner, Debbie phoned and said, "Don't come home - Mississauga is being evacuated and there are police going around telling everyone to leave, and they are making sure you do." She said she was going to a friend's home in Oakville. Since there were three of us, the friends we were visiting did not have enough accommodation for us. We left their home at about 10:30 PM and went to a hotel, but they were booked up. They said that the people from Mississauga were taking up every room in Greater Toronto. I tried a motel and we got their last room. We had my mother with us and had to share the one room. My mother was shocked that she had to sleep in the same room as Elinor and I. The next morning we discovered that Mississauga was completely locked down. No trains were allowed to pass through. The Queen Elizabeth, the Lakeshore, and the Dundas highways were all closed. 250,000 people had been evacuated. I called a few hotels and was told to forget it - there was not a single free room in the Greater Toronto area. We still had my mother with us, and although Elinor and I could sleep on the floor somewhere, we certainly did not want my mother in her late eighties to have to do it. My sister Aileen lived in Richmond Hill, so we drove there. They looked after mother but had no room for us. We drove back to North Toronto and called on Paul, Elinor's brother. They did not have a bed, but Elinor slept on the couch and I slept on the floor. Their dog must have liked the way I tasted, because it spent all night licking my face. The next morning I phoned Debbie and asked, "What did John do?" She said he was not home when she left, so she did not know.

Mother did not have her medication. I called the police and asked if we could go to her apartment to retrieve it. They agreed, but I had to be escorted by the police, and was told where to meet the policeman. I did so and was given five minutes in her apartment to get the medication. I then drove up to Richmond Hill to deliver it. John had been at a Youth Corps meeting on Sunday and had stayed overnight with one of the other Youth Corps organizers. He phoned all of our relatives trying to find out where we had gone, but most lived in Mississauga and had been evacuated too, so they were not home. Eventually he phoned Paul's house and found us there and took a subway to join us. The dog now had two faces to lick and it seemed to prefer John's. Finally on Thursday we were allowed to go home. The reason for the evacuation was due to the rupture of a tank car of liquid chlorine. The city officials convened a committee of twenty or thirty people who claimed to be experts on the dangers of chlorine and the art of evacuations. Although a ruptured chlorine car in the midst of a fire would have had ALL of the chlorine vaporize in the first few minutes of the fire, the committee demanded 100% guarantees that there was no chlorine remaining after the fire burned out - which no one could do. So they asked "what is the worst that could happen" and decided that if the car was still full of chlorine then many people could die if a cloud of chlorine ran across the land. So the only safe thing to do was total evacuation. Safe, but not useful, and avoidable if they had consulted a chemist. Our son Paul (who was in Nairobi) heard about the disaster and phoned to see if we were safe.

In September of 1983 we celebrated our 40th wedding anniversary by holding a party at our house. All of our family attended along with many friends and neighbours. It was a beautiful day and we celebrated it on our patio deck and pool. To also celebrate, the next weekend we climbed up a high hill in Horseshoe Valley where we had a time share and carved our initials and the date on a tree on the hill top. We continued to climb that hill for the next ten anniversaries, including our 50th anniversary.

John E. Burgener

Our anniversary tree in Horseshoe Valley, Ontario.

Our children gave us a trip to Hawaii as an anniversary gift. After the party we went to Hawaii for three weeks. During the first week we stayed in the Royal Hawaiian at Waikiki. It was a very nice hotel with good meals, entertainment, and a private beach. We spent that week enjoying the sights on Oahu. The next week we spent on Kauai, were we stayed in a beautiful hotel called the Royal Palms. While we were there we took a helicopter ride around the island. During the third week we visited Maui and drove up the crater. It was a great holiday.

Debbie married her high school sweetheart, Jeff Heximer, while we lived in the Tecumseh Road house. She planned to be married in St. Christopher's where she had always gone to church. However, the parish priest said that since she was now living in the city, she would have to have the permission of her local pastor for her to be married in St. Christopher's, even though she still attended mass in St Christopher's. When she went to do this, she discovered that the local priest, Father Fullerton, was a classmate of mine, and he wanted her to be married by him. Debbie agreed and the wedding was at St. Vincent De Paul, performed by Father Fullerton on September 28, 1985. The reception was at The Sutton Place Hotel, which was owned by the company Jeff worked for. They gave us a very reasonable price for the top floor ballroom and they upgraded the meal. It was a beautiful wedding.

Deborah and Geoffrey's Wedding.

John was the last to get married. He met Paula Foley through a recommendation from a friend of Jocelyn's (Peter's wife). The wedding was at St Christopher's with Paula's brother, Father Fred Foley, assisting. John and Paula's wedding reception was held in the Tecumseh house. They had a barbecue of T-bone steaks for the dinner and only two talks. The rest of the evening was music, dancing, and chatting. A large tent was set up in the backyard, and with the house it worked out very well. Our grandchildren were at the reception, and one grandson, who was about six years old, had picked up a glass of beer and was walking around like the adults, holding the glass in his hand, no doubt feeling very big. He was not drinking it. One of the guests came to me and said, "There is a child drinking beer - you must stop him!" I replied, "Yes, I know he is carrying a glass of beer, but he is not drinking it - he is just wanting to feel big." She then said, "Are you not going to stop him?" I replied, "I see no reason to." At that point she declared that she would not stay in a house that allowed children to drink alcohol. I suggested in that case she should leave.

John and Paula's Wedding.

Chapter 19

NEW TECHNIQUES, MOBILE LABS, GROWING THE BUSINESS

TSL developed many new approaches to analytical procedures. TSL was involved in activities as diverse as solving problems in evaluating the durability of the paint used in road markings, working out how to have plastic coatings stick to car bumpers, improving the safety of imported bottled drinking water, and in general developing better methods of analyzing materials.

TSL's offices at 1301 Fewster Dr.

ICP DEVELOPMENT

Probably the most successful innovation in geochemical analysis we developed was our whole rock geochemical analysis mentioned above using an inductively coupled argon plasma spectrometer (ICP). This technique did an analysis that added up to 100%. Major constituents along with the minors were determined with accuracy better than the slow labour intensive wet chemical methods. The chemical methods would require many man-days of effort, while the ICP required a few minutes. When we introduced this procedure we received samples from around the world. One of our big customers was the Geological Department of Japan. Other labs later copied our techniques. I believe ours, with an RSD of 0.5% at 98% confidence level, was the best rock analysis possible up until the time I retired.

BRANCH LABORATORIES

TSL had several branch laboratories. The first was in Vancouver. We bought the mining division of Superintendents, a Swiss company that was heavily involved in cargo inspection. We upgraded it and transferred John Van England from Toronto. He later set up a lab in Spokane Washington named TSL Laboratories, as a branch of Vancouver. We also had branches in Saskatoon, Manitoba, and Kirkland Lake, Ontario, also called TSL Laboratories. The Saskatoon and Kirkland Lake Laboratories are still operating. The other two are no longer operating.

One day a young man walked into the lab and said that he was interested in setting up a lab in Central America. He wanted to know what we could do for him. He was a chemist from England who had come to Canada because he was fed up with the control the unions had on English industry. He had a job at International Nickel and found the same union problems there. He subsequently went to Central America and settled in Honduras, working for a government lab, but he wanted to set up an independent mining lab. He hoped to have a spectrograph but did not have the money to buy a new set-up and he wondered if we could get him a used one. Two months before, an Ontario Department of Health Lab was closed down. Some years before, TSL sold that lab a complete spectrographic lab. Now the lab equipment was up for sale by a disposal department. We offered $3000 and they accepted it, so we did actually have a used set-up available. The chemist and I came to an agreement that for $20,000 we would supply a complete spectrographic lab set up in Honduras with me facilitating ten days of training there. He would pay shipping and handle customs and any legal problems. We were to ship the equipment and he would advise us when ready for installation and training. He would pay $10,000 up front and the rest when I left for Honduras. It was a good deal for both of us.

About six months later I got the call and flew to Honduras with standard materials, charts, and books. Raymond met me at Tegucigalpa Airport and drove me to his lab a few miles out of the city. He had constructed a nice building and had a good chemical set-up and a very well organized geochemical lab. He had two technicians and wanted me to train him and them. The first three days were spent setting up the equipment. The next seven working days were an intensive course on spectrographic analysis for mineral exploration. Both Raymond and his technicians were good students. I stayed at his home, which was a nice tropical-style house. He had married a charming Honduran girl and he took me to meet her parents. They were peasants but they had a house in a village (perhaps with his help) in an area set up by the government. It was a three roomed cement block building with running water on a ¼ acre plot of land where they could grow food and raise chickens or a pig. I thought it was a very good solution to rural poverty.

One night as we sat on Raymond's porch we could hear an odd noise. He suddenly jumped up, ran off the porch, and found that ants were emptying a bag of corn he had bought to feed his ducks. There was a stream of ants each carrying a kernel of corn across his property, across the road, and into a field. There was another steam coming back. By the time we discovered it, half his corn was gone.

On Sunday he took me to Mass at the cathedral in Tegucigalpa. The cathedral was filled with many people standing outside. He drove me around to see the surrounding country. It was hilly with some mountain areas. There was a lot of jungle, but other areas with meadows had century plants. Some areas were cultivated. The United Nations was building a super highway from Tegucigalpa to the airport. As he pointed out, they hardly needed a highway (never mind a superhighway) as there were few cars in Honduras and very few planes landed. It was of minimum benefit to Honduras. Those benefiting were the UN officials who were living like lords. It was a waste of money when so many other things were needed. It was an interesting two weeks. As I left, his wife gave me a large carved wooden key as a key to the Honduran people's heart.

MOBILE LABS

TSL set up a lab for a Canadian mining company in the Sultanate of Oman. I sent one of our chemists, Walter Grondin, to set it up and train the operators. The air route was through Jordan. It happened that the day he landed one of their frequent revolutions occurred. All night there was machine gun fire outside the hotel. He slept on the floor against a brick wall as protection against flying bullets. By daylight the machine gunning stopped. When he asked at the desk, they said that was usual - the gunners do not want to be seen so they do their shooting at night. He got safely to Oman. There he was warned not to drink alcohol or talk to any women. On the flight back a person tried to light a fire in the aisle to cook his food.

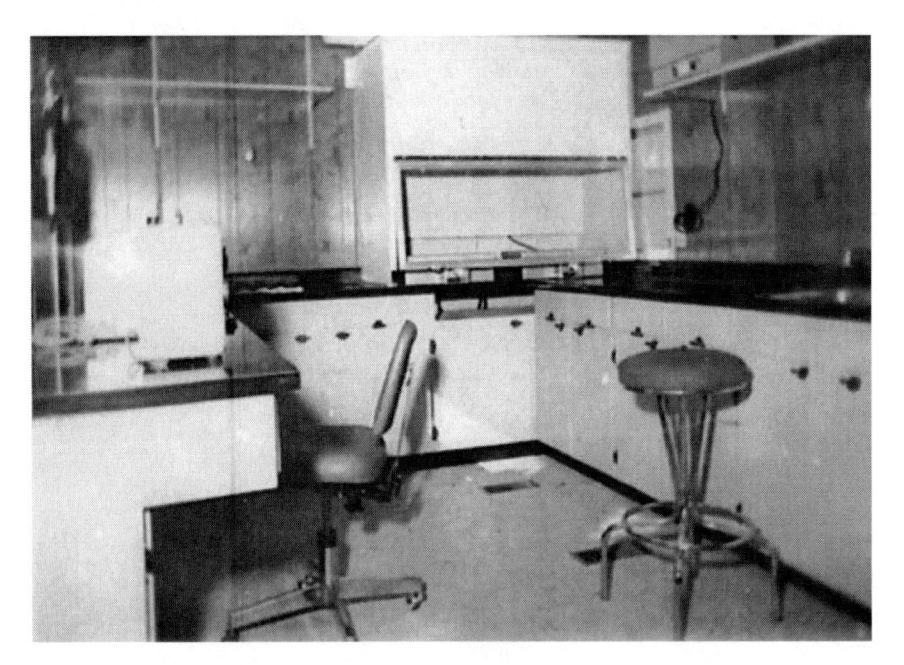

Interior of an onsite lab.

My son John was involved with several of these labs. In 1980 we set up a lab in Uranium City, in northern Saskatchewan. He drove the company's 1967 Chevy van and trailer lab combination up to Uranium City on a winter ice road across Lake Athabasca. He had been delayed starting while trying to assemble the equipment for the trailer lab, so he arrived at the start of the ice road the last day it was open. The ice road was over 300 miles long, using river beds as roads, and some ploughed sections through the scrub forest. It was a cold trip, with the temperature hovering at around minus 50° F. The old trailer could not handle the cold and rough roads and one of the wheel's springs broke. While pondering what to do, the last convoy of freight trucks passed heading south. There would be no more vehicles in either direction traveling on the road until the next year. That a convoy was passing by this late was a miracle. One truck was a flatbed transport and the driver generously offered to turn around and carry the trailer on to Uranium City, but he needed his fuel covered. John offered all of his cash on hand - $500 - and the driver accepted. He took the trailer the remainder of the way. If John had not been able to have the trailer carried by the flatbed truck, the trailer would have sunk into the river bed in the next week or two's thaw and would have never been seen again. When they arrived at Uranium City the old Chevy Van was on its last liter of gas. If the trailer's spring had not broken and the flatbed not carried it the rest of the way, John would have run out of gas long before he reached Uranium City. There were no gas stations along the way – he would have had to walk the last 100 or so miles at 50 below and left both the van and trailer behind to sink in the lake or rivers.

Trailer Truck Mobile Lab.

John also set up and operated our Yellowknife Lab. The mobile lab in Idaho, set up by our Spokane branch, got into trouble and was bailed out by John.

He set up and operated the complete lab in Nairobi for two years. He was not anxious to go, but once he was there he enjoyed it.

Over the years we offered many contract and mobile on-site assay laboratories. These included Ungava Bay in the Arctic, Uranium City in northwestern Saskatchewan, Yellowknife in the Northwest Territories, Bancroft and Gowganda in Ontario, Whitehorse in the Yukon, Cold Lake in Manitoba, James Bay and Gaspé in Quebec, and Moncton in New Brunswick. We also set up labs in the mountains of Idaho, as well as in Honduras, Kenya, and the Sultanate of Oman.

TSL AND COMPUTERS

Over the years as computers developed, TSL applied them to laboratory operations. In the early seventies we bought our first computer: a Wang. It had 5 kilobits of memory, no disc memory, and no software. You had to write your own software in machine language and for printout you used a teletype. I wrote the software for our payroll and some laboratory calculations, and used it for several years. The next computer was a Digital PDP-8, which was part of the ICP spectrometer. It also used a teletype to communicate. The software was in punched tape and had to be read by teletype into the computer at 110 baud (110 bits per second). To start the tape reading we needed to hand toggle in the start routine. Modern computers run at mega or gigabits per second. A gigabit is 1 billion bits per second, so the speed of modern computers is vastly greater than what the spectrometer had. It generally took four to six hours to turn on the PDP-8 and load in the programs. In 1978 or 1979 John convinced me to get a better computer that was easier to program to replace the PDP-8. We bought a used Digital PDP-11 for about $25,000. The PDP-11 had to be housed in a separate room and kept at a constant temperature. It had 80 megabytes of disc memory, but the discs were in a round case about ten inches thick and twenty inches diameter. The memory disc was mounted in a cabinet 3.5 feet high by 2.5 feet square. The computer was in a six foot high cabinet. Separate monitors were connected to the computer. This was a big computer with a total of 128 kilobytes of memory. The memory was hand-wired magnetic cores, with thousands of individual wires in each memory board. The maintenance on the computer cost us $1,500 a month. The PDP-11 ran 100 times faster than the PDP-8. It was still slow compared to today's computers, but a lot faster than the PDP-8. John tied the PDP-8 to the PDP-11 and wrote the software necessary to have the spectrometer send its results to the PDP-11. Then the PDP-11 was used to process the data and report the results. With it we could run and report 500 whole rock samples each day. Our competition took about one hour per sample, so a good chemist would be able to only do about eight a day. With mining exploration needing the data only available with whole rock analysis, we had a huge advantage over our competition and we rapidly became the most significant lab in the world for whole rock analysis.

The next computers in the early eighties were the Commodore Pets, which included a keyboard and monitor and disc storage. The Basic language was developed and writing software was easier. I wrote software in Basic for our payroll on the Pets, and all of our front office reports and invoices were done with the Pets for many years before we switched to PCs. At TSL we wrote all our own software.

Then the personal computers came into use with memories and overall capabilities equal to the PDP-11. For the cost of maintenance we could buy a new PC every month, so we switched to PCs. Every section of the lab could have its own PC and they could be networked. The large computer became useless. We tried to sell it and ended up selling it for the gold contacts in the hardware. As we slowly added more PCs to the lab, our main chemist came to John and threatened to quit if he put a PC on his desk. He did not want these new things interfering with his work. About two years later he came back to John and threatened to quit if he did not get a PC on his desk. It was unfair that everyone else had one and he didn't.

***

ENVIRONMENTAL ISSUES

TSL became involved in a number of environmental issues and I was amazed at how little the media were interested in the truth. The fish in the Don River were dying. It was determined that they were dying from lack of oxygen in the water, obviously caused by pollution. There were some factories on the river and the media and environmentalists were condemning them. TSL had contracts to check the effluent from these factories and knew they were not the cause. I sent one of my staff to rent a boat and paddle up the river to find the cause. He found it. The farmers on the river were dumping their surplus produce into the river. As the vegetables decomposed they used up the oxygen. On advising the media of this, it was not reported. They still quoted the environmentalists, who were blaming the factories. Neither had investigated the facts, but they all claimed authority.

On another occasion we had been asked to check the leaking of contaminates from the Love Canal into the Niagara River. A TV station heard about it and asked if we would be willing to be interviewed on TV. We agreed. The interviewer finally asked for our opinion of the contamination. As soon as it became apparent that we were saying we found no problem, they announced a transmission difficulty and stopped the interview. Obviously the objective was not to report the facts but to promote an agenda. The financial editor of the Toronto newspaper, The Globe, asked to interview me. I agreed and the interview took place. He asked me several times how much had we done for International Nickel and I replied that we had done nothing. When his article was published, the headline stated that TSL, a Toronto lab, was carrying on a major environmental research program for International Nickel. I phoned him and he said he knew that we had not done any work for International Nickel, but it made good reading. That is not news - it is fiction. I received a letter from the company condemning me for my dishonesty. I was surprised that the company believed the newspapers.

FAILURE ANALYSIS STORIES

Some of the investigations our industrial failures group carried out were almost amusing. One example was the truck manufacturer who was having production shifts where 100% of the truck bodies had wrinkled paint. It would occur for a day and at other times for several days, but then it would revert back to normal for several weeks. Paint suppliers were stymied. The plant engineers could find no cause. TSL was called. I sent Peter Mladenovich (who was my best trouble-shooter) to spend a day or two in the plant. We suspected that the problem was in the drying process. It was winter and the factory was not overheated. Peter hung around watching for something that could affect the drying. As the midnight shift came on, Peter saw one of the personnel walk over to the access door into the drying tunnel and open the door. When asked why, he was told that the working area was very drafty and was often too cold. When this door was opened, it warmed the area up. The employee was quite proud of his discovery. Thus Peter had discovered the cause of wrinkling: the open door had lowered the temperature in the drying tunnel and created a wind that wrinkled the paint. That employee worked on rotating shifts. When the work area was cold and he was on the shift, the paint would be wrinkled. At the end of his shift the door was sometimes closed, and other times left open. So there had been no discernible pattern to the wrinkling.

Another similar case was in regards to a manufacturer of electric stove heating elements. They were having 100% failure on power testing. No one could find the cause. On studying the failed heating elements it was apparent that some carbon was present. Nothing used in the manufacture contained carbon. Again, Peter spent time on the premises watching. A silicon plug was inserted in the final step of assembly. Peter noticed that the operator who inserted the plug was applying something to the plug before inserting. He asked the operator why he put this material on the plug. He was told that greasing the plug allowed it to go in much easier. The operator was pleased with his innovation. The grease was carbonizing on heating and it shorted the element. In many cases we worked on, the root of the problem was an employee improving a procedure without understanding the effects.

On another occasion I got a call from the Royal Canadian Mounted Police lab in Ottawa. Their equipment was not working and they needed data for a trial that was in process. They had dispatched an airplane to pick me up and bring me to Ottawa to service the equipment. The plane would be at the Toronto Island airport in thirty minutes. I asked if they had checked the fuses. They replied yes. If nothing worked it had to be a power problem. I suggested that they check the main fuse. They came back and said yes, someone had thrown the main circuit breakers and the equipment was now working. In almost all cases of such failures it is expected to be technical and more difficult than it actually is. So often the simple cause is overlooked.

TSL often got calls from offices where it was claimed that their personnel were getting headaches or feeling sick. We would send in a team with hard hats, chromatographs, and other atmosphere testing equipment mounted on carts. Sometimes we did find air problems such as exhaust gas and other pollutants. In most cases we found no problem. However, the problem usually disappeared after our tests were completed. In one case we did find natural gas contamination in low amounts and traced the contamination to the subbasements. This was a new building and natural gas had not been detected, but it must have excavated close to a deposit. The building management was warned and the basements were ventilated while having regular checks. After a couple of years the gas stopped leaking into the building.

There were a few cases where the problem persisted after our survey had found nothing. We suggested putting plants around the office and this eliminated the headaches in every case. Plants not only make an environment more pleasant, they are good pollutant absorbers.

INSURANCE CASES

TSL had a number of interesting insurance cases. A cargo ship had a violent explosion in a hold while in the middle of the Atlantic. Fortunately the ship made it to Halifax. The ship owners blamed the shipper. The shipper retained us to find the cause. The shipment was scrap aluminum produced in machining operations. We found that the aluminum cargo in another hold was wet but not with seawater. This hold had a vent, whereas the hold that exploded was sealed. Aluminum that does not have a microscopic coating of oxide will react with water to form aluminum oxide, setting hydrogen free. The aluminum cuttings would have oxide-free surfaces. We also found that it was raining when being loaded. The wet aluminum in a sealed hold released enough hydrogen to cause an explosion. The ship should have ventilated the wet aluminum.

We were involved in several fire insurance cases. One was a fire in a store in a mall. The fire marshal accused the owners of setting the fire. There appeared to be no cause for the fire, and thus it must have been set. The owners ask TSL to investigate. The fire had started in a room filled with cardboard boxes piled almost up to the ceiling. Although the room had a ceiling mounted gas furnace there was no apparent reason for a fire to start. Of course it would be easy to start a fire in such a room with a small pile of newspapers, without leaving any trace of them. The fire damage to the walls decreased from the ceiling to the floor. Obviously the fire had started at the top and burned down. If it had started at floor level, the fire damage to the walls should have been the same at all levels. We speculated that a spark must have come from the furnace and started the fire on the top. The fire marshal agreed that it did not make sense that the owners would have climbed up to the top to set the fire, as one would not expect the fire to leave such evidence.

TSL also did stack effluent sampling. One of our personnel climbed up the stack and took a sample of the gasses or dust coming from the chimney. The person who did this could not be afraid of heights. On one occasion a new man, who claimed that heights did not bother him, got half way up a stack and froze. He would not move up or down, he just hung on. Most stacks have loops that prevent one from falling. Our foreman climbed up to try to help him down but he would not move. Finally we had to get firemen who had to put a ladder up. It took three firemen, one below him one above him, who had to climb from their ladder through the loops and onto the chimney ladder to break him loose. With a harness they let him down.

Chapter 20

THE LATER YEARS

As the business became more established I took more time off to enjoy life. Elinor and I both enjoyed the mountains and the Rockies, and every year for several years we drove to Calgary to visit Peter and family. We often attended the Calgary Stampede as VIPs since Peter was involved with the Stampede. On several occasions we also drove to Spokane to visit the lab there. These were long drives, but we always treated them as part of a holiday, enjoying what the route had to offer.

At the rail, at the Chuck Wagon Race.

A Broader Vision

The five bedrooms in our Tecumseh house were often filled with visiting family. Jocelyn would bring her children and spend a few weeks every summer. We welcomed their visits. It was great having the grandchildren with us. It also allowed the grandchildren to meet and know their cousins. Paul and Suzanne lived in Milton for ten years and then in Mississauga and often visited us.

Jocelyn and family on a summer visit at Tecumseh.

In the spring or the fall we often spent a week or so in Myrtle Beach. It was half the way to Florida, and while the climate was not as warm, it was warm enough. It is not as crowded in the spring and fall as Florida and there are a number of theatres with interesting shows. There is also a huge outlet mall, which the women love. There are also many great seafood restaurants and a number of other attractions; it is a great place for a break. In 1989 we went down in the fall, right after a hurricane. The devastation was unbelievable. The houses at Pawleys Island were washed away. Boats were inland as much as ¼ mile. All the trees for miles inland had their tops blown off. It was reported that a school was used as refuge in the storm and a tidal wave had washed over it. People inside saw the water rise up the windows and cover the building and then settle down. It must have been very frightening. The hotels along the beach had their first floors washed out. The hotel we usually stayed in was closed as the first floor including the lobby and the dining room were completely washed out. The famous beach at Myrtle Beach was washed away and by the time we got there they were rebuilding the beach with continuous lines of dump trucks bringing sand, along with huge earth movers that were spreading it. The next year when we retuned the beach was restored.

We often went to Hilton Head. It has a warmer climate and is a very pretty island. We stayed at the Hilton Hotel Timeshare, which is a very nice place, and of course we always visited Harbour Town, with the many yachts in its circular bay. There are also some good restaurants there. On one occasion, as we went in to a restaurant for lunch, a large power yacht was fuelling up and after lunch it was still fuelling. I went over and looked at the fuel meter and saw that it was at $3,800.

The divorced wife of Carlton Joyce (the former employee who ended up with Wear Check) lived on Hilton Head and we visited her in her multi-million dollar home on the water. She had a private dock that her son used when visiting in his big sailboat. I guess Carlton did all right with Wear Check.

ANOTHER FAMILY TRIP TO EUROPE

In 1987 Peter decided to take his family to Europe and invited us to accompany them. He bought a Volkswagen minibus and we met them in Paris. We drove through France visiting many castles and unique towns. We stayed for three days at a castle built in the eleventh century. The proprietor only spoke French, although some of the staff spoke English. This was good for Peter's children since they had all been schooled in French Immersion. It was operated as it had been in the eleventh century.

All guests ate all meals together in the huge dining hall. After dinner everyone went to the lounge and chatted while sipping liqueurs. It was a different experience. Fresh bread was baked every day, taken out of the ovens, and placed in a heap on the kitchen floor. The castle's big dog would climb up and lay on the pile of fresh warm bread, and no one objected. I guess that was the way it was in the eleventh century.

At Avignon we danced on the bridge as the song "Dansant sur la pont d'Avignon" while others watching probably thought we were nuts. While eating lunch at a sidewalk cafe in Avignon we were startled by a crow falling from the sky, which landed dead on our table. We visited the Dordogne Caves and saw the prehistoric paintings. While looking at them it occurred to me that they were the kind of drawings a modern child would make. Of course, the drawings may have meant to be instructions to others rather than art. The Dordogne Caves are now closed to the public.

Castle built in 1100, where we stayed during Peter's family trip to Europe.

We continued south to the Mediterranean. Peter had to fly home for business and left his family at a resort on the Mediterranean until he returned to continue the trip. We left Peter's family at this point and rented a car. We drove on the eastern side of France to Mount Blanc, where we spent a couple of days in a nice hotel overlooking the big snow-covered mountain. Then we continued on to Grindelwald in Switzerland, where we spent a few days. We made another trip up the Jungfrau, then went to Paris, and then flew home. We enjoyed the enthusiasm of the grandchildren as we traveled with them, and their enthusiasm in the new things they were seeing and doing. It was a great family trip.

SOME MEDICAL COMPLICATIONS

On a visit to a timeshare in South Carolina I fell down a set of stairs that had a door at the bottom. I ended up all tangled up against the door. When the door was opened I fell out on the floor. I twisted both knees so badly I could not stand up. The ambulance took me to the hospital where they said nothing could be done and I would probably not walk for some months. They loaned Elinor a wheelchair and said, "Take him home." Fortunately we were traveling with Bob and Madeleine Welter so they got me back to the timeshare. There was no way I could drive back home. Bob and Madeleine had their own car so they could not drive us home and Elinor did not want to drive so far. We phoned John and he flew down and drove us home. I only left the car once on the way and that was to sleep in a motel. Fortunately the hospital had loaned us a wheelchair, but it was a struggle to get me in and out of the car. After a few weeks I was able to use crutches, but I was on them for several months. We shipped the wheelchair back to the hospital. My knees have given me trouble ever since.

Since Elinor was a young woman she had been troubled with a peculiar sort of fainting. She would suddenly lose her balance for a second and then she would quickly recover. It was getting worse, however. She went to our doctor, who sent her to a specialist, who sent her to another specialist, and so on. This went on for four years and got us nowhere. We were in Florida for a holiday and she had a particularly bad episode, lasting several seconds - enough to make her fall. I decide that I was fed up with chasing doctors and phoned the Cleveland Clinic and asked to stop in on our way home. We got an appointment in three days instead of three months, as it would have been in Canada. When we got there they had reserved a room for us at the hotel and said for Elinor to come back the next day at 8:00 AM. In two days Elinor saw more specialists than she had seen in four years in Canada. The second evening they had a conference with us and explained there was no cure for her ailment; it was not life-threatening, and it would get worse in old age. They gave her some exercises that would help, again emphasizing that it was not a cure. In two days we knew were we stood and at total cost of $1,500. We probably spent more than that in traveling expenses in Canada, not to mention the four years of futile pursuit for answers. Canada's poor medical care is to be expected. For everyone to get the same treatment, you must push everything to the lowest common denominator. Canada's medical system discourages the exceptional and rewards the mediocre.

Chapter 21

RETIREMENT

When John finished the across Africa and Asia trip, he began to work with me full time. A few years later Paul returned from Kenya and also began to work with me at TSL. With both John and Paul helping develop the company, TSL expanded its services into environmental testing, general industrial testing (including accelerated weathering), metallurgical testing and industrial failure analysis. As we expanded, we remained at the state of the art. We were the first laboratory to install an HP computer-controlled chromatograph. We had computer-controlled physical testing equipment. We were the only Canadian laboratory that had the Standards Council of Canada approval on 2000 procedures. No other lab in Canada had more than 500 procedures approved, even today as I write this. TSL was also a Department of National Defense approved laboratory and a General Motors approved laboratory. TSL was without peer and was the most versatile commercial laboratory in Canada. TSL always kept up with the state of the art equipment, such as our computer-controlled chromatograph, which could detect a part per trillion of pesticides. A part per trillium is 1 gram in 1 million kilograms.

I retired in 1988 and sold the business to Paul, John, and two long-term senior employees, Walter Grondin and Dan Biliski, who expanded the business. They added nuclear testing and expanded industrial testing. A few years later, a group of accountants, who were assembling a national laboratory business, approached TSL with their plan and offered to buy the company and merge it with others to become the largest lab in Canada.

TSL was sold to them in 1990. The new owners did not listen to the technical staff, resulting in some unwise expansions. They had previously bought a laboratory in Northern Ontario. It was one that I had turned down several years before when offered the chance to buy it. Its facilities were junk, and even if it changed ownership, its building would be condemned because of lead contamination. The accountants paid several million dollars for it assuming that it was in excellent condition. When they bought TSL, the TSL staff pointed out the problems. Instead of closing the junk lab, they used TSL personnel and money to try to fix the mess, and at a cost to TSL, not to the other lab. They had also acquired a lab in Vancouver, but it too was poorly run and was losing money. Again, they tried to use TSL resources to fix that lab. John and Paul objected to staff, equipment, and supplies being charged to TSL and used in the other labs, and they tried to get the other labs to allow them to run the companies properly. They were fired for trying. Soon TSL's profits disappeared and the company went into bankruptcy two years after they took it over. The shortage of cash meant that they never paid Paul and John the remaining 75% of the purchase price, which was due two years after the initial down payment. The various subsections were sold to their managers or to other labs, but TSL itself died. What was probably Canada's most advanced laboratory closed. The spin-off companies are still in operation, with Activation Laboratories now larger than TSL was, and Wear Check still a successful international business.

John presently runs a company, Burgener Research Inc., that makes nebulizers for ICP spectrometers. His company is a spin-off from the nebulizers developed by him and Guy Legere to do the Whole Rock analysis. He vastly improved the original design and obtained four patents on new atomizing techniques. He now sells about 2,500 nebulizers a year and calculates that more labs use his nebulizers than any other.

I believe that the struggles that Elinor and I endured when we started were worthwhile. After the first two years we made a reasonably good living. We had a greater freedom than would have been possible working for any company. With this freedom we were able to do things with our children that would not have been possible otherwise. Also, I was always able to do what I thought was ethical and was not forced to follow dictates from some boss. I provided a living for more than 100 employees, some of whom spent most of their working lives at TSL. Several of our employees arranged their working hours to suit their school children's hours. They worked from 9:30 AM to 3:00 PM.

A Broader Vision

One chemist chose to work from 5:00 AM to 1:00 PM. I was happy to treat employees as human beings. It also provided a place of training for quite a few skilled and motivated people who later moved on to good positions in other businesses. In addition to my immediate employees, the derivatives of TSL are providing employment to several thousand in jobs that would not exist but for TSL. TSL introduced spectrochemistry to Canada and sold and installed 80% of the installations in Canada until Jaco merged with Fisher and our dealership was canceled. In recent years the spectrographs have been replaced with spectrometers. The difference between them is that a spectrograph used photographic film to record the results and the newer systems use electronic devices, similar to digital cameras, to record the results. Overall, in over forty years of running the lab, we did millions of analysis on every type of sample. I expect that almost every person alive today has been influenced by my work and the development of spectrometric analysis. Almost everything we eat, drink, wear, or use today is analyzed at some point before it is sold. Most of those analyses are spectrometric.

***

When I retired we sold our house and bought a condominium being built in Clarkson. Although it had an indoor and outdoor pool, it was not the same as our own back yard, so a cottage seemed worth considering. Not finding one that suited us, we decided to buy a lot and build our own. After all, having built one house and modified two others, why not build another? We found a reasonably priced lot at Sunset Bay on Georgian Bay. It was near Penetanguishene and was a two hour drive from the condo. The waterfront lots were four times the price, and as the shore is rocky there was no great advantage to a waterfront lot, so we bought across the road from the water. We arranged with the developer to build a 1500 square foot, two bedroom cottage.

Peter, being an architect, pointed out that to make a two story cottage would not cost that much more and would allow more room for friends and family. He submitted a design that made it a very comfortable and attractive cottage. Our plan was to have the builder finish the outside. I would get my exercise by finishing the inside, with help from family and friends. Of course we had the usual problems with the builders. When I showed the contractor the plans, he said, "This has been designed by an architect, and what the hell does an architect know about cottages?" He stated that it was impossible to build it the way Peter had designed it. When I told Peter, he said it was designed as a post and beam structure with a roof that allowed sky lights. Obviously the local builders were not very knowledgeable. So he redesigned the roof but left the post and beam structure intact. The builder built the walls as supports. He did not understand a post and beam structure. To support the pillars, the plans called for concrete pads 24 x 24 and 3 inches thick; the builders poured pads 12 x 12 and 2 inches thick. They also put in two layers of concrete blocks less than specified and started to build the structure.

Our cottage on Georgian Bay.

Fortunately we discovered the discrepancies. At the same time, the building inspector condemned the building. He insisted that it had to be torn down, saying that the small support pads would break under the load and that the building would collapse. I hoped to use the cottage in my lifetime and it looked like we were in for a long haul of legal battles and delay. I went to see the inspector to see what could be done. He said that the two layers of cement blocks could be put in without a problem by jacking up the structure. The pads were a different problem since the structure was already being supported by the pads. In the meantime, the builder poured the basement floor and decided to pour an eight-inch thick floor instead of a four-inch floor. When I found out he had gone ahead and poured the floor, I was really annoyed. However, he

A Broader Vision

pointed out that an eight inch floor was stronger than pads, and if he put thicker pillars around the originals, supported on the floor, we would have better support than called for. I called the inspector and he agreed, but he wanted to run some tests on the strength of the concrete; these tests passed. The missing two layers of blocks were installed. The builder said he fired the foreman who had made all the errors. The other problem was to get the builder to finish the job. It was quoted for completion in July. At the end of September the house was still missing windows and a deck. I finally advised the builder that I was hiring another builder to complete the job and that I would not pay him the remaining $25,000. He could sue me and I would use every trick possible to delay, and drag it out for years, and I would probably win. The next day he showed up and stayed and finished the job.

When we sold our house, we set the closing date for July. The condo was supposed to be finished in June and the cottage was meant to be completed in July. However, neither place was available to be lived in. Having anticipated this, we planned a holiday. When we returned at the end of August, we had no place to live. We were homeless people of no fixed address. Fortunately my daughter had room for us. A month later her husband was transferred to Edmonton, so they had to move. Again we were homeless, since the condo was still not finished. In fact it was not finished until December. We covered the missing windows in the cottage with plastic and I had arranged to get the plumbing done so that water and a toilet were installed. We therefore decided to camp out in the cottage. The first few nights we slept in sleeping bags on the floor until the excess furniture in storage was delivered (bearing in mind that we'd moved from a five bedroom house to a two bedroom condo). By December when we moved into our condo, the cottage had electricity, plumbing, two bedrooms dry walled, temporary kitchen cupboards, a refrigerator, a kitchen stove and a wood stove. By the summer of 1990 the cottage was quite livable, with some trim yet to be finished. With four bedrooms, a large living/dining room with couches, and an equally large recreation room with couches, we had room for many visitors at a time. Since the cottage was beside Awenda Provincial Park, we had all the advantages of the park, including four excellent swimming beaches.

John E. Burgener

Our boat.

To further enhance the cottage we bought a 21-foot Bowrider powerboat that had a maximum capacity of nine adults. This boat allowed the grandchildren to water ski and we made many excursions to Giant's Tomb Island, where there were excellent beaches for swimming. We often just cruised around the picturesque 30,000 islands in Georgian Bay. On Labour Day Penetang held a poker run for speed boats in the Penetang Bay, bringing thirty or more big boats that were 500 horsepower or better. Some of these boats were reaching top speeds of 100 miles per hour. We often went out in our boat to watch the races. It was thrilling to have a stream of boats screaming by at those speeds. There was always a helicopter flying along with them, probably in case of trouble. On one occasion we were anchored with several other boats at the entrance to the bay and racers were screaming around us. One boat decided to go through the anchored boats to shorten his path. It appeared to be headed for my boat. I thought we were about to die, but he missed us and screamed past my boat less ten feet away. At these high speeds the boats are barely touching the water and there is practically no wake.

We enjoyed the cottage and boat for more than sixteen years, and enjoyed many family gatherings, as well as visits by friends and relatives. Besides working on our cottage, much traveling was done. We drove out to Calgary and the Rockies and back several times during those sixteen years. I was a hard driver and could cover the 2200 miles from our condo to Peter's house in three days. On one of these trips we camped along the forest fire control road on the east side of the Rockies. It truly is wild; the road is a fire control route and not a tourist route. One evening as we were about to set up our tent, I noticed a puma standing on a rise looking at us and wagging its tail - no doubt appraising us for its supper. We decided to move on to another location some miles away.

Our 50th wedding anniversary.

In September 1993 we celebrated our 50th wedding anniversary at Paul and Suzanne's house. It was a great party with all of our family present, along with many friends. We also celebrated by taking a cruise in the Mediterranean. We had reserved for a table for eight, but somehow our reservation got lost and we ended up at a table for four. The other couple was unfriendly and they asked to have another table. They moved us instead, since we did not have a reserved table. We ended up at a table for eight, but we were alone. However, a couple of younger women who were traveling together had reserved for the late sitting but there was no table available, so they moved them to the early sitting and put them at our table. We became friends and they really went out of their way to look after us. They were our constant companions on the whole cruise, even taking the same land excursions we took. This cruise was in the Mediterranean on a ship that was scheduled to be refurbished. One night we ran into a violent storm and the old ship creaked and groaned all through the night. If it was going to break up, I prayed it would not happen before daylight. It survived the storm. We docked at a Greek port, whose name I can't remember, but there was an ancient open-air theatre and one of the entertainers from the ship stood on the stage and sang her heart out. The acoustics were good and so was she.

Guests at our 50th wedding anniversary celebration, held at Paul's house.

TIMESHARE HOLIDAYS

We had four weeks of timeshare and made great use of the exchange options. The timeshares were two bedroom units, so we always had company. Our friends the Welters also had timeshare, so between us we had five weeks every year. We visited many places in Canada and the USA that we would never have visited without timeshare. On one of our autumn timeshare trips we stayed at Charleston in South Carolina and decided to go home along the Blue Ridge Parkway. It was a beautiful drive and for the first couple of nights we stayed in beautiful hotels. The third day we visited some sights in the area and started north in the late afternoon. The weather predictions were calling for snow in the mountains in a couple of days, so we decided to drive until 7:00 or 8:00 PM and then stop for the night to get further north before the snow arrived.

A Broader Vision

We did not run into snow - we ran into freezing rain. It was raining and freezing so hard that we were down to the speed of crawling. It was not possible to keep the windshield clear so I was hanging out my window with Bob hanging out the passenger window to make sure we stayed on the road. We were on top of the mountain, there were no side roads, and it was probably forty miles to the next motel. We continued crawling along for several hours, and by now it was dark. There were no other cars on the road. We finally came to a side road where a police car was parked. As we approached a policeman got out and signalled us to stop, which I had planned to do anyway. He said that four miles ahead there was a motel that was closed for the winter, but it had been opened because of the ice storm. He said there were quite a few cars like us crawling along and it was expected that drivers would have taken the side road, hoping to get out of the ice. However, the side road was worse because it was hilly, and cars would get stuck at the bottom of the hills, so that was why he was there.

We carried on for the four miles and were happy to drive into the motel parking lot. They assigned us a room and offered some canned food for dinner. After many hours of struggling we were glad of anything. All night we could hear branches falling off trees because of the weight of the ice. When parking I had chosen a spot away from the trees. I hoped my car would still be drivable in the morning. Fortunately my car was not hit, but other cars in the parking lot had damage. There were about thirty cars in the lot. At about 3:00 PM the police said the roads were safe to drive on and so they let us go. Fortunately we did not run into snow and we enjoyed the rest of the way home.

✱ ✱ ✱

In 1996 we traveled to Switzerland with my sister Jennie and her husband Jim. We supplied the time share and Jim supplied the rental car. Although Elinor and I had been to Switzerland several times, we always had a specific place that we wanted to see, or we otherwise had a compelling reason to go. This time we had two weeks and we were going to see all we could. We landed in Zurich and boarded a train for Andermatt. The Glacier Express travels from Zermatt to St. Moritz. Andermatt is half way. Andermatt is a pretty mountain village with typical Swiss houses in a valley completely surrounded by mountains. Swiss cows with their bells could be heard and seen grazing all throughout the area. You could also see the rows of snow fences protecting the village from avalanches. The snow on the mountain side usually averages more than seven feet deep. We spent the night in a pretty hotel and after a good breakfast we boarded the red and white Glacier Express. The coaches have large windows both on the side and in the roof so you can see the mountains. The coach seats are in a red fabric facing one another with a table between. They are very comfortable. There was also a running commentary broadcast in clearly understandable English and German. When we left Andermatt the train climbed up the side of a mountain passing a gondola lift on the way and then descended down the other side.

As we traveled along we were in rugged mountainous country, passing through valleys with quaint villages. These villages featured a steepled church nestled amongst a collection of houses. In other places we passed through wide plateaus with several such villages, all of them the very picture of peace and tranquility. I reflected that it was no wonder that the Swiss have been able to find refuge from the wars that surrounded them. Some of the mountains were covered with rugged rock; others are partially treed while others have snow covered peaks. I was struck by how wonderful it must be to live in such beauty. We also passed through some larger towns that were again surrounded by mountains. The towns were clean and neat and appear to be well ordered, although many of the buildings were hundreds of years old.

In one town we passed through there was a monastery that was built in 800 A.D. that was still in use; it was surrounded by houses that are were centuries old but the buildings looked as good as if they were built in the twentieth century. We saw some glaciers but it was August so there was not a lot of snow cover. We crossed the Rhine River, which was several hundred feet below us as we crossed from one mountain to another. In the late afternoon we arrived at St. Moritz, and there we disembarked. St. Moritz is a peaceful and picturesque mountain town.

We spent the night in a nice hotel. The next day we rented a car and started our own independent tour of Switzerland. We drove south into Italy, then back to Switzerland at Lugano, and then through the excessively long (and rather depressing) nineteen kilometer tunnel under the Gotthard Pass. It was evening as we drove through this tunnel, and as we had to pass through Andermatt we decided to spend another night there. The next morning there was a cattle auction and the square was filled with cows. One had to be careful where one stepped. We drove through the Valleys on our way to our timeshare at Leysin.

A Broader Vision

On the way we passed the Rhone Glacier. On the east side the Rhone River starts, and on the west side, the Rhine River starts. At Aigle, just before we reached Lake Geneva, we left the main road, passed an imposing castle, and proceeded up a mountain road through miles of vineyards, reaching Leysin about half way up the mountain. The timeshare was a very nice two bedroom apartment on the side of the mountain with a spectacular view into the valley and up the mountain. This was our headquarters for the next two weeks. Leysin was a village with all the essentials, including a co-op grocery store, locally called "the coop". Churches, a private finishing school, and school for training hotel managers were there. There was also a gondola lift up to the mountain top to a rotating restaurant. The mountaintop was also used by para-gliders for launch. During our stay we enjoyed a lunch at the rotating restaurant and watched the para-gliders jump off the mountain. They would land in Leysin and take the gondola back up.

Castle of Chillon, Switzerland.

Although Jim and Jennie had been to Switzerland on a bus tour, they had not seen very much. Our first excursion was to Montreux to visit the Castle of Chillon, which Jennie and Jim had not seen before. Byron's poem about the prisoner of Chillon made it famous. I saw the place where the prisoner was chained. It was cruel and I hope that this sort of treatment will never happen again. This is probably a futile hope because today in many places of the world human torture is still being practiced. We spent most of the day enjoying the castle. After leaving we drove into the mountains on the north side of the lake and revelled in some spectacular views.

The Matterhorn, Switzerland.

Our next excursion was to Zermatt to see the Matterhorn. We drove south to the Valleys, through them to Visp, and then south along a mountainside to Tash. A train took us the rest of the way, since only electric vehicles were allowed in Zermatt - standard automobiles were not permitted. We spent the day there. It was a charming village with many old houses that were probably hundreds of years old, and of course there were many new houses. It was a tourist town and had all the modern conveniences. It had a spectacular setting in the mountains with the Matterhorn, which is a unique peak standing by itself. There was a beautiful Catholic church built in the thirteenth century and other lovely buildings. We had our lunch in Burgener's Restaurant and visited Burgener's mountain and ski shoe shop. There was also a Burgener hotel. At Burgener's shoe store we compared notes: the shopkeeper had a great-great-uncle named Alexander Burgener. He was a famous mountaineer who died on the Matterhorn. My father had the same great-uncle.

After Zermatt we visited Grindelwald, where we had visited several times, and we were happy to introduce Jim and Jennie to such a unique and memorable experience. It was one of the few places in Switzerland where there is an easily accessible glacier. It has the cog rail up to Switzerland's highest mountain the Jungfrau, and the Eiger and Monk peaks. The glacier came down to the valley and one could walk along the gorge to its face. The mountaintop restaurant at First was worth the visit. It was a pleasant valley.

We spent the night in Grindelwald and the next day in the area around Grindelwald. In the next valley known as Louterbrunon a huge glacier came right down to the valley. One could walk inside the glacier and view a river flowing inside from the melting ice. This valley also had two plateaus on the side of the mountains, called verandas, that were big enough to accommodate communities. To go to these communities one had to use a gondola lift. We visited these communities, and then went to Interlacken, which was a pretty town between two lakes. Next we visited the beautiful Lake Thun and the village of Thun, near where my father was born. Another veranda called Beatonburg was visited next. This veranda is large enough to have roads to it and on it. It is half way up the mountains and extends for many miles. We had supper there and checked into a hotel for the night. At sunset we were above the clouds and could watch the so-called "click", which occurs when the setting sun turns the mountaintops into glowing crimson and gold peaks for a brief moment. It was beautiful to observe. In the morning we were above the clouds and could enjoy the gold and red tones of the rising sun on the mountains. I understood why people would choose to live on a veranda.

We passed through many other interesting and beautiful places, but it would take a whole book to adequately describe them all.

The next trip was to Bern, the capital of Switzerland. It was a big, ancient, and yet modern city, with broad boulevards and narrow winding streets. The older parts of the city were the most interesting. This is the location of the famous and historic clock tower, which has the brass figurine that struck the bell with a hammer to mark the hours. It also showed the phases of the moon. The streets in the older part had statues and figures in the middle and in many places the sidewalks were covered. Window flower boxes of red geraniums added to the beauty. On the winding streets, the reticulated street cars had four bends. The newer streets had electric buses supplied by overhead wires. The ancient bear pit, the cathedral, and the Aare River were all visited. Of course the government buildings, the theatres, and museums were all worth seeing. It was a great city to visit.

The last place we visited was the medieval village of Gruyère. It was a complete village surrounded with a wall. It had a square and a market area where volume measures of different sizes were carved in stone. There were ancient apartments/flats built around the square with the castle at the end; a wall surrounded the entire area. There were carved dates on some of the buildings going back to 1517. The ramparts around the town had roofs, as did the turrets in the ramparts. The castle was beautifully furnished with intricately carved furniture. The walls of some of the rooms in castle were painted in panels like wall paper, while others had beautiful scenes or birds. The fireplaces were huge - 6 feet high and 10 feet wide - and in many cases the wall that held the fireplace was decorated with scenes of celebrations or of knights battling. Behind the fireplaces on the back wall of the fireplace there was a large tank filled with water that heated up, retaining heat for hours after the fire was finished.

There was a chapel inside the walls and a big church outside the walls with a graveyard. The apartments were still occupied. In the castle a wheelchair was displayed that had a gear system, so it could be moved by turning a crank. There was a dog house that looked like a mountain chalet. It was an amazing village on a hill. We visited a few other places including the Aigle Castle, which appeared to have been built to protect the vineyards. The day we visited the Aigle Castle a group of students from the hotel school were also visiting. The professor leading the group allowed us to accompany them. It was an interesting tour. Two days later we drove to Geneva and flew home. It was a great visit.

OUR 60TH WEDDING ANNIVERSARY

In 2003 our son John had a party to celebrate our 60th wedding anniversary. Our entire family had grown to include eleven grandchildren, three daughters-in-law, and one son-in-law, plus a boyfriend and a girlfriend of our grandchildren that were all present. A grandson and his girlfriend came from Australia and of course many came from western Canada, where most of our family lived. It was a great celebration. All of our children honoured Elinor and me, all with deep emotion, even to the extent of not being able to finish their speech. We have a wonderful family. Many of our relatives and many friends, some from Arvida days, celebrated with us. We also celebrated our 65th wedding anniversary while we lived in Nelson, BC. Our son Peter arranged the celebration in Calgary. Several of our friends from Mississauga attended the celebration. It was a great celebration as only Peter can arrange, with a trip the next day to a special lunch at the Banff Springs Hotel in the mountains.

Our complete family at our 60th wedding anniversary.

BIRD WATCHING

Elinor was interested in birds and started us bird watching. For several years in early May we went to Point Peelee on Lake Erie, Ontario, with the Welters, Paul's wife Suzanne's parents. Point Peelee is a point of land that juts into Lake Erie. The Point has huckleberry trees that keep their berries all winter and fall off when the new blossoms appear. They are also late in getting leaves. In the spring it is a flyway for thousands of birds. They eat last fall's berries. Spring offers ideal conditions for bird watching and many people come to see the birds in that location. There is a nice hotel with an indoor swimming pool and a good restaurant, which is a great place to rest after a day of bird watching. Bob and I worked at getting photos while Elinor and Madeleine added to their life lists of birds. Elinor had a life list of close to one hundred that she had identified. Our next door neighbour on Springhill, Dr. John Kingleyside, had a life list of hundreds of birds. We often saw him at Point Peelee. He traveled extensively to study birds. We also traveled to a number of sites in Canada and the USA. On several of our trips out west we tried to see the yellow-winged black birds that are supposed to be in Manitoba, but we never saw them. There is a swamp near Lake Huron where every year hundreds of swans come and stay a few days. We asked a friend who has a cottage nearby to let us know when they arrived. We got the call and drove to the swamp. Sadly, they left about an hour before we got there.

Bird watching at Point Peelee.

Another time we were on a cruise and were told that in certain swamps in Trinidad one could see Red Ibis. We went out of our way to see them and when we got there, there were none. The driver did not mention that they only came to the swamp in the evening. He drove us there in the morning. When we complained, he said, "You wanted to see where the Red Ibis can be found. This is where they are found." We did see some huge snakes, but no birds.

On another occasion we drove into the Okefenokee Swamp in northern Florida and southern Georgia and took an air boat (a boat powered by an airplane motor and propeller) to an Indian camp on an island. We did not see any exotic birds, but we saw lots of alligators.

The last few years our bird watching was limited to the birds on our feeders at the cottage.

Chapter 22

CRUISES

In 1972 we took our first cruise. Elinor saw a cruise advertised for seven days at $500 per person and said that she would love to go on a cruise. I was not anxious to do this, but if Elinor wanted to, I would go along. She arranged things and next thing I knew, we were on a Costa cruise out of Miami. I did not consider lying in the sun on a deck or around a pool to be very interesting so I took a briefcase of work with me so that I would not completely waste the week. The first day out I found a shady spot and opened up my briefcase. After about ten minutes Elinor came along with several others. They took the papers I was studying and shoved them in the briefcase and said. "You are on this cruise to enjoy yourself - not to work!" Then they dragged me off to play some game. I must admit that I did not open the briefcase again on that trip; I had a wonderful time and I only lounged on the deck when I was exhausted. As it turned out, I became hooked on cruises after all.

On that cruise there was Mass every morning and we met an interesting couple there. They had one daughter who was severely handicapped. They took her on cruises because it was an easy way for her to travel. Elinor, being an avid bridge player, found a couple to play bridge with. The husband suggested that we play for ten cents a point. Elinor was about to agree but I said, "Let's just make it a friendly game." At ten cents a point, one could lose a lot of money. I should have had more faith in Elinor. We won every game we played with big scores. We also entered a bridge tournament and won that. On the final day the captain gave out prizes to the various winners and Elinor was presented with a cup that sat in a prominent place in our house. After that trip

A Broader Vision

we were both hooked on cruises, visiting many interesting places and meeting interesting people.

On a cruise in the Baltic we visited Russia and spent a day in St. Petersburg visiting the many places of interest. Elinor bought a small box made of a paper-like material that was beautifully decorated. I bought a cap in Finland. In Norway, Elinor heard of a store that sold some curio she wanted and we took a taxi to it. It was late afternoon and after our purchase the store closed. We went out to take a taxi but none came by and now the stores were closed. It was foolish to not have asked the store to call a taxi. In an hour our ship was leaving and we were several miles from the dock. We were afraid we would not make it back in time. Fortunately we saw a policeman and asked him to help us. He called a taxi for us and we made it back to the ship.

Elinor in Norway on a Scandinavian Cruise.

On a cruise to the eastern Caribbean with Jim and Jennie (my sister), we as usual asked for a table of eight. At the table there was a relatively young man and wife. The other couple at the table were not very talkative and seemed to be more interested in keeping to themselves. The young couple, by contrast, were lively and talkative. We took several land excursions with them. However, the wife always wanted to sit in the front of the vehicle and occasionally I wished to sit in the front to get pictures. Finally I got a chance to sit in the front and the wife had to take a back seat. To my horror it turned out that the wife was seriously crippled and had real difficulty getting in a back seat. I had noticed at dinnertime that he helped his wife, but I thought he was being courteous. I jumped out so she could have the front seat but she was already part way in and it was more difficult to move her again. Needless to say, I took the back seat after that. It turned out that he was a professor at the University of Montreal and his specialty was spectroscopy. In fact, he was using equipment that TSL had sold. They were a very nice couple and we communicated with them for several years.

Photo on a cruise.

A Broader Vision

As a girl Elinor had been interested in horses and over the years she collected horse figurines that ranged from Royal Doulton to inexpensive brass. She had anything that ranged from an item that was a mere few inches tall to a horse figure made of leather that stood about a foot and a half high. This horse was bought in Rome on a Mediterranean cruise from a street hawker. Elinor saw the horse and said she wanted it for her collection. It was big and would not fit in a suitcase. I would have had to carry it on the plane home. In fact, it was so big that it would not fit in her horse collection cabinet. The hawker, recognizing Elinor's interest, followed us along as we walked around Rome. He quoted a price of $70, which diminished my interest. As we were about to enter the Coliseum, Elinor made a last plea and the hawker dropped the price to $30, so I bought it and carried it home. Elinor found a place for it in a corner of our living room. I later saw a smaller version of the same horse figurine in Canada for sale at $200. On a visit to Virginia in the USA, Elinor found a horse figurine carved out of coal. Her collection consisted of one hundred and fifty figurines, some of which were signed pieces of art.

Cruising gave Elinor the chance to collect unusual items for her horse collection and her curio cabinet. She did have some exceptionally unusual items, though: an elephant carved out of ivory, which she bought at a Chinese exhibit, and several Hummel figurines of pre-war vintage. She also had several Royal Doulton pieces - some bought in London - and she also obtained an Irish glass horse, which she bought on a visit to Ireland. On a visit to Venice during a cruise she bought some Murano glass. On a cruise stopping in Venezuela, she discovered a Murano glass branch in the back country. We took a trip through terrorist territory to visit it, being assured that we would not be bothered if we visited the Murano factory. She also had a collection of forty collector's plates and many other unique collectables.

When Elinor became sick and we moved to Nelson, her collection was broken up. Most of her horse collection was taken by our granddaughter Samantha, but I have no idea what happened to her other collections.

***

While on another cruise I met an older chap at the martini bar whose interests were similar to mine, and after a couple of times he suggested that we have dinner with him at one of the special dining rooms so our wives could meet. We did so, but his wife had also invited a retired general. The general was a stuffed shirt and an ass. The next day at the martini bar he apologized and said that his wife was from a military family, and any high ranking officer was a god to her no matter how stupid. He suggested we do it again but without any military presence. We did so and had a pleasant meal. Unfortunately our wives were not compatible. Nonetheless, we continued to enjoy martinis together.

In 2000 we flew to Manaus, Brazil, at the junction of Amazon River and the Negra River - a thousand miles upstream from the ocean. Manaus was a big city with a population of two million and it had a very fancy opera house. Electronics and oil refineries were its main business. There was a road from other cities in Brazil but it required an all-terrain vehicle. It was really only assessable by water or air. There were small communities around it on the Negra and Amazon rivers. The Amazon water was muddy brown and the Negra was black. The two streams ran side by side for hundreds of miles before they mixed. This is apparently because the Amazon is heavy with silt and the Negra is almost silt free. We took some small boat trips on the Amazon to some of the communities. The houses were built on stilts or on rafts because in the rainy season the river could rise as much as twenty feet. We also went on a jungle hike along well used paths. Walks were also offered where one would have to use a machete. Further down the river there was another city called Santarim, which was more modern despite having no connecting roads. The river was the highway and everyone had a boat of some kind. There were floating service stations on the river where gasoline could be bought and minor repairs made. Tractor trailers were used around the town, but the trailers were moved up and down the river on barges.

On this cruise we met a couple who were basically living on cruises instead of in a retirement home. They had been on this ship for eight weeks and when we docked in Fort Lauderdale, they were booked on another ship. I thought this was an interesting way to live and it was actually no more expensive than living in a retirement residence. We cruised back to Fort Lauderdale, stopping at Trinidad on the way.

While on a Mediterranean cruise we took a shore excursion to Florence. The bus let us off and told us to meet back at 5:00 PM in order to return to the ship. When the group gathered to return, a man said he had been separated from his wife and had not been able to find her. He feared she had an accident or took sick. On this cruise every bus had a member of the crew, which is exceptional for the industry. The crew member told the bus to wait while she checked with the police and hospitals. This took some time and we all agreed to wait. Finally at 8:00 PM it was decided that the bus should return to the ship and that the crew member would stay in Florence. Another passenger and his wife offered to stay with her and said he would pay any expenses. It was 9:00 PM when we got back to the ship; the ship was supposed to sail at 8:00 PM. However when we got back to the ship, it was discovered that the wife was already on board: she had taken a taxi.

MANAUS: Population 2 million

Amazon and Negra do not mix!

Manaus Opera House

Manaus on the Amazon River.

In 2008 Elinor and I, along with our daughter Deborah and Elinor's caregiver Sarah Madigan, sailed from San Diego to Hawaii and returned to Vancouver. Even though Elinor was confined to a wheelchair, we were able to make some interesting shore excursions. The ships staff took her down the gangplank and of course got her back on the ship. Elinor enjoyed the cruise. As we cruised, albatrosses were frequently seen. We have twice sailed through the Panama Canal.

The last time we went on cruise was in October 2010, when Elinor and I sailed from Vancouver to Fort Lauderdale. It was our second trip through the Panama Canal. We were accompanied by our daughter Deborah and daughter-in-law Jocelyn. Dementia was catching up with Elinor, but she enjoyed the cruise. We met a young man who was accompanying his grandfather, and he decided that he should also look after me. Although I had two other women with me - Debbie and Jocelyn - he felt that they were too busy looking after Elinor to give me due attention. We certainly met some very nice people on cruises. From Fort Lauderdale we flew to Mississauga, where John had bought a condominium for us. Unfortunately it was Elinor's last cruise: in late November of 2011, she fell and broke her pelvis - an accident from which she did not recover. My wife of more than 68 years died on January 6th, 2012.

We took twelve cruises together. We cruised the north, the east, the west, and the south Caribbean. We have sailed from Vancouver to Hawaii and back. We cruised the Amazon from Manaus to Fort Lauderdale. Twice we sailed through the Panama Canal. The Mediterranean, the Adriatic, the Baltic, and the east coast of North America from Montreal to Fort Lauderdale, as well as the west coast of North America from Alaska to Panama had all been seen via cruise ship by Elinor and me.

Chapter 23

MEDICAL COMPLICATIONS

In 1997 Elinor had a colonoscopy on the Friday morning before the Civic Holiday weekend (August 1). On that same Friday evening, we went to the cottage to spend the long weekend there. Saturday morning when Elinor got up, she complained of pain in her abdomen. She said it was not bad and that it was probably something she had eaten. However, it continued to worsen as the day progressed. After lunch she said it was getting worse and that maybe we should go to the emergency. I drove her to Penetanguishene hospital. It was a small hospital and it is now closed by our government controlled Medicare. This was a caring hospital run by a religious community where you did not have to wait in the emergency room for five or six hours. By early afternoon it was determined she had a perforated colon and needed an emergency operation right away. The hospital was not equipped to perform the operation and started calling other hospitals. No one would take her. They called the doctor at his cottage - the same doctor who had obviously caused the perforation by the colonoscopy - but he said while he was qualified to do the operation, he was not on call, and therefore was not allowed to do it. I wondered if that was true. The hospital called every major hospital in southern Ontario and no one would take her. The doctor said that it was absolutely essential that she have the operation within the next few hours or she would die. I called our son John to alert the family.

By now it was getting on to midnight and there was a change of shifts. A new doctor came on shift and, reviewing Elinor's case, said he knew of a caring doctor in Orillia who could do the operation. He called the doctor at his home and he agreed to perform the operation. He said to send her over right away and that he would be waiting for her. By the time she got to Orillia it was about 1:30 AM. Doctor O'Connor was waiting for her and stated that at this late time her chances were very poor that she would survive the operation; however, she had no chance without it. By now our son John had joined me. We said the rosary and continued praying. At about 5:00 AM the doctor came out and said she had survived the operation and that the next four hours were critical. He also said that she appeared to be a strong woman and that he was very optimistic. John and I stayed with her the remainder of the day, and by evening she recognized us and appeared to be recovering. Paul was vacationing in Nova Scotia when he heard of Elinor's operation and he and Suzanne immediately left and drove back, arriving two days later. On going immediately to see Elinor they found her reading a book in bed and she said that "Jack had just gone to lunch so go have lunch with him. I am fine being here reading". Indeed she was recovering. In the small hospital in Orillia she was allowed to remain for ten days while she healed. On the eleventh day I drove her to the cottage and we resumed our normal living.

I always regarded doctors as professionals who accepted the responsibility of doing the job even if inconvenient. It is hard to believe that every operating room in southern Ontario was so booked up that a really urgent operation could not be performed. It was a holiday weekend. Before our government controlled medical system took over, a hospital was a place to go to in order to be healed. The healing hospitals operated by religious communities have all been shut down in favour of large, impersonal, bureaucratic, inefficient institutions. In many cases now, the hospital is simply a repair shop. Once the repair is done they ship you out. If you have an emergency during a holiday weekend, you will probably not be helped.

The majority of people can afford to cover the usual medical expenses. If the health plan covered annual medical expenses of greater than, say, 3% of your annual income, the vast majority could handle that. A major operation or multi-year cancer treatment in excess of 3% of annual income would be covered by the government, and would not become a burden. With such a system a nominal charge could be applied to all medical visits. For example, a $25 charge at the hospital emergency would, I believe, greatly reduce the wait times. From my many hours sitting in the emergency room I have observed that many (if not most) people waiting are not in urgent need, but since it costs

A Broader Vision

them nothing to see a doctor, they figure that they might as well get checked. The argument is that the poor can not afford the expense. However, the income tax system identifies the poor so they can be issued a medical card just like we all have now.

In 2005 Elinor had a peculiar attack and ended up in the hospital. It was decided that she should have an MRA. The morning she was to have it, she was very upset. She always was very claustrophobic and the MRA frightened her. I told the MRA staff that I thought she better not go through with it. They said they would give her a sedative. As I went with her to the MRA department I could see the terror in her eyes and again suggested they cancel it. I went back to wait in her room when I heard the emergency call, "Code Red in MRA." I rushed down but they would not let me in. After waiting about an hour, they admitted that she went into cardiac arrest and had been resuscitated. She remained in the ICU lingering between life and death for three days. Finally she recovered. However, she did suffer brain damage. As a result, among other things, she became terrified of falling. Although able to walk, she would not walk without assistance and ended up confined to a wheel chair. I continued to get her to walk short distances while I supported her, in order for her to get exercise. Elinor needed assistance in her daily life after that. We arranged a caregiver service in which a lady would come every morning to help Elinor get dressed for the day and to spend some time with her. Although we had some very good caregivers, the company frequently sent a new person. They usually had no experience with elders and I ended up being the prime caregiver and was the one training their staff. We had many doctor appointments, but most doctors would have us wait for hours in their waiting rooms before seeing us for a minute or two. Our main activity became waiting in doctors' offices. Elinor was becoming less aware and less able to be active through it all. One of the novice caregivers had no idea of how to help her get out of bed and Elinor fell and tore her leg on the nearby wheelchair. We rushed her to the hospital to stitch the severely bleeding gash on her leg. Fortunately the ambulance paramedics slowed the bleeding, but she had to wait for over eight hours before a doctor arrived. It needed twenty stitches. Then we had to wait another eight hours for an ambulance to return us to the apartment. She was unable to stand to get into a car.

In 2008, while walking with my help, she suddenly collapsed. I called 911 and she was taken to the hospital, where they said her hip had disintegrated.

They immediately replaced it. Although the operation was a success, she got an infection. The geriatric team of the hospital decided that since she was ninety two years old, she had to go to a nursing home. I pointed out that I could look after her. They insisted that she had to go. I refused and they said I was abusing a senior and that they would have me arrested if I stood in the way. Alternately, they would leave her in my care if I had twenty-four hour nursing care, a hospital bed, and a mechanical lift. I arranged all of this and got her out of the hospital. Our son Paul, who was living in Nelson, BC, suggested that we move to Nelson. He had a big house and had room for us. He said there was good medical service in Nelson. Nelson was a very pleasant place to live and many doctors chose to live there. He claimed the ratio of residents to doctors was 800 to 1 as compared with Ontario where the ratio was 7000 to 1. While gathering some data on Honduras, I noted with interest that the resident to doctor ratio was 4500 to 1. From a medical point of view, Ontario is worse than an undeveloped country. Fed up with the wait times and the poor medical service in general in Ontario, I charted an ambulance plane and flew Elinor to Nelson, BC. The pilot did not like the idea of landing at an airport surrounded by mountains with unpredictable weather and instead landed at a mountain-free airport four hundred miles from Nelson. The ambulance company arranged for ground ambulance to take us the four hundred miles. At about half way to Nelson the ambulance driver announced that we had to change ambulances because this was the end of his territory. We transferred to another ambulance. Before we reached Nelson we had to go through a mountain pass. When we got to the pass it was snowing and the driver did not want to drive through the pass in a snowstorm. She called for a different driver. We waited by the side of the road for an hour for the new driver. We finally arrived in Nelson. We flew from Toronto to the mountains in four hours, but it took ten hours from the plane to Nelson.

Nelson is a pretty town. It was founded more than a hundred years ago as a mining town. The mines are closed but it has a beautiful location in a valley with a lake and mountains on each side. The town has many restaurants, since it is visited by many in the summer. It has all the necessary stores and facilities, including a lakeside park that is filled with flowers in the summer. The valley extends for many miles with other towns and villages along the lake and rivers. It is an interesting place to live, with excellent medical facilities. Elinor had another peculiar attack while in Nelson. She was taken to the emergency and was treated and back home in less than an hour. We felt that it was a good place to settle.

Caption: Elinor and I in Nelson, BC.

Paul retired in July, 2012, from his work as an engineer working on assignments for the National Research Council of Canada. His assignment in southern British Columbia was up at the end of 2008 and he planned to retire in Nelson. He had already started to build his retirement home. Unfortunately the 2008 economic crash occurred and with uncertain economic times he decided he better take his next assignment. It was in Calgary, thus he had to move, so we all moved to Calgary. Although two of our sons and three grandchildren lived in Calgary, we had none of our friends there. Calgary was not an easy place to get around if one did not drive and my vision had deteriorated to the point that I could not drive. It seemed that wherever you went in Calgary you had to drive on a freeway. To compensate for my inability to drive I bought a scooter. At the apartment we had when we first arrived in Calgary, it was possible to use a scooter. It was a nice apartment with three bedrooms and three bathrooms. It was also possible to have a live-in caregiver. She was a young woman that we had found in Nelson who was studying to be a nurse. Sarah Madigan was an exceptionally good caregiver for Elinor.

Sarah Madigan with Elinor.

Unfortunately the landlord would not renew the lease since he wanted to sell the apartment. It was not likely we would easily find another apartment like the one we had, and Sarah wanted to continue her studies, so we decided to move to a retirement residence. Most residences wanted to put Elinor in their nursing area. This also meant that we would be separated since nursing sections were only designed for one person per room. I have not found anywhere in Ontario, Alberta, or BC a retirement residence with nursing care that allows a couple to live together and have the nurse come to the room on whatever floor we are on. It is always a special floor for nursing care and only one person per room. I had no intention of doing that. Peter was able to find one that allowed Elinor to live with me and not have her in a nursing section. It was an excellent residence, but it was isolated. To leave the area one had to use a freeway. A scooter had very little use.

A Broader Vision

While living here Elinor came down with a severe case of bronchitis and had to go to the hospital. The hospital said Elinor had a swallowing problem and could not be allowed to eat or drink in case she choked. They advised that because she was 92 years of age and struggling that she should go to a hospice. I knew for some time that she had a problem with swallowing and that there was a risk that she could choke to death. However, she was not choking so why condemn her to death, and why force us to sit around and wait for it? As we had experienced in Mississauga, the doctor here would not sign her out. So I got another doctor (who had also seen her) to sign her out. The doctor who originally said that Elinor had to go to a hospice was very annoyed that I questioned her wisdom. I expected that if either of us had to go to the hospital and ended up in her care that we would end up in a hospice.

Our son John in Mississauga offered to buy a condo attached to a retirement residence if we wanted to return to Mississauga. As mentioned earlier, in October of 2010 Elinor and I, along with our daughter Deborah and our daughter-in-law Jocelyn, cruised from Vancouver to Fort Lauderdale and flew to Mississauga to look at John's condo. At that time we saw that it was very attractive and the location was near our friends. We moved in and with the help of caregivers for Elinor, we lived an independent life in a condo attached to a retirement centre. Although Elinor occasionally choked, she did not choke to death. Unfortunately Elinor fell in our apartment and fractured her pelvis. It was a very painful fracture from which she did not recover. She died on January 6, 2012, in her 95th year.

Chapter 24
REFLECTIONS

My mobility being somewhat reduced, I have more time to reflect. When I think back on my life, I realize that God had a big influence throughout. I first realized it when I made my decision to take math and physics at the university. I knew that math, physics, and chemistry was the course I should take, because that was what God wanted me to take. It was a tough course, and if there were times I doubted, I still knew on a fundamental level that I would make it if I didn't give up. There were many instances in my life when I knew that things would work out. In every case, I had prayed prior to the decision I made, and the action I should take was made known, sometimes by circumstances and others by just knowing what I should do. God speaks to us in many ways. My sister Jennie bringing Elinor up to my back room as I worked on my "ear" is but one example. Jennie could have told her that I was working on an exhibit, but she had worded it in such a way that Elinor was especially intrigued. Another example is in the timing of Elinor's tonsil removal and her toboggan accident, where she was the only one injured, spending ten days in the hospital, working together with the perfect timing of my three months in Kingston, when Peggy Jack was in too much of a hurry for marriage. These circumstances were all directed to cause Elinor to be my wife and I thank God for directing me so.

I reflect as well on our adoption of Deborah and how we all prayed hard for direction on this very serious choice. Events subsequently unfolded revealing providence: When planning the business and holiday trip to the east I had not originally included Quebec City. A late enquiry caused it to be included, which led us to stop at Sainte Anne-de-Beaupré Shrine. When we first saw Debbie, her name was Deborah Anne, and I knew that she was to be our daughter.

God has directed me to live a successful and useful life. Whenever problems occurred I asked God for help. The ThermoCarb, although not the success I had hoped for, was still not a failure. The pin tubes are still being sold. Wear Check is a success, now employing 3500 people, a worthwhile result of my efforts. In fact, many things I was prompted to do were primarily for the advantage of others. I was active in the Social Forum. In Arvida I arranged for a daily 5:15 pm Mass so people walking home from work could attend. I also started a boys club for teens to give them something to do. When we moved to Pine Avenue, I organized an altar boys club and a men's organization to attend to some of the parishes' material needs. I participated in raising funds for St. Mary's new church. I was on the committee to raise funds for the building of St. Christopher's church. At St. Christopher's, I served as chairman of the Holy Name society and was the first Parish Council chairman. I was an usher and minister of communion. As chairman of the parish Share Life committee, we raised over two million dollars during the years of my chairmanship. In 2000 I was on the committee to raise funds for St. Christopher's renovations. As well as participating in church activities, I helped form the Canadian Spectroscopy Association and supported it for fifteen years. I helped form the Canadian Testing Association and was chairman for several years. I supported this Association for many more years as well.

My vision of a good life has been that both family and God were more significant than money or fame. To live as I felt one should, I have made many choices that were difficult, but necessary. I have struggled often to survive, yet always kept God and my family as the focus and always enjoyed the daily life and the good results that came from my efforts. For the most part, my life has been successful and joyful. This too comes from following what I believed to be the right paths not the easiest paths. I believe that what I was able to accomplish has helped improve life for all people. I believe that should be true for anyone who keeps their focus on serving God throughout their lives, that their work will help everyone else, and their lives will be satisfying and joyful.

Elinor participated and was active in everything I did. She was also very involved in organizing the Catholic Women' League and was chairman in both St. Mary's and St. Christopher's. She helped organized the Girl Guides in St. Christopher's and was involved in the set up of the Church Community

Volunteers. She participated in raising funds for The Canadian Cancer Society and the Heart and Stroke Fund. She also acted as a DRO in elections and canvassed for the Liberal Party.

Although Elinor's activity in the last few years was curtailed by brain damage and dementia, we never considered separating and putting her in a nursing home. We lived an active life together in the presence of God for more than 68 years. Unfortunately she fell and broke her pelvis while I was finishing this book and she did not recover. Incidentally, she did not choke to death as was feared. Although she has passed on, she is still present to me. I know that she is watching me and pointing out the corrections I have to make. I confidently look forward to being with her again.

Printed in Canada